The Divide

THE DIVIDE

Global Inequality from Conquest to Free Markets

Jason Hickel

W. W. Norton & Company
Independent Publishers Since 1923
New York • London

First published by The Random House Group Ltd. in Great Britain under the title
The Divide: A Brief Guide to Global Inequality and its Solutions

For information about permission to reproduce selections from this book, write to
Permissions, W. W. Norton & Company, Inc., 500 Fifth Avenue, New York, NY 10110

For information about special discounts for bulk purchases, please contact
W. W. Norton Special Sales at specialsales@wwnorton.com or 800-233-4830

Manufacturing by Quad Graphics, Fairfield
Production manager: Anna Oler

Library of Congress Cataloging-in-Publication Data

Names: Hickel, Jason, 1982– author.
Title: The divide ; global inequality from conquest to free markets / Jason Hickel.
Description: First American edition. | New York : W. W. Norton & Company, 2018. |
"First published in 2017 by The Random House Group Ltd. in
Great Britain under the title THE DIVIDE: A Brief Guide to
Global Inequality and its Solutions." |
Includes bibliographical references and index.
Identifiers: LCCN 2017052787 | ISBN 9780393651362 (hardcover)
Subjects: LCSH: Equality. | Globalization.
Classification: LCC HD82.H4393 2018 | DDC 330.9—dc23
LC record available at https://lccn.loc.gov/2017052787

W. W. Norton & Company, Inc.
500 Fifth Avenue, New York, N.Y. 10110
www.wwnorton.com

W. W. Norton & Company Ltd.
15 Carlisle Street, London W1D 3BS

1 2 3 4 5 6 7 8 9 0

for the wretched of the earth

Contents

Preface

Beginnings

I grew up in Swaziland – a tiny, landlocked country near the eastern seaboard of southern Africa. It was a happy childhood, in many ways. As a little boy I ran around barefoot through sandy grassland with my friends, unhindered by fences or walls. When the monsoon rains hit we would sail tiny bark boats through the dongas, welcoming the wet. We climbed trees and plucked mangoes and lychees and guavas to snack on whenever we grew hungry. During lazy afternoons I would sometimes wander up the hill from our little bungalow along the dirt track towards the clinic where my parents worked as doctors. I still remember the cool of the polished concrete floors and the breezy shade of the courtyard. But most of all I remember the queue – the queue of patients winding out of the door, some sitting on wooden benches, others on grass mats, waiting to be seen. To me, it seemed that the queue never ended.

As I grew older, I began to learn about things like TB and malaria, typhoid and bilharzia, malnutrition and kwashiorkor – scary words that were nonetheless familiar and well worn among our family. Later still I learned that we were living in the middle of the worst epidemic of HIV/AIDS anywhere in the world. I learned that people were suffering and dying of diseases that could easily be cured, prevented or managed in richer countries – a fact that to me seemed unspeakably horrible. And I learned about poverty. Many of my friends came from families that scraped together meagre livelihoods on subsistence farms subject to the constant caprice of drought, or who struggled to find work while living in makeshift shelters in the slums outside Manzini, the country's biggest city.

They were not alone. Today, some 4.3 billion people – more than 60 per cent of the world's population – live in debilitating poverty, struggling to survive on less than the equivalent of $5 per day. Half do not have access to enough food. And these numbers have been growing steadily over the past few decades. Meanwhile, the wealth of the very richest is piling up to levels unprecedented in human history. As I write this, it has just been announced that the eight richest men in the world have as much wealth between them as the poorest half of the world's population combined.

We can trace out the shape of global inequality by looking at the distribution of income and wealth among individuals, as most analysts have done. But we can get an even clearer picture by looking at the divide between different regions of the world. In 2000, Americans enjoyed an average income roughly nine times higher than their counterparts in Latin America, twenty-one times higher than people in the Middle East and North Africa, fifty-two times higher than sub-Saharan Africans and no less than seventy-three times higher than South Asians. And here, too, the numbers have been getting worse: the gap between the real per capita incomes of the global North and the global South has roughly tripled in size since 1960.

*

It is easy to assume that the divide between rich countries and poor countries has always existed; that it is a natural feature of the world. Indeed, the metaphor of the divide itself may lead us unwittingly to assume that there is a chasm – a fundamental discontinuity – between the rich world and the poor world, as if they were economic islands disconnected from one another. If you start from this notion, as many scholars have done, explaining the economic differences between the two is simply a matter of looking at internal characteristics.

This notion sits at the centre of the usual story that we are told about global inequality. Development agencies, NGOs and the world's most powerful governments explain that the plight of poor countries is a technical problem – one that can be solved by adopting the right institutions and the right economic policies, by working hard and accepting a bit of help. If only poor countries would follow the advice of experts from agencies like the World Bank, they would gradually leave poverty behind, closing the divide between the poor and the rich. It is a familiar story, and a comforting one. It is one that we have all, at one time or another, believed and supported. It maintains an industry worth billions of dollars and an army of NGOs, charities and foundations seeking to end poverty through aid and charity.

But the story is wrong. The idea of a natural divide misleads us from the start. In the year 1500, there was no appreciable difference in incomes and living standards between Europe and the rest of the world. Indeed, we know that people in some regions of the global South were a good deal better off than their counterparts in Europe. And yet their fortunes changed dramatically over the intervening centuries – not in spite of one another but *because* of one another – as Western powers roped the rest of the world into a single international economic system.

When we approach it this way, the question becomes less about the traits of rich countries and poor countries – although that is, of course, part of it – and more about the relationship between them. The divide between rich countries and poor countries isn't natural or inevitable. It has been created. What could have caused one part of the world to rise and the other to fall? How has the pattern of growth and decline been maintained for more than

500 years? Why is inequality getting worse? And why do we not know about it?

*

From time to time I still think back to that queue outside my parents' clinic. It remains as vivid in my mind as if it were yesterday. When I do, I am reminded that the story of global inequality is not a matter of numbers and figures and historical events. It is about real lives, real people. It is about the aspirations of communities and nations and social movements over generations, even centuries. It is about the belief, shaken with doubt from time to time but otherwise firm, that another world is possible.

At one of the most frightening times in our history, with inequality at record extremes, demagogues rising and our planet's climate beginning to wreak revenge on industrial civilisation, we are more in need of hope than ever. It is only by understanding why the world is the way it is – by examining root causes – that we will be able to arrive at real, effective solutions and imagine our way into the future. What is certain is that if we are going to solve the great problems of global poverty and inequality, of famine and environmental collapse, the world of tomorrow will have to look very different from the world of today.

The arc of history bends towards justice, Martin Luther King Jr once said. But it won't bend on its own.

PART ONE

The Divide

One

The Development Delusion

It began as a public-relations gimmick. Harry Truman had just been elected to a second term as president of the United States and was set to take the stage for his inaugural address on 20 January 1949. His speechwriters were in a frenzy. They needed to whip up something compelling for the president to say – something bold and exciting to announce. They had three ideas on the list: backing for the new United Nations, resistance to the Soviet threat and continued commitment to the Marshall Plan. But none were very inspiring. In fact, they were downright boring and the media was bound to ignore the speech as yesterday's news. They needed something that would tap into the zeitgeist – something that would stir the soul of the nation.

Their answer came from an unlikely source. Benjamin Hardy was a young, mid-level functionary in the State Department, but as a former reporter for the *Atlanta Journal* he had a knack for a good headline. When he stumbled across a memo requesting fresh ideas for the inaugural address, he decided to pitch his boss a wild thought: 'Development'. Why not have Truman announce that his administration would give aid to Third World countries to help them develop and put an end to the scourge of grinding poverty? Hardy saw this as a sure victory – an easy way, he wrote in his pitch, 'to make the greatest psychological impact' on America and 'to ride and direct the universal groundswell of desire for a better world'.

Hardy's bosses shut him down. It was a risky, out-of-the-blue idea, possibly too new to make much sense to people; it wasn't worth experimenting with it in such an important setting. But Hardy was determined not to let the opportunity pass. He managed to fake his way into the White House, gave a rousing defence of the idea to Truman's advisers and – with a little bit of careful manoeuvring by supporters on the inside – his plan ended up as an afterthought, 'Point Four', in Truman's draft. Truman approved it.

It was the first inaugural address ever to be broadcast on television. Ten million viewers tuned in on that cold January afternoon, making it the largest single event ever witnessed up to that time. More people watched Truman's address than watched the inaugural addresses of all his predecessors put together. And they loved what he had to say. 'More than half the people of the world are living in conditions approaching misery,' he proclaimed. 'Their food is inadequate. They are victims of disease. Their economic life is primitive and stagnant.' But there was hope, he said: 'For the first time in history, humanity possesses the knowledge and skill to relieve the suffering of these people. The United States is pre-eminent among nations in the development of industrial and scientific techniques . . . our imponderable resources in technical knowledge are constantly growing and are inexhaustible.' And then the clincher: 'We must embark on a bold new program for making the benefits of our scientific advances and industrial progress available for the improvement and growth of underdeveloped areas . . . It must be a worldwide effort for the achievement of peace, plenty, and freedom.'

Of course, there were no actual plans for such a programme – not even a single document. It was included in the speech purely as a PR gimmick. And it worked. The media went crazy – papers from the *Washington Post* to the *New York Times* glowed with approval. Everyone was excited about Point Four, and the rest of the speech was forgotten.

*

Why did Point Four so capture the public imagination? Because Truman gave Americans a new and powerful way to think about the emerging international order. The dust was settling after the Second World War, European imperialism was collapsing and the world was beginning to take shape as a collection of equal and independent nations. The only problem was that in reality they were not equal at all: there were vast differences between them in terms of power and wealth, with the countries of the global North enjoying a very high quality of life while the global South – the majority of the world's population – was mired in debilitating poverty. As Americans peered beyond their borders and began to notice the brutal fact of global inequality, they needed a way to make sense of it.

Point Four offered them a compelling narrative. The rich countries of Europe and North America were 'developed'. They were ahead on the Great Arrow of Progress. They were doing better because they *were* better – they were smarter, more innovative and harder working. They had better values, better institutions and better technology. By contrast, the countries of the global South were poor because they hadn't yet figured out the right values and policies yet. They were still behind, 'underdeveloped' and struggling to catch up.

This story was deeply affirming for Americans; it made them feel good about themselves, proud of their achievements and their place in the world. But perhaps more importantly, it gave them a way to feel noble too – it gave them access to a higher, almost cosmological purpose. The developed countries would stand as beacons of hope, as saviours to the poor. They would reach out and give generously of their riches to help the 'primitive' countries of the South follow their path to success. They would become heroes, leading the way to a world of unprecedented peace and prosperity.

In other words, Point Four explained the existence of global inequality and offered a solution to it in one satisfying stroke. And for this reason it wasn't long before it was picked up by the governments of Western Europe as well. As Britain and France were withdrawing from their colonies, they needed a new way of explaining the gross inequality that persisted between themselves and the people they had ruled for so long. The story of development – that the nations of the world were simply at different positions along the Great Arrow of Progress – offered a convenient alibi. It allowed them to disavow responsibility for the misery of the colonies, and it was more palatable than the explicit racial theories they had relied on in the past. What is more, it allowed them to shift their role in the eyes of the world: graciously relinquishing imperial power, they would turn to aiding their fellow man.

It was an incredibly beguiling tale to Western ears. It wasn't just another story – it had all the elements of an epic myth. It provided a keystone around which people could organise their ideas about the world, about human progress and about our future.

The story of development remains a compelling force in our society to this day. We encounter it everywhere we turn: in the form of charity shops like Oxfam and Traid, in TV ads from Save the Children and World Vision, in annual reports published by the World Bank and the International Monetary Fund, and every time we see the world's nations ranked by GDP. We hear it from rock stars like Bono and Bob Geldof, from billionaires like Bill Gates and George Soros, and from actors like Madonna and Angelina Jolie, khaki-clad and mobbed by eager African children. We get it in the form of Live Aid concerts and celebrity fundraising singles like 'Do They Know It's Christmas?', which somehow manages to crop up every year. Every major university offers degree programmes in development, and a whole class of professionals has emerged to staff the thousands of NGOs that have sprung up over the past few decades. Development is everywhere. And it comes with its own rituals that millions upon millions of people can participate in: buying TOMS shoes, giving a few dollars a month to sponsor a child in Zambia, or sacrificing summer holidays to volunteer in Honduras.

It probably wouldn't be a stretch to say that almost everyone in the Western world has at some point encountered or even participated in the story of development. It is ubiquitous. And it has become an enormous industry, worth hundreds of billions of dollars – as much as all the profits of all the banks in the United States combined.

*

The development story is so deeply ingrained in our culture that we take it almost completely for granted. It seems manifestly true. For much of my young adult life I passionately believed in it. When I left Swaziland for university in the United States, I was confronted by a completely different world to the one in which I had grown up: a world replete with excess – enormous houses, giant cars, slick new roads and cavernous shopping malls. But I was unable to put Swaziland behind me. Casting about for explanations for and solutions to the profound material differences between the two worlds I straddled, I found answers – and hope – in the story of development.

During my final year of university, I moved to Nagaland, a remote state in a far-flung corner of north-east India, to work with a local microfinance organisation. I found it exciting and rewarding – being part of the development story gave me a sense of value and purpose far beyond anything the corporate world had to offer. It made me feel as though I was part of something important. It made me feel noble.

Eager to continue working in the field, I later returned to Swaziland to take up a job with World Vision, one of the world's largest development NGOs. Based in the village of Mpaka, a dusty outpost on a road that traverses the lowveld between Manzini and the border of Mozambique, I threw myself into a range of projects – everything from water systems to healthcare – and once again I felt the rush that came with being part of the development story. But after my initial excitement faded, I found myself confronting some difficult questions. We had dozens of projects across that tiny country, representing millions of dollars of charity and many years of work – and World Vision was only one of many NGOs tackling the very same problems, bolstered by a steady flow of aid from donor countries in the global North. But on the whole, nothing really seemed to be changing. Why did most people in Swaziland remain so poor, despite this effort? It felt as though we were shovelling sand into a bottomless pit.

World Vision had hired me to help analyse why their development efforts in Swaziland were not living up to their promise. The reason, I discovered, was that their interventions were missing the point. Their story about the world – borrowed more or less verbatim from Truman – led them to assume that all that Swazis needed was a bit of charity to help them out. World Vision went about caring for dying AIDS patients, setting up income-generation schemes for the unemployed, teaching new techniques to farmers and paying for children's education. But, as helpful as these projects were, they did nothing to address the actual causes of the problems. Why *were* AIDS patients dying? Over time, I learned that it had to do with the fact that pharmaceutical companies refused to allow Swaziland to import generic versions of patented life-saving medicines, keeping prices way out of reach. Why were farmers unable to make a living off the land? I discovered that it was related to the subsidised foods that were flooding in from the US and the EU, which undercut local agriculture. And why was the government unable to provide basic social services? Because it was buried under a pile of foreign debt and had been forced by Western banks to cut social spending in order to prioritise repayment.

The deeper I dug, the more I realised that the reason poverty persisted in Swaziland had quite a lot to do with matters that lay beyond Swaziland's borders. It gradually became clear that the global economic system was organised in such a way as to make meaningful development nearly impossible. These findings troubled me. But when I pointed them out to one of World Vision's managers, I was told that they were too 'political'; it wasn't World Vision's job to think about things like pharmaceutical patents or international trade rules or debt. If we started to raise those issues, I was told, we would lose our funding before the year was over; after all, the global system of patents, trade and debt was what made some of our donors rich enough to give to charity in the first place. Better to shut up about it: stick with the sponsor-a-child programme and don't rock the boat.

Frustrated and disillusioned, I left World Vision and went back to studying, determined to learn everything I could about the deeper structural determinants of poverty – not just in Swaziland, but across the global South. I needed to understand why so much of the world continues to live in grinding poverty, despite decades of 'development', while a few countries enjoy almost unimaginable wealth.

What I learned along the way is that the story we've been told about rich countries and poor countries isn't exactly true. In fact, the narrative we're familiar with is almost the exact opposite of reality. There is a very different story out there, if we are willing to listen to it. It will completely change the way we think about the world. It will change the way we think about why poverty exists. It will change the way we think about progress. It will even change the way we think about our own civilisation, about our everyday lifestyles, and about what the world should look like in the future.

Anthropologists tell us that when the structure of a core myth begins to change, everything else about society changes around it, and fresh new possibilities open up that weren't even thinkable before. When myths fall apart, revolutions happen.

The Myth Begins to Crumble

One of the reasons that the development story has been so compelling to people is that it has at its core a narrative of success – a bit of heartening good news in a world full of bad. Thanks to the generous aid of rich countries, the story goes, we have made remarkable strides in our fight against global poverty, and human want will soon be relegated to the dustbin of history. This hopeful story has inspired people for many decades and won the development industry millions of eager recruits. But in recent years public enthusiasm seems to have waned; people are beginning to pack away the streamers and quietly exit the party. Development agencies have produced report after report of hand-wringing analysis about the fact that people no longer believe that development is working. Drawing on survey data, the UK development umbrella group Bond recently reported that 'efforts to eradicate poverty appear to many members of the public to have failed, and scepticism about the effectiveness of aid and global development initiatives has risen'.

Development agencies find this trend difficult to understand. As far as they're concerned, development has been an outstanding success, scoring improvements in areas like child and maternal mortality and inching us towards a world without poverty. And indeed there have been some impressive achievements. For example, the number of children dying from preventable causes has declined from 17 million in 1990 to less than 8 million in 2013. And the likelihood of mothers dying during childbirth has declined by 47 per cent during the same period. These statistics are certainly worth celebrating. But the development industry wants the public to believe that these gains are tantamount to the overall success of the development project, and the public just aren't buying it. There may be some small wins around the edges, they feel, but on the whole things don't appear to be getting much better, and may even be getting worse. The development industry has repeatedly failed to deliver on its grand promises to End World Hunger or Make

Poverty History – so why give them any more money? Why let them encourage false hope?

And they're right. Take hunger, for example. In 1974, at the first UN Food Summit in Rome, US Secretary of State Henry Kissinger famously promised that hunger would be eradicated within a decade. At the time there were an estimated 460 million hungry people in the world. But instead of disappearing, hunger got steadily worse. Today there are about 800 million hungry people, even according to the most conservative measures. More realistic estimates put the figure at around 2 billion – nearly a third of all humanity. It is hard to imagine a greater symbol of failure than rising hunger, especially given that we already produce more than enough food each year to feed all 7 billion of the world's people, with plenty left over for another 3 billion.

What about poverty? For many years, the development industry has told us that absolute poverty has been steadily declining. In 2015, the United Nations published the final report of the Millennium Development Goals – the world's first major public commitment to reduce poverty – claiming that the poverty rate had been cut in half since 1990. This official good-news narrative ricocheted through the media and was repeated endlessly by NGOs. But it is very misleading. First, almost all of the gains against poverty have happened in one place, China. Second, the good-news story relies on proportions instead of absolute numbers. If we look at absolute numbers – the original metric by which the world's governments agreed to measure progress – we see that the poverty headcount is exactly the same now as it was when measurements began back in 1981, at about 1 billion. There has been no improvement over thirty-five years.

And that's according to the lowest possible poverty line. In reality, the picture is even worse. The standard poverty measure counts the number of people who live on less than a dollar a day. But in many global South countries a dollar a day is simply not adequate for human existence, to say nothing of human dignity. Many scholars are now saying that people need about four times

15

that in order to have a decent shot at surviving until their fifth birthday, having enough food to eat and reaching normal life expectancy. So what would happen if we measured global poverty at this more realistic level? We would see a total poverty headcount of about 4.3 billion people. That's more than four times what the United Nations would have us believe, and more than 60 per cent of humanity. We would also see that poverty has become *worse* over time, with more than 1 billion people added to the ranks of the poor since 1981. Imagine the entire population of the United States and then triple it. That's how much global poverty has grown over the past few decades. These numbers represent almost unimaginable human suffering.

And all the while, inequality has been exploding. In 1960, at the end of colonialism, per capita income in the richest country was thirty-two times higher than in the poorest country. That's a big gap. The development industry told us that the gap would narrow, but it didn't. On the contrary, over the next four decades the gap more than quadrupled: by 2000, the ratio was 134 to 1. We can see the same pattern if we take a regional view. The gap between the United States (the world's dominant power) and Latin America, sub-Saharan Africa, South Asia and the developing countries of the Middle East and North Africa has roughly tripled between 1960 and today. This is hardly a tale of 'catching up'. And of course global inequality is even worse at the level of individuals. In early 2014, Oxfam reported that the richest eighty-five people had come to accumulate more wealth than the poorest 50 per cent of the world's population, or 3.6 billion people. The following year things had already become worse – and so too the year after that. And in early 2017, as the World Economic Forum met in Davos, Oxfam announced that the richest eight people had as much wealth as the poorest 3.6 billion.

It would be difficult to overstate how devastating these facts are to the success narrative that the development industry seeks to propagate. No story can survive very long when it runs so obviously against the grain of reality. Eventually something has to give.

The industry is scrambling to respond to this existential crisis. NGOs, watching their donor base recede, are working around the clock to turn the tide of defection. Many of them have hired expensive public relations agencies to help them combat negative perceptions and get people back on board with the old story. The stakes are high, for if the story of development collapses, so too will our certainties about the present order of the global economy. If people begin to accept that, despite many decades of development, poverty has been getting worse rather than better, and the divide between rich and poor countries is growing rather than closing, then it will become clear to all that there is something fundamentally wrong with our economic system – that it is failing the majority of humanity and urgently needs to be changed. The official success story has helped keep people on board with our existing system for a long time. If that story falls apart, so too will their consent.

Why Are Poor Countries Poor?

When I first started teaching at the University of Virginia in 2005, I would begin my classes each term by asking students to brainstorm answers to the question: Why are poor countries poor? Their responses were more or less the same each year. You can probably guess them. There were always a few who thought it had something to do with people being lazy, having too many children or holding 'backwards' cultural values. Others guessed that it had to do with corruption or bad governance or poor institutions; or perhaps with environmental problems like poor soils unsuited to productive farming and climates that incubate tropical diseases. And some believed that poor countries were poor because they just *were*. Poor countries are just naturally poor, they assumed, and no one is really to blame for it. After all, poverty is the normal first stage of development. Poor countries are like children; they just haven't grown up yet. They haven't *developed*.

It is a line of thinking that comes straight out of Truman's

17

speech. After all, the story that he spun into being calls us to see the countries of the world as a series of unconnected individuals, like runners on a track racing in their own separate lanes. Some runners are behind, others are ahead; some runners are fast, others are slow. Maybe it has to do with institutions or governance or climate – but regardless of the reason, the important thing is that they are each responsible for their own achievement. So if rich countries are rich, it's down to their own talent and hard work. If poor countries are poor, they have no one to blame but themselves. This approach encourages us to think with a kind of 'methodological nationalism' – to analyse the fate of each nation without ever looking beyond its borders.

It was a somewhat strange move on Truman's part. By casting the fates of poor countries and rich countries as separate and unconnected, his story ignored the obvious relationships between them. It airbrushed away the long and fraught history of entanglement between the West and the Rest, along with the political interests at stake. Truman wasn't ignorant of that history. He knew that the United States had been violently intervening in Latin American countries since the 19th century in order to secure access to the continent's raw materials. Indeed, the US military was invading and occupying states like Honduras and Cuba even as late as the 1920s and 1930s – during Truman's own career – at the behest of American banana and sugar companies.

And of course, European powers had been controlling vast regions of the South since as early as 1492. Indeed, Europe's Industrial Revolution was only possible because of the resources they extracted from their colonies. The gold and silver they siphoned out of the mountains of Latin America not only provided capital for industrial investment; it also allowed them to buy land-intensive goods from the East, which freed them to transfer their own labour power from agriculture to industry. Later, they came to rely on sugar and cotton – produced by enslaved Africans – that was shipped in from their colonies in the New World, grain from colonial India and natural resources from colonial Africa, all of which provided the energy and raw materials they needed to secure their industrial dominance. Europe's development couldn't have happened without colonial loot.

But it came with devastating consequences for the colonies. The plunder of Latin America left 70 million indigenous people dead in its wake. In India, 30 million died of famine under British rule. Average living standards in India and China, which had been on a par with Britain before the colonial period, collapsed. So too did their share of world GDP, falling from 65 per cent to 10 per cent, while Europe's share tripled. And mass poverty became an issue for the first time in history, as European capitalism – driven by the imperatives of growth and profit – prised people off their land and destroyed their capacity for self-sufficient subsistence. Development for some meant underdevelopment for others. But all of this was carefully erased from the story that Truman handed down.

*

Point Four was originally articulated for Western audiences – it explained global inequality in a way that absolved Western nations of any culpability. But during the 1950s and 1960s the governments of the United States, Britain and France realised that it could have power beyond their borders as well, and they began to wield it as a weapon in their foreign policy arsenal.

They were worried about the progressive ideas that were bubbling up across the global South in the aftermath of colonialism. The leaders of the new independent nations were rejecting Truman's story about global inequality. Drawing on insights from thinkers such as Karl Marx, Aimé Césaire and Mahatma Gandhi, they pointed out that underdevelopment in the global South was not a natural condition, but a consequence of the way Western powers had organised the world system over hundreds of years. They wanted to change the rules of the global economy to make it fairer for the world's majority. They wanted to stop foreign states and corporations from plundering their resources, to take control of their own abundant raw materials and to build their own industries without Western interference. In short, they wanted justice – and they saw this as a basic precondition for development.

As far as the Western powers were concerned, this was a dangerous movement that had to be stopped, for it threatened to disrupt their economic dominance. They needed a way to defuse the anger of the people. And they found it in the work of American economist Walt Whitman Rostow. Rostow – an academic who moonlighted as a foreign policy adviser to President Dwight Eisenhower – argued that underdevelopment was not a political problem, but a technical one. It had nothing at all to do with colonialism or Western intervention, but rather to do with internal problems. If poor countries wanted to develop, all they needed to do was accept Western aid and advice, implement free-market policies and follow the West's path to 'modernisation'. By telling a story of poverty that focused on domestic policies, Rostow's theory not only sought to pull people's attention away from the unfairness of the global economic system, it erased that system from view.

Rostow published his theory in 1960 in *The Stages of Economic Growth*. He advertised the book as a 'non-communist manifesto' and it quickly became popular at the highest levels of policy in the US government. During the 1960s and 1970s, the government peddled Rostow's theory across the global South as a containment strategy – a way of depoliticising the question of global inequality. It proved to be such a promising tool that President Kennedy hired Rostow into a senior role at the US State Department, and President Johnson later promoted him to national security advisor. Following Truman's lead, Rostow turned the development story into a public-relations exercise, although this time it was targeted not only at American ears, but also at the rest of the world.

However, Rostow's story failed to work as planned. Across the global South, newly independent countries were ignoring US advice and pursuing their own development agenda, building their economies with protectionist and redistributionist policies – trade tariffs, subsidies and social spending on healthcare and education. And it was working brilliantly. From the 1950s through the 1970s, incomes were growing, poverty rates were falling and the divide between rich and poor countries began to close for the first time in history. And we shouldn't be surprised; after all, global South countries were using the exact same policies that Western countries had used during their own periods of economic consolidation.

The United States, Britain, France and other Western powers were not pleased with these developments. The policies that global South governments were rolling out undermined the profits of Western corporations, their access to cheap labour and resources, and their geopolitical interests. In response, they intervened covertly to overthrow dozens of democratically elected leaders across the South, replacing them with dictators friendly to Western economic interests who were then propped up with aid. For anyone who was paying attention, these coups gave the lie to the story told by figures like Truman and Rostow, and proved the point that the leaders of the global South had been trying to get across all along. Indeed, Western-backed coups were being carried out even as early as the 1950s – including in Iran and Guatemala – while Rostow was busy writing his book. Close as he was to the Eisenhower administration, which perpetrated those first coups, Rostow knew full well what was going on. Indeed, he may have been involved in the US-backed coup against the leader of Brazil in the 1960s, which took place during his tenure in the State Department.

Yet despite these attacks the South was still rising and continuing to push for economic justice. In the halls of the United Nations, governments of the South argued for a fairer international order, and they were succeeding. Given the new rules of global democracy, the North seemed powerless to stop the rise of the South. But in the early 1980s that suddenly changed. The United States and Western Europe discovered they could use their power as creditors to dictate economic policy to indebted countries in the South, effectively governing them by remote control, without the need for bloody interventions. Leveraging debt, they imposed 'structural adjustment programmes' that reversed all the economic reforms that global South countries had painstakingly enacted. In the process, they went so far as to ban the very policies that they had used for their own development, effectively kicking away the ladder to success.

Structural adjustment – a form of free-market shock therapy – was sold as a necessary precondition for successful development in the global South. But it ended up doing exactly the opposite. Economies shrank, incomes collapsed, millions of people were dispossessed and poverty rates shot through the roof. Global South countries lost an average of $480 billion per year in potential GDP during the structural adjustment period. It is now widely acknowledged by scholars that structural adjustment was one of the greatest single causes of poverty in the global South, after colonialism. But it proved to be enormously beneficial to the economies of the North.

As structural adjustment forced open markets around the world, a new system emerged in the mid-1990s to govern the international economy. Under this new system – run by the World Trade Organization – power would be determined by market size, so the rich countries of the North would be able to enshrine policies to suit their own interests even if it meant actively harming the interests of the South. For instance, global South countries would have to abolish their agricultural subsidies, but the United States and the European Union would be allowed to continue paying subsidies to their own farmers, enabling them to undercut the market share of global South producers in the one sector in which they are supposed to have a natural competitive advantage. Today, power imbalances like these, enshrined in the Uruguay Round of the WTO, are estimated to cost poor countries at least $700 billion each year in lost export revenues.

*

If we bring history back into the analysis, the story of global inequality begins to take on a far more complex and even sinister hue. The whole idea that rich countries are the saviours of poor countries begins to seem more than a bit naive. The problem is not that poor countries are having difficulty hoisting themselves up the development ladder; the problem is that they are being actively prevented from doing so. The development industry likes to refer to poor countries by the passive adjective 'underdeveloped'. But perhaps it would be more accurate to make the term a transitive verb, 'under-developed': to have had one's development intentionally obstructed, undone or reversed by an external power. After all, as we will see, poverty doesn't just exist. It is *created*.

Aid in Reverse

When I teach this history in the classroom, I find that it quite often makes some students feel uncomfortable. Yes, they reply, terrible things happened in the past, but we live in a fairer, more compassionate world. And for evidence they invariably invoke the aid budget, pointing out that rich countries give poor countries about $128 billion in aid each year.

It is a powerful idea. Together with grand claims about global poverty reduction and the assumption of methodological nationalism, the growing size of the aid budget sits right at the centre of the official development story. The idea of aid has been with us since at least Truman, but its continuing power in our world today is largely down to the efforts of one man: the American economist Jeffrey Sachs, former director of the Millennium Development Goals and special adviser to UN Secretary General Ban Ki-moon. Sachs, affable and good-looking – a refreshing departure from the stereotypical technocrat – has become the aid evangelist of our age and a kind of rock star in the process, bagging two appearances on *Time*'s list of the world's 100 most influential people. His bestselling 2005 book, *The End of Poverty*, made a simple and compelling argument. Nobody is to blame for the continuing poverty of poor countries, he said. It's just down to natural accidents of geography and climate and these can easily be overcome. If rich countries would just increase their foreign aid contributions to 0.7 per cent of GDP, we would be able to eradicate global poverty in only twenty years. All poor countries need is enough to pay for essential agricultural technologies, basic healthcare, clean water, primary education and electricity, and they'll be on their way up the ladder of development.

What matters here is not the content of the proposal (with which few would disagree), but the story that it implies. Not only are rich countries not responsible for causing underdevelopment in poor countries, as Rostow once insisted; they are in fact reaching out across the divide with loving concern. Sachs' ideas gave life to the aid narrative for a new generation and were celebrated by the governments of most of the world's rich countries; indeed, many increased their foreign aid disbursements accordingly. The aid narrative was useful because it overrode any suggestion that Western powers were in any way responsible for causing the suffering of the South. The US and Britain had just invaded Iraq, at least in part in order to secure access to the region's vast oil reserves, and the Bush administration had just helped topple the progressive government of Jean-Bertrand Aristide in Haiti and tacitly supported a coup attempt against Venezuela's Hugo Chávez, continuing the long history of aggressive intervention that Eisenhower had set in motion in the 1950s. But the flow of aid would stand nonetheless as irrefutable proof of Western benevolence. It was a matter of perception management.

If we look more closely, however, even this dimension of the development story crumbles into incoherence. It's not that the $128 billion in aid disbursements doesn't exist – it does. But if we broaden our view and look at it in context, we see that it is vastly outstripped by the financial resources that flow in the opposite direction. By comparison, the aid budget turns out to be a mere trickle.

At the end of 2016, the US-based Global Financial Integrity (GFI) and the Centre for Applied Research at the Norwegian School of Economics published some truly paradigm-shifting data. They tallied up all of the financial resources that get transferred between rich and poor countries each year: not just aid, foreign investment and trade flows, as previous studies have done, but also other transfers like debt cancellation and remittances and capital flight. It is the most comprehensive assessment of resource transfers that has ever been made. They found that in 2012, the last year of recorded data, developing countries received a little over $2 trillion, including all aid, investment and income from abroad. But more than twice that amount, some $5 trillion, flowed out of them in the same year. In other words, developing countries 'sent' $3 trillion more to the rest of the world than they received. If we look at all years since 1980, these net outflows add up to an eye-popping total of $26.5 trillion – that's how much money has been drained out of the global South over the past few decades. To get a sense of the scale of this, $26.5 trillion is roughly the GDP of the United States and Western Europe combined.

What do these large outflows consist of? Well, some of it is payments on debt. Today, poor countries pay over $200 billion each year in interest alone to foreign creditors, much of it on old loans that have already been paid off many times over, and some of it on loans accumulated by greedy dictators. Since 1980, developing countries have forked over $4.2 trillion in interest payments – much more than they have received in aid during the same period. And most of these payments have gone to Western creditors – a direct cash transfer to big banks in New York and London.

Another big contributor is the income that foreigners make on their investments in developing countries and then repatriate. Think of all the profits that Shell extracts from Nigeria's oil reserves, for example, or that Anglo American pulls out of South Africa's gold mines. Foreign investors take nearly $500 billion in profits out of developing countries each year, most of which goes back to rich countries. Then there are the profits that ordinary Europeans and Americans earn on their investments in stocks and bonds they hold in the global South, through their pension funds, for example. And there are many smaller outflows as well, such as the extra $60 billion per year that developing countries have to pay to foreign patent owners under the WTO's agreement on intellectual property rights

(TRIPS) in order to access technologies and pharmaceuticals that are often essential to development and public health.

But by far the biggest chunk of outflows has to do with capital flight. GFI calculates that developing countries have lost a total of $23.6 trillion through capital flight since 1980. A big proportion of this takes place through 'leakages' in the balance of payments between countries, through which developing countries lose around $973 billion each year. Another takes place through an illegal practice known as 'trade misinvoicing'. Basically, corporations – foreign and domestic alike – report false prices on their trade invoices in order to spirit money out of developing countries directly into tax havens and secrecy jurisdictions. Developing countries lose $875 billion through trade misinvoicing each year. A similarly large amount flows out annually through 'abusive transfer pricing', a mechanism that multinational companies use to steal money from developing countries by shifting profits illegally between their own subsidiaries in different countries. Usually the goal of these practices is to evade taxes, but sometimes they are used to launder money or circumvent capital controls.

Three trillion dollars in total *net* outflows per year is twenty-four times more than the annual aid budget. In other words, for every dollar of aid that developing countries receive, they lose $24 in net outflows. Of course, this is an aggregate figure; for some countries the ratio is larger, while for others it is smaller. But in all cases net outflows strip developing countries of an important source of revenue and finance that could be used for development. The GFI report finds that increasingly large net outflows (since 2009 they have been growing at a rate of 20 per cent per year) have caused economic growth rates in developing countries to decline, and are directly responsible for falling living standards.

*

What this means is that poor countries are net creditors to rich countries – exactly the opposite of what we would usually assume.

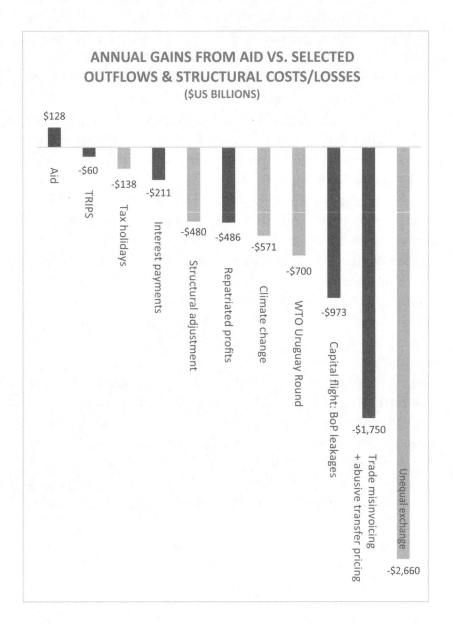

ANNUAL GAINS FROM AID VS. SELECTED OUTFLOWS & STRUCTURAL COSTS/LOSSES
($US BILLIONS)

$128 — Aid

-$60 — TRIPS

-$138 — Tax holidays

-$211 — Interest payments

-$480 — Structural adjustment

-$486 — Repatriated profits

-$571 — Climate change

-$700 — WTO Uruguay Round

-$973 — Capital flight: BoP leakages

-$1,750 — Trade misinvoicing + abusive transfer pricing

-$2,660 — Unequal exchange

Comparing aid to various outflows (dark grey) and structural costs/losses (light grey).

But when we consider the aid budget in its broader context, we should look not only at outward flows but also at the losses and costs that developing countries have suffered as a result of policies devised by rich countries. For instance, when structural adjustment was imposed on the global South during the 1980s and 1990s, they lost around $480 billion each year in potential GDP. That's nearly four times the size of today's annual aid budget. More recently, imbalances in the World Trade Organization have caused losses of $700 billion per year in potential export revenues, outstripping the aid budget by a factor of six.

But perhaps the most significant loss has to do with exploitation through trade. From the onset of colonialism through to globalisation, the main objective of the North has been to force down the cost of labour and goods bought from the South. In the past, colonial powers were able to dictate terms directly to their colonies. Today, while trade is technically 'free', rich countries are able to get their way because they have much greater bargaining power. On top of this, trade agreements often prevent poor countries from protecting their workers in ways that rich countries do. And because multinational corporations now have the ability to scour the planet in search of the cheapest labour and goods, poor countries are forced to compete to drive costs down. As a result of all this, there is a yawning gap between the 'real value' of the labour and goods that poor countries sell and the prices they are actually paid for them. This is what economists call 'unequal exchange'. In the mid-1990s, at the height of the structural adjustment era, the South was losing as much as $2.66 trillion in unequal exchange each year (in 2015 dollars) – a hidden transfer of value that amounts to twenty-one times the size of today's aid budget and dwarfs the flow of foreign direct investment.

There are many other structural losses and costs that we could take into account. For example, ActionAid reports that multinational corporations extract about $138 billion from developing countries each year in the form of tax holidays. This figure alone outstrips the global aid budget. Remittances sent home by immigrant workers are slashed by exorbitant transaction fees, cost-ing families $33 billion each year. Global South economies lose about $27 billion in GDP each year because aid disbursements are so volatile, making it very difficult for them to plan investment and manage their budgets. Then there are forms of extraction that are more difficult to quantify, such as the 162 million acres of land (more than five times the size of England) that has been grabbed in global South countries since 2000. And then, of course, there are the damages that developing countries suffer due to climate change – caused almost entirely by rich countries – which are cur-rently estimated to cost $571 billion per year.

The point here is simple: the aid budget is diminutive, almost ridiculously so, when compared to the structural losses and out-ward flows that the global South suffers. Yes, some aid goes a long way towards making people's lives better, but it doesn't come close to compensating for the damage that the givers of aid themselves inflict. Indeed, some of this damage is caused by the very groups that run the aid agenda: the World Bank, for example, which prof-its from global South debt; the Gates Foundation, which profits from an intellectual-property regime that locks life-saving medi-cines and essential technologies behind outlandish patent pay-walls; and Bono, who profits from the tax haven system that siphons revenues out of global South countries.

This is not an argument against aid as such. Rather, it is to say that the discourse of aid distracts us from seeing the broader pic-ture. It hides the patterns of extraction that are actively causing the impoverishment of the global South today and actively impeding meaningful development. The charity paradigm obscures the real issues at stake: it makes it seem as though the West is 'developing' the global South, when in reality the opposite is true. Rich coun-tries aren't developing poor countries; poor countries are effec-tively developing rich countries – and they have been since the late 15th century. So it's not only that the aid narrative misunderstands what really causes poverty, it's that it actually gets it *backwards*. Just as in Truman's time, aid serves as a kind of propaganda that makes the takers seem like givers, and conceals how the global economy actually works.

Perhaps Frantz Fanon, the famous philosopher from Martinique and leading thinker of Algeria's anti-colonial struggle, put it best:

> Colonialism and imperialism have not settled their debt to us once they have withdrawn from our territories. The wealth of the imperialist nations is also our wealth. Europe is literally the creation of the Third World. The riches which are choking it are those plundered from the underdeveloped peoples. So we will not accept aid for the underdeveloped countries as 'charity'. Such aid must be considered the final stage of a dual consciousness – the consciousness of the colonised that it is their due, and the consciousness of the capitalist powers that effectively they must pay up.

Frantz Fanon recognised that poverty in the global South is not a natural condition any more than is the wealth of the West. Poverty is, at base, the inevitable outcome of ongoing processes of plunder – processes that benefit a relatively small group of people at the expense of the vast majority of humanity. It is delusional to believe that aid is a commensurate, let alone honest and meaningful, solution to this kind of problem. The aid paradigm allows rich countries and individuals to pretend to fix with one hand what they destroy with the other, dispensing small bandages at the same time as they inflict deep injuries, and claiming the moral high ground for doing so.

*

A few years ago I had the opportunity to visit the West Bank in Palestine. On one particularly hot afternoon, my hosts drove me down into the Jordan Valley to interview some farmers there about water issues. Along the way, bumping along a gravel track, we came across a huge white sign jutting out of the desert rocks. The sign announced a USAID initiative 'to help alleviate recurring water shortages' by adding a new well in the area. It was branded with the American flag and bore the proud words: 'This project is a gift from the American People to the Palestinian People.'

A casual observer might be impressed: American taxpayer money offered generously, in the spirit of humanitarianism, to assist impoverished Palestinians struggling to survive in the desert. But Palestine doesn't have a shortage of water. When Israel invaded and occupied the West Bank in 1967, with the backing of the US military, it asserted total control over the aquifers beneath the territory. Israel draws the majority of this water – close to 90 per cent – for its own use in settlements and for irrigation on large industrial farms. And as the water table drops, Palestinian wells are running dry. Palestinians are not allowed to deepen their wells or sink new ones without Israeli permission – and permission is almost never granted. If they build without permission, as many do, Israeli bulldozers arrive the next day. So Palestinians are forced to buy their own water back from Israel at arbitrarily high prices.

This is not a secret. It is happening out in the open, and the farmers I spoke to know it all too well. For them, the USAID sign only adds insult to injury. It's not that they lack water, as USAID implies; it's that the water has been stolen from them. And it has been stolen with US support. In 2012, just two months before my visit, the United Nations General Assembly adopted resolution 66/225, calling for the restoration of Palestinians' rights to their own water. One hundred and sixty-seven nations voted in favour of the resolution. The United States and Israel voted against it.

I tell this anecdote not just as an example of how aid often misses the point, but to illustrate a much larger truth. Poor countries don't need our aid; they need us to stop impoverishing them. Until we target the structural drivers of global poverty – the underlying architecture of wealth extraction and accumulation – development efforts will continue to fail, decade after decade. We will continue to watch the poverty numbers rise, and the divide between rich and poor countries will continue to grow. This is a difficult truth to swallow for the millions of well-meaning people who have been sold on the development story. It can be scary to grapple with the collapse of a core myth. At least it was for me. But it also opens up a world of exciting new possibilities, and clears the way to a different kind of future.

Two

The End of Poverty . . . Has Been Postponed

Everything faded into mist. The past was erased, the erasure
was forgotten, the lie became truth.

George Orwell, *1984*

On a cool September day in 2000, the world's heads of state
gathered at the United Nations headquarters in New York to sign
one of the most important international agreements in modern
history: the Millennium Declaration. It was a monumental occa-
sion. For the first time, world leaders had committed themselves to
a full range of development aspirations. And the main objective –
the one that captured the world's attention – was a pledge to cut
global poverty and hunger in half by 2015.

After the meeting in New York, UN staff buckled down to the
work of formulating the aspirations of the Millennium Declaration
into a series of eight concrete, measurable targets called the Millennium Development Goals. Goal 1 was to cut poverty and hunger in
half, but there were a number of others: to achieve universal primary education, to eliminate gender disparity in education, to

reduce child mortality by two-thirds, to reduce maternal mortality by three-quarters, and to reverse the spread of AIDS and malaria. Poor countries themselves would be responsible for meeting these targets (the assumption being that poverty had to do with domestic policies) with the help of aid and other forms of assistance from rich countries.

After the launch of the MDGs, a well-funded PR campaign kept the programme prominent in the public imagination and high on the global policy agenda. It quickly became the biggest coordinated international effort of the 21st century. Each year the UN published a report updating the world on progress towards the goals. And only twelve years in, with their deadline still three years away, they claimed success on Goal 1. They announced that poverty rates had already been cut in half, and that the goal of halving hunger was close to being achieved.

The announcement came as a shock to many. At the time, the world was still mired in the worst economic crisis in nearly a century. As Western economies had contracted, export industries in the global South dried up and employment fell. To make matters worse, the poorest had been hit by unprecedented spikes in the price of food. If anything, analysts were expecting there to be *more* poverty and hunger. Nevertheless the media seized the story and ran with it. Soon after the UN's report, *The Economist* ran a widely shared article with the headline: 'A Fall to Cheer: for the first time ever, the number of poor people is declining everywhere'. That same year, Charles Kenny published *Getting Better: Why Global Development Is Succeeding*, with a glowing foreword by Bill Gates. Gates himself published a public letter in 2014, opening with the words: 'By almost any measure, the world is better than it has ever been.' And the Swedish academic Hans Rosling continued to make his earnest presentations with shiny visual gimmicks illustrating how the plight of the poor keeps improving. Rosling's TED Talk, 'The Best Stats You've Ever Seen', has been viewed more than 10 million times. The UN's poverty-reduction figures quickly became some of the most repeated statistics in the world.

This is what I call the 'good-news narrative' about poverty. It is a comforting story, a welcome contrast to the depressing tales that often fill the daily news cycle. After all, it feels good to take a step back and realise that things are not as bad as they seem – that in the broad scheme of things, the world is gradually getting better. It is a story that vindicates our civilisation and affirms our deepest and most powerful ideas about Progress.

It also serves as a potent political tool. The good-news narrative enjoins us to believe that the global economic system is on the right track. It implies that if we want to eradicate suffering, we should stick with the status quo and refrain from making drastic changes. For anyone who has an interest in maintaining the present order of distribution – the global 1 per cent, for instance – the good-news narrative is a useful story indeed. Sometimes this argument is quite explicit. In early 2015, the *Spectator* published a blog post with the title: 'What Oxfam doesn't want you to know: global capitalism means less poverty than ever'. It led with the MDG statistics on the reduction of extreme poverty, followed by a graph showing the declining proportion of undernourished people in developing regions. The author argued that all the attention we've been focusing on social inequality and wealth accumulation among the richest 1 per cent is misplaced. The 1 per cent may now have more wealth than the combined population of the entire rest of the world, but that's OK because the very system that has made them so rich has also reduced poverty in developing countries. 'We are, right now, living through the golden age of poverty reduction,' the author wrote. 'Anyone serious about tackling global poverty has to accept that whatever we're doing now, it's working – so we should keep doing it. We are on the road to an incredible goal: the abolition of poverty as we know it, within our lifetime. Those who care more about helping the poor than hurting the rich will celebrate the fact – and urge leaders to make sure that free trade and global capitalism keep spreading. It's the only true way to make poverty history.'

Of course, even if we take the good-news narrative at face

value, it tells us nothing about whether these gains are the direct result of the rapid extension of free-market capitalism across the globe, as the *Spectator* article asserts. Indeed, it is possible that they have happened in spite of it. But what is clear here is that when it comes to the question of global poverty, the political stakes are high. If poverty is falling faster than ever, that would be a strong argument in favour of our existing economic system. If poverty is falling a little bit, but not as quickly as it was before, then maybe our system isn't quite as good as it could be. And if poverty is not falling at all but rather rising, that would be a good reason to change the system altogether. With these kinds of questions on the table, it is crucial that we have the facts straight.

Some of the claims made by the MDGs are strong and deserve to be celebrated. The number of deaths among children under five declined from 12.7 million in 1990 to 6 million in 2015. That means there were 18,000 fewer children dying each day. This is a remarkable improvement. The same is true of maternal mortality, which declined by an impressive 45 per cent during the MDGs. Primary school enrolment is up. And HIV and malaria infection rates have declined markedly. While the UN technically fell short of reaching its targets on these fronts, the numbers are nonetheless evidence of substantial progress.

But the headline assertion of the good-news narrative, the claim that poverty and hunger have been cut in half, rests on much shakier ground. If we look more closely, the real story about global poverty is not quite as rosy as we have been led to believe. In fact, it is nearly the opposite of the official narrative. How did this happen? What is going on? And what might a more accurate story of global poverty and hunger look like?

The Great Poverty Disappearing Act

To understand what's wrong with the story of poverty reduction, we have to start at the beginning. The first multilateral agreement to reduce global poverty was signed in 1996, when the world's heads of state met at the World Food Summit in the beautiful city of Rome. The commitment back then was a bold one: 'We pledge our political will and our common and national commitment to achieving food security for all and to an ongoing effort to eradicate hunger in all countries, with an immediate view to reducing the number of undernourished people to half their present level no later than 2015.' It is crucial to note that the goal was to halve the *absolute* number of undernourished people. The Rome Declaration focused specifically on hunger rather than income as the key dimension of poverty, but it set an important precedent for the *type* of target – in terms of parameters and ambition – that the world would pursue.

Four years later, when the world's leaders gathered to sign the Millennium Declaration in New York, they set out an explicit goal on income poverty – the first of its kind. There was enormous fanfare surrounding this new pledge, but those who were watching closely found little to celebrate, for the goalposts were subtly shifted from the ones laid out in Rome. The new commitment was to halve 'the *proportion* of the world's people whose income is less than one dollar a day and the *proportion* of people who suffer from hunger' from the baseline year of 2000. By switching from absolute numbers to proportions, the target became easier to achieve, simply because it could take advantage of population growth. As long as poverty was not getting much worse in absolute terms, it would automatically appear to be getting better in proportional terms. At the time, there were 1,673 million people in poverty. To cut the *number* of poor in half would mean reducing the poverty headcount by 836 million people. But to cut the *proportion* meant reducing it by only 669 million people – a significantly easier goal to achieve. It was a masterful piece of statistical theatre, and almost nobody noticed.

That was just the beginning. Shortly after the Millennium Declaration was adopted, the UN rendered it into the Millennium

Development Goals that we know so well today. During this process, the poverty goal (MDG-1) was diluted yet again – this time behind closed doors, without any media commentary at all. First, they changed it from halving the proportion of impoverished people in the whole *world* to halving the proportion in *developing countries only.* Because the population of the developing world is growing at a faster rate than the world as a whole, this shift in the methodology allowed the poverty accountants to take advantage of an even faster-growing denominator. On top of this, there was a second significant change: they moved the starting point of analysis from 2000 back to 1990. This gave them much more time to accomplish the goal, extended the period of denominator growth *and* allowed them to retroactively claim gains in poverty reduction that were achieved long before the campaign actually began. This backdating took particular advantage of gains made by China during the 1990s, when hundreds of millions of people were lifted out of extreme poverty, and deceptively chalked them up as a victory for the Millennium Development Goals.

This new round of statistical theatre shrank the target by even more than the first round. The goal of the Millennium Declaration was to cut the number of poor by 669 million people. But MDG-1 pledged to cut the number of poor by only 490 million. There's another way to think about this change. The world's governments initially decreed that there should be no more than 1,004 million people living in poverty in 2015; that was to be the absolute cap, and anything more than that was deemed to be morally unacceptable. But they later decided to adjust the cap *upward* to 1,327 million, essentially declaring it would be acceptable for 323 million *additional* people to suffer from extreme poverty in 2015. This also meant that they permitted themselves to be much less aggressive in the fight against poverty: while the initial goal required an annual rate of poverty reduction of 3.35 per cent, the final goal allowed for a much more leisurely rate of only 1.25 per cent. In comparison, the new goal would need hardly any effort to achieve.

There is something highly questionable about the ethics behind MDG-1, given that it rests on such a flexible understanding of moral acceptability. But for those who are committed to promoting the good-news narrative, it has been remarkably useful. By redefining the goal, the Millennium Campaign is now able to claim that poverty has been halved when in fact it has not.

TABLE 1   Diluting the poverty goal.

	Baseline year	Baseline poverty count (millions)	Promised reduction by 2015 (millions)	Proportion reduction by 2015 (%)	Annual rate of reduction (%)
Millennium Declaration	2000	1673	669	40	3.35
MDG-1	1990	1817.5	490	27	1.25

Source: Adapted from Pogge, 'How World Poverty is Measured'.

The good-news narrative about poverty reduction only works because the goalposts have been shifted. But that's not the only sleight of hand to be concerned about.

*

What counts as poverty – the 'poverty line' – is normally calculated by each nation and is supposed to reflect the total cost of all of the essential resources that an average adult needs to subsist. For most of recent history, it has been understood that poverty lines are not really comparable across contexts: what counts as poverty in Somalia is not the same as what counts as poverty in Chile. Nonetheless, there was a big push to try to find some kind of common denominator that would make it possible to measure the poverty rate across the world with a single methodology. Martin Ravallion, an Australian economist at the World Bank, was the first to make this a reality. In 1990 he noticed that the poverty lines of a few of the world's poorest countries clustered around $1.02 per day. It seemed reasonable, he thought, to assume that this would be a good low-end threshold for measuring absolute poverty. On Ravallion's recommendation, the World Bank adopted the dollar-a-day line as the first-ever international poverty line (IPL).

But the IPL proved to be somewhat troublesome. Using this line, the World Bank was forced to announce in its 2000 annual report that poverty was *rising*. 'The absolute number of those living on $1 per day or less *continues to increase*,' the report read. 'The worldwide total rose from 1.2 billion in 1987 to 1.5 billion today and, if recent trends persist, will reach 1.9 billion by 2015.' This was alarming news, and projected a troubling future trend. Not only that, it also suggested that the structural adjustment programmes imposed by the World Bank and the IMF on global South countries during the 1980s and 1990s in the name of 'development' were actually making things worse. This posed serious problems for the World Bank. If poverty reduction was going to be the method by which we measured global economic progress, then it was clear that structural adjustment would have to be scrapped, and the World Bank would have to acknowledge a very costly mistake. This would mean halting the process of forced market liberalisation and privatisation around the world, which was bad news for the multinational corporations – and the global South elite – who benefited so much from it. It was a dramatic moment that looked set to consign the World Bank's radical free-market policies to the dustbin of history.

But not long after the report was released, the World Bank's story changed. In 2001, the Bank's president, James Wolfensohn, delivered a speech in which he stated that the forced imposition of free-market policies had actually *reduced* poverty in the developing world: 'Over the past few years,' he announced, 'better policies have contributed to more rapid growth in developing countries' per capita incomes than at any point since the mid-1970s. And faster growth has meant poverty reduction: the proportion of people worldwide living in absolute poverty has dropped steadily in recent decades, from 29 per cent in 1990 to a record low of 23 per cent in 1998. After increasing steadily over the past two centuries, since 1980 the total number of people living in poverty worldwide has fallen by an estimated 200 million.'

What was curious about Wolfensohn's speech was that he acknowledged that per capita incomes had been growing faster up until the mid-1970s, technically admitting that the World Bank's structural adjustment programmes had slowed progress during the 1980s and 1990s. But at the same time he claimed that poverty had nonetheless been reduced during those decades – and that's the part of the story that captured everyone's attention. The media went along with it, pivoting from questioning the Bank's policies to celebrating its success against poverty. That was in 2001. Then, three years later, the Bank published its new official figures, which stated that poverty reduction was even more successful than Wolhfensohn had suggested – twice as successful, in fact: a grand total of 400 million people were rescued from extreme poverty between 1981 and 2001. The story just kept getting better.

How did the World Bank's poverty numbers change so suddenly from a rising trend to a falling one? To put it simply, they changed the international poverty line. In 2000, they shifted it from the original $1.02 level to $1.08. While the new poverty line looks slightly higher than the old one, in reality it was just 'rebased' to new purchasing power parity (PPP) calculations, which are updated every few years to compensate for depreciation in the purchasing power of the dollar. If the purchasing power of the dollar goes down, people need more dollars to buy the same stuff as before. So the poverty line needs to be periodically 'raised' to account for this. But in this case they didn't raise it quite enough to account for purchasing power depreciation. So the new $1.08 poverty line was actually *lower* in real terms than the old $1.02 line. And lowering the poverty line made it appear as though fewer people were poor than before. When the new line was introduced, the poverty headcount fell literally overnight, even though nothing had actually changed in the real world.

This new poverty line was introduced in the very same year

that the Millennium Campaign went live, and it became the campaign's official instrument for measuring absolute poverty. With this tiny alteration, a mere flick of an economist's wrist, the world suddenly appeared to be getting better.

The IPL was changed a second time in 2008, to $1.25. The World Bank's economists claimed that this new line was roughly equivalent to the earlier one, in real terms, but watchdogs like Yale professor Thomas Pogge and economist Sanjay Reddy at the New School in New York pointed out that the data was simply not comparable. Once again, the number of absolute poor changed overnight, although this time it went up – by 430 million people. At first glance this seems like it must have been shockingly bad news – a decisive blow to the good-news narrative. But there was a bright side, as far as the World Bank was concerned: the poverty reduction *trend* started to look significantly better, at least since the baseline year of 1990. While the $1.08 line made it seem as though the poverty headcount had been reduced by 316 million people between 1990 and 2005, the new line inflated the number to 437 million, creating the illusion that an additional 121 million souls had been saved from the jaws of poverty. Once again, the Millennium Campaign adopted the new poverty line, which allowed it to claim yet further gains.

*

There is yet another sleight of hand at the centre of the poverty story that is often overlooked. Remember that the Millennium Development Campaign moved the baseline year back to 1990, which allowed them to claim China's gains against poverty. What happens if we take China out of the equation? Well, we find that the global poverty headcount *increased* during the 1980s and 1990s, while the World Bank was imposing structural adjustment across most of the global South. Today, the extreme poverty headcount is exactly the same as it was in 1981, at just over 1 billion people. In other words, while the good-news story leads us to believe that poverty has been decreasing around the world, in reality the only places this holds true are in China and East Asia. This is a crucial point, because these are some of the only places in the world where free-market capitalism was *not* forcibly imposed by the World Bank and the IMF. Everywhere else, poverty has been stagnant or getting worse, in aggregate. And this remains evident despite the World Bank's attempts to doctor the figures.

What Happened to Hunger?

The good-news narrative of the MDGs seeks to direct all our attention to the question of poverty. But what about hunger – the other big goal of the Millennium Declaration? For a long time we didn't hear much about the hunger issue, probably because the world's governments were clearly failing to achieve this goal – the number of hungry people in the world had been steadily *rising* during the MDG period. When heads of state first pledged in 1996 to cut hunger in half before 2015, there were 788 million hungry people in the world. In 2009, there were 1,023 million, or about 30 per cent more. This trend has long been a thorn in the side of the powers that be. After all, one of the best ways to test the success of an economic system is to assess progress against hunger. If the hunger numbers are static – or, worse, on the rise – it is difficult to argue that something isn't fundamentally wrong.

Of course, when the Millennium Campaign pushed the base year back to 1990, the hunger trend appeared to get a little better. And diluting the goal to focus on proportions instead of absolute numbers helped a little bit too. But even with these changes, in 2009 the hunger headcount was still 21 per cent worse than it was in 1990. The UN was forced to concede defeat, publishing a report admitting that the hunger goal was going to be impossible to achieve: instead of decreasing, 'hunger has been on the rise for the past decade'.

It seemed a disaster. But then, out of the blue, in 2012 the UN agency responsible for calculating the hunger numbers, the Food and Agriculture Organization (FAO), suddenly began telling the exact opposite story. With only three years to go before the expiry of the MDGs, the FAO announced an 'improved' methodology for counting hunger. And the revised numbers delivered a rosy tale at last: while 23 per cent of people in the developing world were undernourished in 1990, the UN was pleased to announce a reduction to 15 per cent. The goal still hadn't been accomplished, of course, and in terms of absolute numbers there wasn't much to write home about: over twenty-five years they had managed to cut hunger from 1 billion people to 800 million. And almost all of this reduction had happened in Asia; in Africa, the number of undernourished people had increased. But at least now the UN could at last claim some progress on a global level. The 2013 report of the MDGs announced: 'Progress in reducing hunger has been more pronounced than previously believed, and the target of halving the percentage of people suffering from hunger by 2015 is within reach.'

How did they pull this off? How did they turn a story of crisis into a story of progress? It all had to do with the new methodology. The new model was designed not to reflect the impact of economic crises, so the numbers did not show the massive spike in hunger that followed the food-price crisis of 2007 and the financial collapse of 2008. In addition, the FAO revised their estimates of countries' food supplies, and 'relaxed' their assumptions about people's access to calories. They also adjusted the hunger threshold downwards, and in such a way that the trend appeared to improve more rapidly than under previous measurements. All of this made the hunger story look much better than it had before. Media outlets ran the new story without scrutinising the methodological changes.

Methodological twists aside, the other major problem with the UN's hunger numbers has to do with the definition of hunger itself. The UN counts people as hungry only when their calorie intake becomes 'inadequate to cover even minimum needs for a sedentary lifestyle' (i.e. less than about 1,600 to 1,800 calories per day) for 'over a year'. The problem is that most poor people don't live sedentary lifestyles; in fact, they are usually engaged in demanding physical labour, so in reality they need much more than the UN's calorie threshold. The average rickshaw driver in India, for example, burns through about 3,000–4,000 calories per day. The FAO itself recognises this flaw. Its 2012 report admits that 'many poor and hungry people are likely to have livelihoods involved in arduous manual labor'. It calls its core definition of hunger 'narrow', 'very conservative', focused on only 'extreme caloric deprivation' and thus 'clearly insufficient' to inform policy. It acknowledges that most poor people actually require calories sufficient for 'normal' or even 'intense' activity.

So what happens if we measure hunger at these more accurate levels? We see that between 1.5 billion and 2.5 billion people are hungry, according to the FAO's own data. This is two to three

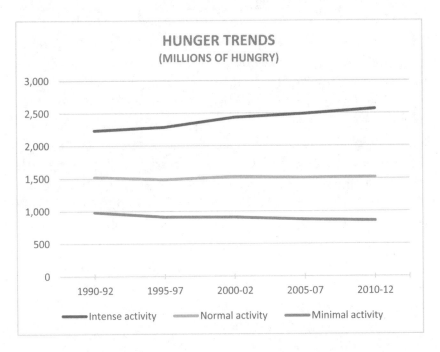

Source: Food and Agricultural Organisation, *State of Food Insecurity 2012*.

times higher than the Millennium Campaign would have us believe. And the numbers are rising, even according to the FAO's questionable new methodology.

But even these estimates aren't quite good enough. Another problem with the FAO's definition is that it only counts calories. So people who have serious deficiencies of basic vitamins and nutrients (a condition that affects some 2.1 billion people worldwide) are not counted as undernourished as long as they can get enough calories to keep their hearts pumping. People who suffer from parasites, which inhibit food absorption rates, also fall through the cracks, since what counts is calorie intake, not actual nutrition. And people who are hungry for months at a time are not counted as hungry, since the definition of hunger only captures hunger that lasts for over a year. The FAO writes: 'The reference period should be long enough for the consequences of low food intake to be detrimental to health. Although there is no doubt that temporary food shortage may be stressful, the FAO indicator is based on a full year.' In other words, the FAO's definition presupposes, without invoking any supporting evidence, that eleven months of hunger is not detrimental to human health.

In light of all this, it is safe to say that the narrative of the Millennium Development Goals dramatically underestimates the scale of global hunger. Again, the idea here seems to be to simply keep people alive, just to satisfy the metrics, while caring little about the kinds of lives they are able to live. And this tragedy persists in the face of what has surely become one of the most repeated facts of our time: that we collectively produce enough food each year to feed everyone in the entire world, at 3,000 calories per day. Hunger is not a problem of lack. It is a problem of distribution. A disproportionate amount of the world's food ends up flowing to rich countries, where much of it ends up as waste. In the US and Europe, consumers bin up to half the food they purchase. The UN finds that cutting global food waste by only a quarter and redirecting it to where it is needed most would solve global hunger in a single stroke.

Thomas Pogge likes to point out that the real metric of poverty reduction actually has nothing to do with proportions, and nothing to do with absolute numbers either. 'The morally relevant comparison of existing poverty,' he says, 'is not with historical benchmarks but with present possibilities: How much of this poverty is really unavoidable today? By this standard, our generation is doing worse than any in human history.'

A More Honest View of Poverty

Let's go back to the claim made by the Millennium Development Goals, that 1 billion people live in absolute poverty today. That's a staggering number no matter how you look at it, and a trenchant indictment of our global economic system. But a growing number of scholars are beginning to insist that the picture is actually even worse than this. They are beginning to question whether the dollar-a-day threshold is the right poverty line to be using in the first place. The international poverty line used by the MDGs – $1.25 per day – is based on the national poverty lines of the fifteen poorest countries. Why should we trust the poverty lines of a few extremely poor countries? Why should we believe that these lines are an accurate reflection of what poverty is really like in those countries? What if the bureaucrats who set the national poverty lines don't have access to adequate data? What if the numbers are manipulated for the sake of political image?

Even if we do choose to accept the accuracy of these national lines, using them to calculate the IPL means setting it at rock bottom. And this level tells us very little about what poverty is like in even slightly better-off countries. Take Sri Lanka, for example. In 1990, government authorities conducted a survey that found that 40 per cent of the population fell under the national poverty line. But the World Bank, using the IPL, reported only 4 per cent in the same year. In Mexico in 2010, the government reported a poverty rate of 46 per cent using the standard national line, while the World Bank reported only 5 per cent using the IPL. In other words, in many

47

cases the IPL makes poverty seem much less serious than it really is. India offers another example. Using the IPL, the World Bank estimated that India had 300 million people living in poverty in 2011, and claimed that the proportion of impoverished people had been decreasing steadily over time. But empirical research in India at around the same time showed that 680 million people 'lack the means to meet their essential needs'. Indeed, in 2011 nearly 900 million Indians, or 75 per cent of the population, were subsisting on less than 2,100 calories per day, up from 58 per cent in 1984. So not only does the World Bank dramatically understate the true extent of poverty in India, it also claims there has been a 'reduction' of poverty while hunger has been decisively on the rise.

The same story can be told in many other regions, where living just above the IPL still means living in destitution. In India, a child living just above the IPL has a 60 per cent risk of being underweight. In Niger, babies born to families just above the IPL face an infant mortality risk of 160/1,000, more than three times the world average. Earning $1.25 per day comes nowhere near to providing the 'adequate' standard of living that is supposedly guaranteed by the Universal Declaration of Human Rights, which states: 'Everyone has the right to a standard of living adequate for the health and well-being of himself and of his family, including food, clothing, housing and medical care.'

Even establishment institutions are beginning to recognise this. In 2014 the Asian Development Bank conceded that the $1.25 line was simply too low to be meaningful. It is now considering nudging it up to $1.50 – a level that will at the very least allow for basic nutrition. Even this minor shift would see the number of people in extreme poverty rise by more than 1 billion, and invert the MDGs' poverty reduction trend.

The present IPL theoretically reflects what $1.25 could buy in the United States in 2005. But the US government itself calculated that in 2005 the average person needed at least $4.58 per day simply to meet minimum nutritional requirements, and that is to say nothing of housing and other costs necessary for basic survival. According to British economist David Woodward, living at this level in the UK would be 'equivalent to 35 people living on a single minimum wage, with no benefits of any kind, no gifts, borrowing, scavenging, begging or savings to draw on (since these are all included as "income" in poverty calculations), and no free health service or education (since these are not generally available to the poor)'.

If $1.25 is not sufficient to guarantee basic nutrition, or provide children with a decent shot of not dying before their fifth birthday, then how can we legitimately claim that lifting people above this low line means bringing them out of poverty? If we are to be serious about eliminating poverty in meaningful terms, we need to set a line that at the very least allows people to achieve the lower end of normal human life expectancy, which is about seventy-four years. Recent studies place this 'ethical poverty line' at about $5 per day – four times higher than the standard $1.25 line. This line isn't perfect, because it still ends up comparing contexts that may not be

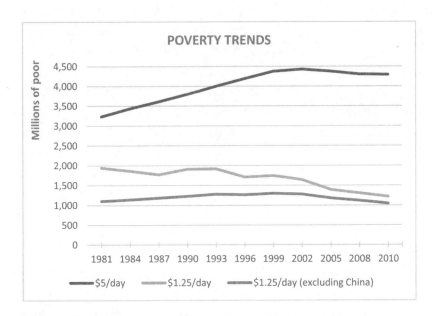

Source: PovcalNet (2005 PPP)

entirely comparable, but it is the best global line that's currently available.

The $5 poverty line enjoys support from a number of sources. Economists Rahul Lahoti and Sanjay Reddy argue that people require about $4.50 per day to cover minimum basic nutrition alone. The New Economics Foundation in London shows that people need about $5.87 per day to reduce infant mortality rates to 30 per 1,000, which is the world average (although still five times higher than in developed countries). As it turns out, $5 per day is the mean average of all the national poverty lines in the developing world. It also accords with the World Bank's own repeated statements that the $1.25 line is 'deliberately conservative', appropriate for only the poorest countries: 'In more developed regions, higher international poverty lines are more appropriate. When comparing poverty rates across countries within the Latin American and the Caribbean region, the $4 a day poverty line provides a more meaningful standard. For the Eastern European and Central Asia region, the $5 a day poverty line is often used.' Some organisations are calling for an even higher poverty line. ActionAid, for instance, wants us to use $10 per day, which is the upper boundary suggested by the World Bank and the income necessary to cut infant mortality down to 20 per 1,000 (still three times more than in developed countries). Harvard economist Lant Pritchett calls for a poverty line of $12.50 per day as a global minimum standard for human well-being.

What if we were to take these concerns seriously, and measure global poverty at a minimum of $5 per day? We would find the global poverty headcount to be about 4.3 billion people. This is more than four times what the World Bank and the Millennium Campaign would have us believe. It is more than 60 per cent of the world's population. And, more importantly, we would see that poverty has been getting *worse* over time. Even with China factored in, we would see that around 1 billion people have been added to the ranks of the extremely poor since 1981. At the $10-a-day line we see that 5.1 billion people live in poverty today – nearly 80 per cent of the world's population. And the number has risen considerably over time, with 2 billion people added to the ranks of the poor since 1981.

There is a strong consensus among scholars that the $1.25 line is far too low, but it remains in official use because it is the only line that shows any progress against poverty – at least when you include China – and therefore is the only line that justifies the present economic order.

Inequality: Measuring the Divide

Most everyone is worried about inequality these days. We know that income inequality *within* countries has been getting worse over the past few decades; this much is common knowledge, and we have movements like Occupy Wall Street to thank for bringing it to popular attention. But what about inequality *between* countries? On this front, most economists tell us we have nothing to worry about. Yes, there may be a yawning divide between rich and poor countries, but there's also some good news: that divide is narrowing, and fast.

Economists typically measure income inequality between countries using the Gini index, a method devised by Italian statistician Corrado Gini in 1912. A score of 0 represents total equality, where everyone has exactly the same income. A score of 100 represents total inequality, where one person has everything and everyone else has nothing. In other words, the higher the number the greater the inequality. In 2016 the World Bank's top inequality expert, Branko Milanović, published new data showing that inequality between countries – corrected for population – had declined dramatically over the past few decades, from a Gini index of 63 in 1960 down to 47 in 2013, with a precipitous drop beginning in the 1980s.

The story ricocheted through the media. Just days after Milanović's data was released, conservative commentator Charles Lane wrote a celebratory column in the *Washington Post*. He criticised Pope Francis and US presidential candidate Bernie Sanders for making such a big deal about inequality at the time. Yes, the world's richest 1 per cent have seen their incomes skyrocket, but that's OK, he argued, because the very system that is delivering them their extraordinary wealth is also reducing inequality globally. The US model of free-market globalisation isn't causing inequality, as its critics claim – on the contrary, it is *reducing* it. In fact, the greatest drop in inequality occurred precisely once the United States started pushing free-market policies around the world through structural adjustment and the World Trade Organization. The Cato Institute, a well-known libertarian think tank, picked up on the story too. 'Despite what you might think if you listen to voices prominent in the media . . . there has been a vast *reduction* in poverty and income inequality worldwide over the past quarter-century,' they wrote. 'This is the good news about the world today. Indeed, it's the most important news about our world.'

This story has the benefit of feeling intuitively right. After all, we're aware that countries like China and some East Asian econo-mies have made dramatic leaps towards industrialisation, and have produced large and growing middle classes. And indeed that is exactly the key point. As it turns out, the trend towards greater global equality has been driven entirely by China and East Asia. Take China out of the picture, and the good news narrative melts away. In fact, the economists Sudhir Anand and Paul Segal show that if we take China out of the Gini figures, we see that global inequality has been increasing, not decreasing – up from 50 in 1988 to 58 in 2005. This is important, because – once again – China and East Asia are some of the only places where structural adjustment was not imposed by Washington. Instead of being forced to adopt a one-size-fits-all blueprint for free-market capitalism, China relied on state-led development policies and gradually liberalised its economy on its own terms. It is disingenuous, then, for commenta-tors like Charles Lane and the Cato Institute to build an inequality-reduction narrative that rests on gains from China and chalk it up as a win for Washington's approach to free-market globalisation.

A second problem with this good-news narrative about inequality is that the Gini index is a *relative* measure, and this can be quite misleading. Instead of measuring the gap between the rich and poor, it measures the relative rate at which different incomes are growing. So if the incomes of poor countries increase at a rate slightly faster than the incomes of rich ones, the Gini index shows declining inequality even if the absolute gap between them has grown. Here is an example. If a poor country's income goes up from $5,000 to $5,500 (a 10 per cent increase), and a rich country's income goes up from $50,000 to $54,500 (a 9 per cent increase), the Gini index will show *decreasing* inequality because the income of the poor country is growing faster than that of the rich country, even though the gap between them has *grown* by $4,000. In light of this, many economists reject the Gini index as an overly conservative measure. It is possible to correct for this bias by calculating the *absolute* Gini index. Sudhir Anand and Paul Segal have done exactly that and estimate that global inequality rose from a Gini index of 57 in 1988 to 72 in 2005 – a dramatic increase.

*

There is a third and even more important problem. The World Bank's approach expresses inequality between the world's countries as if they were all anonymous individual units. But if we take a different angle and look at the gap between specific *regions* of the world, a very different story emerges. There are a few ways one can look at this. The best approach is to measure the gap in real terms between the GDP per capita of the United States (as the world's dominant power and a proxy for the rich world) and that of the various 'developing' regions of the global South. Since 1960 the gap between the US and the Middle East/North Africa has grown by 154 per cent, between the US and South Asia by 196 per cent, between the US and Latin America by 206 per cent, and between the US and sub-Saharan Africa by 207 per cent. We can get a sense of what this looks like in the graph on the next page.

Source: World Development Indicators

The graph above focuses on the United States, but if we plotted a line for Western Europe, or even for 'the West' as a broader category, including Australia and Canada and so on, it would rise more or less parallel to that of the United States. From this perspective, the global inequality gap hasn't diminished at all. On the contrary, the gap between poor and rich countries has roughly tripled. Over the past few decades inequality has become so bad that in 2000, Americans earned nine times more than Latin Americans, twenty-one times more than those in the Middle East/North Africa, fifty-two times more than sub-Saharan Africans and a mind-popping seventy-three times more than South Asians. These numbers give us a sense of how unfairly the global economy distributes our planet's wealth.

A Model Made to Fail

This leaves us with some very important questions. Why are the world's governments – and the FAO and the World Bank – so eager to claim victories they have not achieved? Why would they want to make it seem as though poverty and hunger and inequality are being reduced when in fact they are not? It is possible, of course, that some of this has to do with internal pressures. No organisation wants to appear to have failed. But scholars have been questioning the methods used to measure poverty and hunger for many years and suggesting more accurate methods. In light of these calls, why doesn't the UN re-evaluate the data? One likely reason is that if they were to use more accurate measures, then it would become clear that to fix these problems we would need to do much more than just tinker around the edges with a bit of aid here and there. It would require changing the rules of the global economy to make it fundamentally fairer for the world's majority.

But the development industry will not be able to ignore the problem for much longer. In 2015, the economist David Woodward published some rather sobering – even terrifying – analysis of future poverty-reduction scenarios in the *World Economic Review*. His findings are troubling. He shows that given our existing economic model, poverty eradication can't happen. Not that it probably won't happen, but that it physically can't. It is a structural impossibility.

Right now, the main strategy for eliminating poverty is to increase global GDP growth. The idea is that the yields of growth will gradually trickle down to improve the lives of the world's poorest people. But all the data we have shows quite clearly that GDP growth doesn't really benefit the poor. While global GDP per capita has grown by 45 per cent since 1990, the number of people living on less than $5 a day has *increased* by more than 370 million. Why does growth not help reduce poverty? Because the yields of growth are very unevenly distributed. The poorest 60 per cent of humanity receive only 5 per cent of all new income generated by global growth. The other 95 per cent of the new income goes to the richest 40 per cent of people. And that's under best-case-scenario conditions. Given this distribution ratio, Woodward calculates that it will take more than 100 years to eradicate absolute poverty at $1.25 a day. At the more accurate level of $5 a day, eradicating poverty will take 207 years. This is the best we can expect from the business-as-usual trajectory of the development industry. And keep in mind that Woodward's methodology is not able to capture the poorest 1 per cent of the world's population, who will still remain in poverty even at the end of this period. That's 90 million people who will remain in poverty for ever.

This is an extremely optimistic, best-case scenario. It does not account for the slowdown in income growth since the financial crash. It doesn't factor in the spikes in food prices that have effectively wiped out the incomes of the poor over the past few years, or the fact that climate change is already unravelling development gains across the global South. It imagines all of this away, and assumes that no further economic or ecological crises will happen in the next century or two – which is a very big assumption indeed.

As if the epochal timelines here aren't disappointing enough, it gets worse. To eradicate poverty at $5 a day, global GDP would have to increase to 175 times its present size. In other words, we need to extract, produce and consume 175 times more commodities than we presently do. It is worth pausing for a second to think about what this means. Even if such outlandish growth were possible, the consequences would be disastrous. We would quickly chew through our planet's ecosystems, destroying the forests, the soils and, most importantly, the climate. As Woodward puts it: 'There is simply no way this can be achieved without triggering truly catastrophic climate change – which, apart from anything else, would obliterate any potential gains from poverty reduction.' It's a farcical proposition – a cruel joke played at the expense of the poor. And, as if to add insult to injury, achieving this level of growth would mean driving global per capita income up to $1.3 million. In other words, the *average* income would have to be $1.3 million per year simply so that the poorest two-thirds of humanity could earn $5 per day. This gives us a sense of just how deeply inequality is baked into our economic system.

All of this boils down to a simple truth: if we want to have any hope of eradicating poverty without destroying our ability to inhabit this planet, we will need to adopt a completely different economic model – one that provides for a much fairer and more rational distribution of our wealth. Our future depends on it.

Into the Future

When the Millennium Development Goals drew to a close in 2015, they were replaced with another major international commitment – the Sustainable Development Goals. The SDGs have much to recommend them. With seventeen goals in total, they are broader than the MDGs and pay attention not only to human needs but to ecological ones as well. And they improve on the MDGs by taking a more aggressive stance on global poverty and hunger: Goals 1 and 2 – the headline goals – call for the total eradication of extreme poverty and hunger by 2030. This is a welcome commitment, to be sure. But the plan for reducing poverty relies, once again, primarily on increasing global GDP growth, with little attention to distribution or to the ecological consequences of endlessly increasing economic activity. What is more, the SDGs are set to continue measuring poverty at the discredited low-end poverty line, despite widespread objections. And there are no monitoring mechanisms in place to prevent the kind of statistical manipulation that so blighted the MDGs.

The cycle of perception management is simply beginning again. Shortly after the SDGs were launched, the World Bank announced a brand-new poverty line of $1.90 per day. At first glance, it might seem that the Bank has finally admitted that the old line was just too low and has raised it to a more meaningful standard; indeed, many commentators assumed precisely that. But the opposite is true. The Bank didn't raise the poverty line at all – it simply rebased it to the newest purchasing power parity (PPP) calculations, to compensate for depreciation in the purchasing power of the dollar. And once again, the new line is significantly lower than the old one, in real terms. It makes it seem as though there are fewer poor people than before. After rolling out the new poverty line, the Bank suddenly announced that the global poverty headcount had decreased by 100 million people overnight, and that the poverty reduction trend has been declining more rapidly than we used to believe. According to the Bank's new line, the poverty rate dipped below 10 per cent in 2015, crossing a big threshold. Once again, the media repeated the story without bothering to ask questions.

The problem is that PPP revisions are well known for discriminating against poor people. PPP moves relative to the price of consumer goods across whole economies. But people living at national poverty lines do not consume such a broad range of goods; on the contrary, they spend around 70 per cent of their income on food. And it just so happens that the price of food has gone up dramatically since PPP was last revised in 2005, relative to the prices of everything else, which means that while most people are able to buy *more* with their dollars, poor people are actually able to buy *less*. Therefore, if anything, the World Bank should actually be adjusting the real poverty line much higher than the new PPP figures suggest, just to keep at the same level in real terms. But if they do, it would make it much harder for the SDGs to succeed.

In all likelihood, the Bank will continue to revise the poverty line downwards in real terms over the next fifteen years until it shows that poverty has been more or less eradicated. And when 2030 arrives, they will declare that they have succeeded. There will be much media fanfare, and politicians and development leaders will congratulate each other, pleased with a good-news story that will keep the public satisfied and silence any questions about the legitimacy of the global economic order. But meanwhile, back on Earth, some 4.3 billion people will know for a fact that it is a lie.

If the UN is going to declare the end of poverty in 2030, this kind of statistical trickery is exactly what they're going to need. Just before the launch of the SDGs, the World Bank published fresh projections for poverty reduction towards 2030. They are vaguely humorous, albeit in a tragic kind of way. The Bank's indicators show that, assuming sub-Saharan Africa follows all of the Bank's advice and adheres closely to structural adjustment programmes, it will achieve a reduction in poverty from 407 million people in 2008 to 335 million by 2030. That is a long way from zero. Particularly when you consider the fact that in 1990 there were 287 million poor people in sub-Saharan Africa. Take a minute to let this sink in. After forty years of anti-poverty efforts in sub-Saharan Africa, the World Bank projects, bizarrely, that poverty numbers will have been 'reduced' from 287 million to 335 million people. In other words, according to the Bank's own extremely low poverty line, the best that Africans can hope for is that more people will be poor in 2030 than in 1990. That's how well the present system works.

*

I began this chapter by pointing out that the good-news narrative is so important to the world's most powerful governments because it justifies the present economic order and maintains people's consent for it. It would be difficult for them to admit that poverty has actually increased dramatically over the past thirty-five years, for that would call the whole game into question – the single moral justification for the status quo would collapse. But in order to maintain the good-news narrative, they have to limit themselves to a remarkably narrow slice of human history. The Millennium Development Goals, for example, have trained us to forget everything that happened before 1990. That's a convenient date, because the poverty headcount increased steadily during the decade before that, *even according to the World Bank's own $1.25 line.* The 1980s were a decade of severe suffering in the global South, no matter how much you doctor the numbers. Even James Wolfensohn, the president of the World Bank quoted on pages 40–41, admitted that the 1960s and 1970s were better days for developing countries – before the World Bank and the IMF intervened. So what worked so well? And why have we been told to forget about it?

These are questions we need to answer. But in order to really get the full story of global poverty and inequality we have to go back even earlier than the 1960s. Recall that Wolfensohn himself pointed out that poverty had been increasing steadily over the past 200 years, during the rise of industrialisation and the consolidation of Western economic power. Why? What was going on? And why is this not part of the story we have been told?

PART TWO

Concerning Violence

Three

Where Did Poverty Come From? A Creation Story

No one colonises innocently.

Aimé Césaire

The development industry has trained us to think on short time-scales. Today, the dominant narrative about poverty goes back only as far as 1990, the baseline used by the Millennium Development Goals, or 1981 at the earliest, when the World Bank published the first global poverty statistics. As a result, most people know nothing about what happened before then. This lack of historical perspective has been a feature of the development story since its inception. Even Truman's 1949 speech was strangely ahistorical. 'More than half the people of the world are living in conditions approaching misery,' he said, but he offered no suggestions about how this terrible tragedy might have come to pass. A casual listener might have inferred that the US government, and the rest of the Western world, had suddenly discovered poor countries for the first time, as if by accident, having stumbled upon them in some remote corner of the world. If we accept the dominant narrative, we might be forgiven for believing that poor countries have always been poor, and that the gap between rich and poor countries has always existed.

But if we rewind to about 1500, a very different story emerges. At that time, there was little difference between Europe and the rest of the world when it came to the living standards of ordinary people. In fact, people living in South America, India and Asia were in many ways better off than Europeans. Even as late as 1800, life expectancy in England was between thirty-two and thirty-four years – and a dismal fifteen for children born into working-class families. In France, it was between twenty-eight and thirty, and in Germany between twenty-five and thirty-one.

Citizens of the Aztec, Inca and Mayan civilisations were not much better off than Europeans in terms of life expectancy. Like Europeans at the time, they lived in settled communities that were crowded, highly unequal and rife with disease – and they relied exclusively on agriculture for food, which required back-breaking labour and yielded very little nutritional value. But archaeological records show that people in the forager-farmer communities that lived outside these early states were a good deal better off, with life expectancies around 50 per cent longer. They were healthier, stronger, taller and better nourished than their more 'civilised' counterparts in South America – and, indeed, in Europe. They were less likely to die of famine for they had a much more diverse food system: they grew some of their food and foraged for the rest. They worked far fewer hours and the work was lighter. There were no powerful aristocrats or landlords around to force them to work, or to skim their yields for profit. And they were less exposed to the diseases that plagued densely populated societies. In the Americas of the 15th century, such communities were the norm, at an incidence of probably around 80 per cent, while settled agricultural states were the exception.

Evidence from China, Japan and other parts of Asia suggests that people in these regions also lived longer, healthier lives than Europeans did. Indeed, Asia's advantage over Europe in this department lasted until at least 1800. Japan enjoyed a life expectancy of forty-one to fifty-five, China between thirty-five and forty, and parts of South-East Asia around forty-two. In other words, Asians could expect to live as much as ten years longer than Europeans. Asia exceeded Europe in many other key development indicators as well, including superior transport technology, larger cities and better sanitation, public health systems and nutritional standards. And in terms of the balance of global power, Europe in 1500 – just emerging from the Dark Ages – was little more than a backwater, accounting for only 15 per cent of global GDP. By contrast, China and India together controlled 65 per cent of the world economy.

So how did this change? How did a small number of countries in Western Europe become so much richer and more powerful than the rest of the world?

The usual answer to these questions is the one we all learned in school. A series of technological innovations in Britain jump-started the Industrial Revolution that spread through Europe and the United States. The invention of the flying shuttle in 1733 made textile weaving much more efficient, and James Watt's steam engine in 1781 made it possible to build large and powerful machines. Britain's coal fields, which were usefully proximate to the large cities, provided cheap and abundant energy, and because the landscape was relatively flat it was easy to transport both coal and manufactured goods around the country via canals. By virtue of scientific enquiry and geographical accident, Britain was able to build productive industries, and the sale of manufactured goods drove living standards to unprecedented new heights.

This story is powerful in its simplicity, but by focusing only on what happened within Britain's borders, it makes it seem as though these developments occurred in isolation from the rest of the world. Nothing could be further from the truth. In fact, by the time Watt built his steam engine, Britain was already at the centre of a world system that was roughly organised into two zones: the 'core' nations of Western Europe and the young United States, surrounded by the 'peripheral' regions of Asia, Africa and Latin America. And the two zones were in constant interaction, linked by a dense network of connections. Importantly, these interactions were not equitable or mutually agreed – indeed, they were marked by violence and coercion. Europe's industrial innovations are only a part of the story. To really understand how the divide began, we need to go back further.

The Making of the World System

In 1492, Christopher Columbus set sail to discover a new sea route to the Indies. He never made it that far, of course. Victim of shoddy geographical calculations, he was intercepted by a landmass he had not anticipated. When he landed in Cuba, which he insisted was India (stubbornly never admitting otherwise), he encountered a remarkable people – a civilisation very unlike his own. In his journals, Columbus reported that the people were 'so free with their possessions that no one who has not witnessed them would believe it. When you ask for something they have, they never say no. To the contrary, they offer to share with anyone.' They lived in communal buildings, and enjoyed a remarkable degree of equality, even between genders: women were free to leave their partners if they felt they were being mistreated. The people were healthy and strong. Columbus described them as 'well-built, with good bodies and handsome features'. Other observers marvelled at how far they could swim, and noted that even pregnant women were agile and independent, gave birth with ease, and were up and about again shortly thereafter.

Columbus noticed that in addition to being open and generous, the people he encountered were a peaceful lot. 'They do not bear arms, and do not know them,' he wrote. 'When I showed them a sword, they took it by the edge and cut themselves out of ignorance.' Columbus was eager to exploit this vulnerability, jotting a rather ominous note in his journal: 'With fifty men we could subjugate them all and make them do whatever we want.'

During his second expedition, this time with seventeen ships and 1,200 men, Columbus travelled around the Caribbean capturing thousands of indigenous Americans to be sent back and sold in Spain as slaves. But this time his real objective was gold. He had noticed the indigenous people wearing gold ornaments and assumed that the metal must be abundant in the region. Yet he was having a difficult time finding the source, so he resorted to coercive measures. From his base on Hispaniola, the island shared today by Haiti and the Dominican Republic, he forced the local inhabitants – the Arawaks – to bring him a certain quantity of gold every three months. Those who failed to do so would have their hands chopped off or were hunted down and killed. Men were forced to spend their lives in mines, stripping the mountains in search of gold. Up to a third of workers died every six months. Within two years of the Spanish invasion, some 125,000 people had been killed – half the island's population. Most of the remaining inhabitants of Hispaniola were forced into slave labour on plantations. A few decades later, only a few hundred Arawaks remained alive.

One European witness, Bartolomé de Las Casas, reported startling statistics of the slow-motion genocide unfolding in the Caribbean region: 'From 1494 to 1508,' he wrote, 'over three million people had perished from war, slavery, and the mines. Who in future generations will believe this? I myself writing it as a knowledgeable eyewitness can hardly believe it . . .'

Columbus was only the first in a long line of European conquistadors. Shortly after him came Hernán Cortés, who landed in Mexico in 1519, claimed it for the Spanish Crown and proceeded to march inland towards the Aztec capital, Tenochtitlán, where Mexico City now lies. Once again, the indigenous inhabitants of the land responded to their European invaders with hospitality, and their generous gestures are well documented. But Cortés was unmoved. He proceeded with his march, destroying towns along the way and massacring their inhabitants in the squares, conquering by virtue of his superior weapons: cannons, crossbows and horses. When he arrived at Tenochtitlán, Emperor Montezuma welcomed him with marvellous gifts of gold and silver. Cortés imprisoned him in his own palace and took control of the city. By

1521, Montezuma had been killed and the capital plundered of its treasures.

Francisco Pizarro, yet another Spanish conquistador, followed suit. In 1532 he was invited into the Inca capital in Peru by Emperor Atahuallpa, who – protected by an army of 80,000 men – did not consider Pizarro and his soldiers to be a threat. Yet Pizarro, enabled by his weapons, managed to sack the city and capture Atahuallpa. To spare his life, the emperor offered to fill a large room with gold and then to fill it twice again with silver, within two months, for he knew how much the Spanish loved precious metals. As a Nahuatl text from the time put it: 'They lifted up the gold as if they were monkeys, with expressions of joy, as if it put new life into them and lit their hearts. As if it were certainly something for which they yearn with great thirst. Their bodies fatten on it and they hunger violently for it. They crave gold like hungry swine.' Pizarro agreed to the emperor's offer and Atahuallpa proceeded to pile the precious metals high. But it was a trick. Having received the gold and silver, Pizarro executed Atahuallpa after sentencing him in a mock court for the 'crime' of resisting the Spanish invasion.

A few decades later, Europeans discovered the immense network of silver mines centred on Potosi, in what is now Bolivia. Before long the metal came to account for 99 per cent of the mineral exports from the Spanish colonies. Between 1503 and 1660, 16 million kilograms of silver was shipped to Europe, amounting to three times the total European reserves of the metal. And that was on top of the 185,000 kilograms of gold that arrived in Spanish ports during the same period. By the early 1800s, a total of 100 million kilograms of silver had been drained from Latin America and pumped into the European economy – first into Spain, and then out to the rest of Europe as payment on Spain's debts.

To get a sense of the scale of this wealth, consider this thought experiment: if 100 million kilograms of silver was invested in 1800 at 5 per cent interest – the historical average – it would amount to $165 trillion today, more than double the world's total GDP in 2015. Europe had to purchase some of this silver from indigenous

Americans in exchange for goods, of course, but much of it came for free – the product of coercive extraction. It was a massive infusion of windfall wealth into the European economy.

What happened to all of this silver and gold from Latin America? Some of it went to building up the military capacity of European states, which would help secure their political advantage over the rest of the world. But most of it lubricated their trade with China and India. Silver was one of the only European commodities that Eastern states actually wanted; without it, Europe would have suffered a crippling trade deficit, leaving it largely frozen out of the world economy. The silver trade allowed Europe to import land-intensive goods and natural resources that it lacked the land capacity to provide for itself. We can think of this as an 'ecological windfall' – a transfusion of resources that allowed Europe to grow its economy beyond its natural limits at the time, to the point of catching up with and surpassing China and India around 1800. China and India, then, provided a kind of ecological relief to overstrained Europe. Outsourcing land-intensive production also allowed Europe to reallocate its labour into capital-intensive industrial activities – like textile mills – which other states did not have the luxury of doing.

But while Europe benefited from this arrangement, Latin America suffered tremendously. It is estimated that Mexico had a population of up to 30 million indigenous inhabitants before the arrival of the Europeans. The Andean region had a similar number. Central America is thought to have supported around 13 million. The numbers vary by source to some extent, but scholars agree that in 1492 the Latin American region had a combined population of between 50 and 100 million. By the middle of the 1600s, however, the continent's population had been slashed to 3.5 million. In other words, around 95 per cent had been killed.

Much of this genocide played out in the form of massacres perpetrated by the conquistadors. Some of it had to do with the forced dispossession of indigenous Americans and the dismantling of their social and economic systems, which made it impossible for them to subsist. Many also died in slavery, their labour used by Europeans to dig precious metals out of the mountains. Mining was not only exceedingly dangerous, it was poisonous too: the use of mercury to extract silver from the rocks exacted an enormous death toll among miners. And of course much of it had to do with diseases such as smallpox, which Europeans brought with them across the Atlantic – sometimes intentionally, as in cases where infected blankets were distributed as 'gifts' to indigenous Americans. Because indigenous Americans lacked immunity to these foreign diseases, the germs took a heavy toll. Epidemics were as useful to the European conquest as horses and cannons.

*

Indigenous Americans were not the only ones forcibly roped into the expanding empires of Europe. Europeans' labour requirements in the New World were also slaked by slaves from Africa. The slave trade began early in the 1500s, shortly after Columbus's first colony was founded in Hispaniola, and was led by European merchants – at first the Spanish and Portuguese, but later the British dominated – who purchased slaves from the shores of West Africa in exchange for European goods (or, more accurately, goods that Europeans had bought from China and India, paid for with precious metals taken from the New World). Most of these slaves were prisoners of war captured in conflicts between West African states. Once transported to the Americas, they were put to work on European sugar plantations in the Caribbean and in the mines of Brazil. In the 1700s, Portuguese Brazil produced more gold using slave labour than the total volume Spain had extracted from its colonies in the previous two centuries.

By the end of the slave trade in 1853, somewhere between 12 million and 15 million Africans had been shipped across the Atlantic. Between 1.2 million and 2.4 million died en route, in the darkness below the decks of the slave ships, their bodies cast into the sea. It is almost impossible to imagine the scale of the human devastation that these numbers represent.

How much did Western states gain from this enormous quantity of free labour? It is estimated that the United States alone benefited from a total of 222,505,049 hours of forced labour between 1619 and the abolition of slavery in 1865. Valued at the US minimum wage, with a modest rate of interest, that is worth $97 trillion today. And that's just the United States. Right now, fourteen Caribbean nations – represented by the law firm Leigh Day – are in the process of suing Britain for slavery reparations. They have not disclosed how much they seek in damages, but they have pointed out that when Britain abolished slavery in 1834 it paid its slave owners compensation of £20 million for loss of property (paying no compensation to the slaves themselves), which would be the equivalent of $300 billion today. It is worth noting that this figure reflects only the price of the slaves, and tells us nothing of the total value they produced during their lifetimes, nor of the trauma they endured, nor of the hundreds of thousands of slaves who worked and died during the centuries *before* 1834.

Yet the real benefit that Europe derived from the slave economy was not just in the form of value extracted coercively from the bodies of Africans and indigenous Americans. The sugar and cotton plantations of the New World supplied Europe with another ecological windfall, much as silver did. For example, sugar came to account for up to 22 per cent of the calories Britain consumed, which reduced the need for domestic agricultural production and freed up labour power for industrial pursuits. Cotton provided a key raw material for Europe's Industrial Revolution, and without diverting from food production or straining Europe's labour and land capacities. If we add timber imports to sugar and cotton, we see that the New World contributed some 25 million to 30 million 'ghost acres' of productive land to Britain alone – roughly double the size of Britain's own total arable land. These slave-produced imports were one of the single largest factors in spurring Europe's rapid economic development – more significant even than the windfall energy provided by the region's rich seams of coal. Without the ecological windfall from the slave colonies, Europe would not have been able to shift its economic capacity towards industrialisation.

*

Because the Latin American economy was organised by the colonisers to produce only a handful of agricultural products, it was prevented from developing its own domestic industries. Instead, it became dependent on Europe for the manufactured goods it needed. This arrangement proved to be tremendously beneficial to Europe; Latin America was a captive market, providing a steady demand for Europe's industrial exports. Indeed, without the slave colonies of the New World to consume its goods, Europe's industrialisation would have been impossible.

The consequences of this arrangement for the periphery of the world system were immense. As we will see, Latin America would be stuck in a relationship of economic dependency on Europe even into the 21st century, one marked by declining terms of trade, with the price of Latin America's exports falling relative to the price of industrial imports from the West. Africa, for its part, suffered a serious loss of labour power to the Atlantic slave trade. What if the sum of the value produced by African slaves in the New World – worth the equivalent of hundreds of trillions of dollars today – was subtracted from Western wealth and added to the total wealth of Africa? Or even just a proportion of this sum, subtracting, for example, the gains that African kings made through the trade?

Economists often speculate that the global South failed to develop because of a lack of capital. But there was no such lack. The wealth that might have provided the capital for development (precious metals in Latin America and surplus labour in Africa) was effectively stolen by Europe and harnessed to the service of Europe's own development. The global South could *theoretically* have developed as Europe did were it not for the plunder of its resources and labour, and were it not for the fact that it was forced by Europe to supply raw materials while importing manufactured goods. Whether or not they would or should have done so is another matter, of course – after all, much of European-style development required violence towards other lands and other peoples. But the point remains: it is impossible to examine the economic growth of the West without looking at the base on which it drew.

The Great Dispossession

For many decades, the main alternative to the received story of the Industrial Revolution in Europe held that the resources and labour extracted from the periphery of the world system provided the wealth that was necessary for significant capital investment to occur. Adam Smith, the father of modern economics, called this 'previous accumulation' – the initial process of amassing capital that is necessary for capitalism to get going, and without which capitalism cannot exist. Karl Marx called it 'primitive accumulation', perhaps to highlight its barbaric nature, for the process of accumulation was violent: 'The discovery of gold and silver in America, the extirpation, enslavement and entombment in mines of the aboriginal population, the beginning of the conquest and looting of the East Indies, the turning of Africa into a warren for the commercial hunting of black-skins, signalled the rosy dawn of the era of capitalist production. These idyllic proceedings are the chief momenta of primitive accumulation.' Colonial extraction, according to this view, was the driver of accumulation, and accumulation is what made capitalism possible.

As we have seen, however, the real benefit that Europe gained from this first period of colonialism was not just that it allowed for the extraction and direct accumulation of wealth (in the form of value transferred from the New World colonies directly into the coffers of Europe), but rather that it provided ecological windfalls

73

that allowed Europe to pivot towards industrial production, and captive markets where it could sell its manufactured goods. These became the primary forces of accumulation.

But accumulation alone does not explain the rise of industrialisation in Europe. Historians tell us that there were many states that accumulated immense wealth but never became capitalist. In order for capitalism to work, it needs something else: it needs workers. Budding capitalists cannot get very far unless there are people willing to work for them in exchange for wages. We take this for granted today, but there was a time, not so long ago, when it wasn't quite so easy. Up through the Middle Ages, the vast majority of people in Europe – at least outside the city states – wouldn't have *wanted* to work for wages. People didn't need to earn wages in order to live. Most people lived as 'peasants' – in other words, as small farmers cultivating the land to provide for their own needs. And for the most part they were quite happy doing so.

When we think of medieval peasants we usually assume that they must have lived rather miserable lives. And this is true, in many ways: disease was common, nutritional standards were not very high and life expectancy was short – as it was for most people living in settled agricultural societies before the late 19th century. But peasants *did* have the most important thing they needed to guarantee a stable livelihood: they had secure access to land, which they could use for farming crops, grazing livestock, hunting game, drawing water, excavating peat and cutting wood for heating, cooking and shelter. Some had direct rights to their own land, others had the right to use lands owned by lords, and others had access to shared 'commons'. Peasants may not have been rich, but they enjoyed the basic right of habitation – a right that was protected by long-standing tradition and strong laws, such as the 1217 Charter of the Forest in England. It was unthinkable that anyone should not have secure access to the basic resources they needed for survival.

But this traditional security system came under attack in the 15th century – a process that started in England. Wealthy nobles, eager to profit from the highly lucrative wool trade, began a systematic campaign to turn their land into sheep pasture. To do this, they dissolved old feudal obligations and abolished the right of habitation that had protected peasants for so many centuries. They also began to privatise the common land that people relied on for survival, denying them rights of access and fencing the land off for their own commercial use. The 'enclosure' movement, as it came to be known, saw the privatisation of tens of millions of acres over the course of two or three centuries, the displacement of much of the country's population, and the clearance of hundreds of villages. Enclosure was not a peaceful process – it was profoundly violent, as dispossession always is. It required a considerable degree of force – burning villages, destroying houses, razing crops – to prise millions of people off their ancestral lands.

While the wool industry was a major driver of enclosure, the Reformation added impetus to the process. When Henry VIII dissolved the old Catholic monasteries, Church lands were quickly appropriated by the elite. Many of the peasants who lived on them were kicked off. But by far the most powerful driver of enclosure had to do with agriculture. Landlords began to realise that they could skim much more value from peasants if they were able to get them to increase their agricultural output. To do this, they transformed peasants' secure tenure rights into a market for leases, and gave leases only to those who were able to produce the most. Those who were less productive would be kicked off the land and left with no way to survive. This new system – known at the time as 'improvement' – put peasants under tremendous pressure. If they wanted to survive they had to devise ways of extracting ever more yield from their land – far beyond what they needed to live on. They had to increase their workload and intensify their farming techniques. This led to a dramatic increase in agricultural output, but the only real improvement was to the landlords' profits.

The application of this market logic to land and farming marked the formal birth of capitalism. It meant that, for the first time in history, people's lives were effectively governed by the imperatives to intensify productivity and maximise profit. But still, this early form of agrarian capitalism didn't look quite like the form of capitalism we have today. There was another crucial step.

As the enclosure movement advanced across England, peasant riots became widespread. There was Jack Cade's rebellion in 1450, for example, and Robert Kett's rebellion of 1549, both of which had the issue of land rights at their core. In 1607, rebellions erupted across Northamptonshire and quickly spread to Warwickshire and Leicestershire. Thousands of protestors pulled down fences and other barriers that had been erected around enclosed land. The Midland Revolt, as historians call it, culminated in an insurrection at Newton, where peasants ended up in armed combat with the enclosers. They lost. Fifty people were killed, and the movement's leaders were publicly hung and quartered.

Worried that riots like this might coalesce into revolution, the monarchy eventually stepped in to curtail the growing powers of the landlords, defending peasants' traditional rights to common lands. But its efforts were defeated after the English Civil War in the 1640s, which limited the powers of the Crown and allowed the landlord class – which came to control Parliament – to more or less do what they wanted. The 'Glorious Revolution' of 1688 didn't help matters as it only further empowered the landed classes to shape state policy in their own interests. As a result, Parliament itself became a powerful instrument of enclosure, designing legislation that formally extinguished peasants' rights to the commons and enabled 'the clearing of the estates' – a national programme designed to 'sweep' human beings off the elite's newly privatised landholdings. Between 1760 and 1870, some 7 million acres were enclosed by acts of Parliament – about one-sixth of England.

This final episode in the destruction of the English peasant system exactly coincided with the Industrial Revolution. By the middle of the 19th century it was complete: there was almost no common land left and millions of people had been forcibly displaced. The result was a massive refugee crisis, unlike anything we can imagine today – bleaker than our most dystopian science fiction films. Huge portions of England's population had nowhere to go. They had no homes, no land, no food. It was a humanitarian catastrophe: for the first time in history, a significant proportion of the population had no access to any form of livelihood for survival. By the middle of the 1600s, the word 'poverty' had come into common use to describe this new condition, and during the late 18th and early 19th centuries the term became entrenched as a major concept in English-language discourse. This helps us make sense of the extremely low life expectancy found among England's working class in the early 19th century.

The displaced peasants had no way to feed themselves, save for one last option: to sell their labour for wages. Such people were euphemistically referred to as 'free labourers', but this term is quite misleading. True, they were not technically slaves, but wage work was hardly a matter of free choice. Some of the displaced ended up working on the new sheep runs or on the capitalist farms. But most of them moved into towns, pouring into cities like London to scratch out a meagre living. The population of England's urban centres grew at an unprecedented rate and outpaced the urban populations of the rest of Europe, where the enclosure movement had not yet gained traction. These growing cities were not pleasant places to live: the majority of people had no choice but to live in slums, and working conditions were horrible – the hellish backdrop to Dickens' works such as *Oliver Twist*.

This troubled episode in England's history had a silver lining, at least for the country's elite. The impoverished refugees provided the cheap labour necessary to fuel the Industrial Revolution, since they had no choice but to accept the slavery-like conditions and rock-bottom wages of factory work. Factories sprang up to provide inexpensive, mass-produced goods to meet growing consumer demand, using the cheap labour of those who had been displaced. Even small children were sent to Blake's 'dark Satanic Mills' by families desperate to survive. Because employment was relatively scarce, competition among workers drove down the cost of labour, destroying the guild system that had previously protected the livelihoods of craftsmen. Desperate to keep their jobs, workers were under heavy pressure to produce as much as possible and regularly worked for sixteen hours a day – much more than peasants would have spent working on their farms before enclosure. And most of the enormous wealth they produced was appropriated by the factory owners, who gave very little back in wages. This system created a 'trickle-up' effect on a scale that far outstripped what even the most rapacious feudal lord enjoyed. England's industrialists were able to amass wealth unimaginable to even the richest of kings.

The emergence of the landless working class added a final piece to the great transformation of England's economy: they became the world's first mass consumer population, for they depended on markets for even the most basic goods necessary for survival: clothes, food, housing, and so on. It was these three forces – enclosure, mass displacement of peasants and the creation of a consumer market – that provided the internal conditions for the Industrial Revolution. The external conditions, as we have seen, had to do with the colonisation of the Americas and the slave trade.

It is important to grasp the difference between this emerging capitalist system and the various systems that preceded it. Previously, monarchs, conquistadors and feudal landlords directly appropriated wealth from others either by stealing it from them or by forcing them to pay tribute. In other words, they relied on some kind of direct coercive force. But under the new system such direct coercion was no longer necessary. The elite simply relied on the fact that the competitive pressures of the labour market (and the market in leases) would increase workers' productivity at a much higher rate than the one at which their wages increased. This was the basic mechanism of profit, and it served as an automatic conveyor belt for redistributing wealth upwards.

*

We tend to assume that the emergence of capitalism was a natural and inevitable process – as though its basic logic has always existed in human society and gradually matured into the Industrial Revolution. But the historical evidence suggests a very different story. The emergence of capitalism required violence and mass impoverishment, both at home and abroad – a process that left vast swathes of people dispossessed (in the case of English peasants) or enslaved (in the case of Africans and indigenous Americans). Even in England, people didn't welcome this new system with open arms. On the contrary, they protested and rebelled against it, for it violated long-standing cultural expectations about people's basic rights to habitation, to the means of subsistence, to the means of life. The goal of the enclosure movement was not just to displace people from their land, but – much more profoundly – to eradicate these cultural expectations.

Why is this history of England useful to our understanding of global poverty? Because the process of enclosure not only marks the origin of mass poverty as a historical phenomenon, it also illustrates the basic logic of the process that would produce poverty across the rest of the world.

Imperialism's New Logic

The rise of capitalism changed not only the shape of Europe, but also its approach to imperialism. Originally, imperialism had been organised around direct, coercive appropriation of wealth. In some cases – as with the Spanish and Portuguese in the Americas – it focused on stealing precious metals such as gold and silver or on the use of slavery on plantations and in mines. In other cases its goal was securing access to trade routes, as with the French in Canada and the Dutch in South Africa. In all cases, the basic idea was to gain access to existing sources and flows of wealth. But when England got involved in the imperial project, the logic of imperialism changed. And it started in Ireland.

In 1585, English colonisers made their first attempt at reproducing the new system of enclosure and 'improvement' in a foreign territory. They forcibly expropriated the land of Irish peasants and resettled it with farmers trained in the methods of agricultural intensification, directly replicating what was already under way back at home. As in England, this process impoverished vast numbers of people, who were forced to retreat on to small plots of marginal land. Many were left with no hope of survival and migrated to England and Scotland to work as wage labourers – something that had never been necessary before. By the early 1800s, once the enclosure movement had run its violent course over two to three centuries, Irish peasants had so little land for their own use that they were planting only potatoes – the one crop that would yield sufficient calories for them to survive on very small plots.

This dependency on potatoes proved deadly when the potato blight hit in 1845. Over the next seven years 1 million people died – more than 10 per cent of the Irish population – in what became known as the Great Famine. What made this famine so appalling was that it was completely avoidable; it would never have happened if peasants had retained full rights to their ancestral land, where they would have had plenty of space to produce a diversity of crops. In other words, the scarcity that led to the famine was artificially created. But even with the new agrarian system in place, Ireland was still producing plenty of food, in aggregate; the problem was that it was all being siphoned away by the British. Ireland was exporting thirty to fifty shiploads of food to England and Scotland each day during the famine, while the local population starved to death.

Ireland may have been the first experiment in replicating English capitalism through imperialism, but it wasn't the last. This same model was reproduced by English colonisers in the Americas, even using some of the same people who had helped out with the Ireland experiment. How did the English manage to justify the mass dispossession that 'improvement' entailed? For this we largely have the Enlightenment philosopher John Locke to thank. In the late 1600s, Locke – a large landowner in England with stakes in American colonisation – wrote the *Second Treatise of Government*, which developed a new and very powerful theory of property ownership. He stated that while land initially belongs to all people in common, once you 'mix' your labour with it then it becomes your private property. This 'labour theory of property' was used to justify the theft of land in the Americas: since it appeared that no one was engaged in agricultural production, settlers could rightfully appropriate the land as long as they were willing to farm it.

But of course in many cases there *were* people farming the land that English colonisers wanted to take, just as in Ireland. In such cases, Locke claimed that what really counted for ownership was not simply the act of farming, but the *improvement* (i.e. intensification and profit-orientation) of the farming techniques. So settlers who were prepared to apply the principles of English-style agrarian capitalism were justified in appropriating the lands of others. According to Locke, this added to the common good because it would increase overall productivity, even if it meant displacing the land's original inhabitants: it was a contribution to the betterment of humanity, bringing people from the Dark Ages into the light of capitalist civilisation. In other words, once again the idea of improvement came to trump the basic value of human habitation. Indeed, improvement began to assume the status of a religious creed, and its economic principles took on a kind of moral meaning.

But the consequences of this new imperialism were devastating, in the rest of the world even more than in Ireland. In America, the English who settled the north-east in the 1600s were quick to expropriate land from the indigenous population. The governor of the Massachusetts Bay Colony, John Winthrop, acknowledged that Indians lived there but argued that because they had not 'subdued' the land they had no right to it. These land grabs took the English into outright warfare with the indigenous people and culminated in dozens of bloody massacres. In the 1800s, the young United States systematised this land grab by forcibly dispossessing native inhabitants, beginning with the Indian Removal Act of 1830. At the time there were some 120,000 Native Americans living east of the Mississippi River. By 1944, only 30,000 remained; many had been killed, but most had been forced by the US government to move westward. Some 15,000 people perished along the way, on the Trail of Tears. This process of mass enclosure opened up more than 25 million acres for white settlement, clearing the way for tobacco and cotton plantations in the South and intensive grain-farming techniques further north.

*

What unites the Irish and American cases is that both were propelled by the logic of enclosure and improvement. But there is a third example of this that is worth visiting: India. There, the process of enclosure and improvement in the late 19th century led to human suffering on a scale that outstripped that visited on both the Irish and indigenous North Americans, if such tragedies can be compared. It is a story that truly boggles the mind, although it is very little known.

The colonisation of India began in the early 1600s as a corporate affair. It was led by the East India Company, which focused on securing control over trading routes east of the Cape of Good Hope. But the Company's mandate gradually expanded, and by the 1800s it had established direct administrative power over most of the subcontinent, which it eventually handed over to the British government. Wielding this power, the main intervention that the British made in India was to reorganise the farming system, once again according to the logic of improvement.

Unlike in America, in most cases the British didn't resettle the land themselves, but rather forced the Indians to adopt a new agricultural system. Indian farmers were made to cultivate crops for the export market – opium, indigo, cotton, wheat and rice – instead of for subsistence. For many people, making this shift was the only way to survive: it was necessary simply in order to pay the crushing taxes – and debts – that the British had imposed. To further encourage this transformation, the British compelled villages to sell off their grain reserves and did away with systems of mutual support and reciprocity that people had long relied on. They also enclosed common lands at a dizzying pace. Prior to 1870, India's forests had been communally managed; farmers used them to acquire firewood for cooking and heating, and for fodder to feed the cattle they used for ploughing and fertiliser. By the end of the decade the forests had been almost completely enclosed, to be used by the British for building ships and railways. And it wasn't only forests that the British enclosed: common water rights were also privatised and auctioned off with enclosed land, rendered a market commodity for the first time.

Under the British, these centuries-old traditional welfare buffers were destroyed on the basis that they 'interfered' with market forces. The idea was that by stripping them away you could compel Indian farmers to be more productive: cast at the mercy of the market, they would figure out ways to extract ever higher yields from the land. Yet farmers found that the market was rigged against them, for India's tariffs were controlled in London and in the interests of British stockholders. Many smaller Indian farmers were quickly overcome by competition, and their lands appropriated by bigger and more powerful businesses.

These changes were traumatic in their own right. But it wasn't until 1876, when El Niño visited the region with a crushing three-year drought, that the true horror of this new system became apparent. El Niño droughts were not uncommon across the Indian subcontinent during the 19th century and farmers had learned to weather them remarkably well. In lean years they could always rely on their grain reserves to see them through, and the commons, too, were a vital lifeline. But this time they were left without any of these security systems – and the consequences were disastrous. With the forests fenced off, farmers couldn't acquire the fodder they needed to feed their cattle. Cows died en masse, and without their manure agricultural yields deteriorated. And with water sources enclosed, people were unable to use the irrigation systems they normally relied on when the rains failed. All of this made the drought much more deadly than it otherwise would have been.

The human toll was staggering: 10 million Indians died of starvation. As Florence Nightingale observed in 1877, during the second year of the drought: 'The more one hears about this famine, the more one feels that such a hideous record of human suffering and destruction the world has never seen before.' And it kept getting worse. Twenty years later, between 1896 and 1902, El Niño struck again – and this time the death toll was even higher. Nineteen million Indians died of starvation, bringing the total body count to 29 million. Almost 30 million is a difficult number to imagine. Laid head to foot, the dead would stretch the length of England eighty-five times over.

Just as in Ireland, mass starvation in India was completely avoidable. Even in the absence of the traditional support systems that should have protected peasants, the railroads and bridges that the British had built could have been used to feed the population as a last resort by transporting grains from areas of surplus to drought-stricken ones. After all, even during the height of the drought the country had a net surplus of food – there was more than enough to feed the entire population, it just needed to be moved to the right areas. But instead the rail system, obedient to market logic, was used by merchants to ship grain from the hinterlands into central depots where it could be guarded from the hungry and shipped to Europe. Financial speculation on the London Stock Exchange was driving food prices to eye-watering heights, and grain merchants were eager to take advantage of this. In 1877 and 1878, during the worst years of the first drought, they shipped a record 6.4 million tons of Indian wheat to Europe rather than relieve starvation in India. During the period from 1875 to 1900, Indian grain exports increased from 3 million to 10 million tons per year.

The Indian famines of the late 19th century were not a natural disaster, as the British insisted at the time. They were the predictable consequence of imposing a foreign market logic that saw fit to eliminate basic human food security and sacrifice tens of millions of people in the service of profit. The famines had nothing to do with endogenous economic problems; rather, they were caused by India's incorporation into the emerging capitalist world system. As the historian Mike Davis puts it:

We are not dealing, in other words, with 'lands of famine' becalmed in stagnant backwaters of world history, but with the fate of tropical humanity at the precise moment (1870–1914) when its labour and products were being dynamically conscripted into a London-centred world economy. Millions died, not outside the 'modern world system', but in the very process of being forcibly incorporated into its economic and political structures. They died in the golden age of Liberal Capitalism.

Of course, there was nothing 'free' about the free-market system that the British imposed. It was brought in by force, and the rules of trade were rigged by London. The peasants who switched to cash cropping did so under the duress of debt and taxes – including taxes on local irrigation systems and even on the construction of new wells. Just as in England, the creation of a market society required significant violence and social dislocation, and the destruction of centuries-old systems of mutual aid. And, just as in England, people who were dispossessed of their land ended up in the labour market, working for British mills and factories.

How Britain Underdeveloped Asia

The process of colonial enclosure offered development for some and de-development for many others. This effect of colonialism played out not only in the arena of land and farming, but also – and perhaps even more clearly – in industry. In addition to transforming the colonies into exporters of grain and other land-based goods, European powers wanted to turn them into consumers of Europe's growing output of manufactured goods.

From the perspective of the British, the problem with India was that it had relatively strong industries of its own. India's textile industries, for instance, produced some of the finest cloth in the world, making it difficult for Britain to gain dominance in the global textile market. To deal with this obstacle, the British

Colonial Office did everything in its power to hinder and even dismantle India's autonomous industrial development, and sought to ensure that Indian manufacturers would not be able to compete with their British counterparts. They prevented Indians from becoming skilled artisans and they gave British firms preferential treatment in government procurement. In one famous episode, the British set out to destroy India's textile industry by crushing the fingers of the weavers and destroying their looms. But their most potent tool was the use of one-way tariffs, which protected Britain's markets from India's exports while ensuring easy access for Britain's goods into India. It worked: India, once self-sufficient and famous for its exports, was remade into 'the greatest captive market in world history'.

The economic transformation was dramatic. Before the British arrived, India commanded 27 per cent of the world economy, according to economist Angus Maddison. By the time they left, India's share had shrunk to just 3 per cent.

This technique of forcing open the markets of foreign countries had been honed earlier in the century during Britain's engagements with China. In 1793, Britain sent its first official mission to the Chinese empire. Britain was hungry for tea and other exotic goods like porcelain and silk, but could no longer afford to finance them. The Chinese accepted payment only in silver. They didn't need the products that the British offered to trade, and in any case wanted to protect their own industries from the threat of outside competition. British traders were allowed only token access to Chinese markets, their activities restricted to a small trading post in Canton. But Britain's silver was running dry, and British traders had piles of industrial products they were desperate to sell. They needed access to China's markets.

The meeting between the British ambassador and Emperor Qianlong did not go well. The emperor regarded the British as barbarians from an uncivilised land, and was not impressed by the gadgets they brought along as gifts. To clarify his position, he sent a letter to King George III – perhaps one of the most famous letters ever written.

> As your Ambassador can see for himself, we have not use for your country's manufactures . . . Our Celestial Empire possesses all things in prolific abundance and lacks no product within its borders. There is therefore no need to import the manufactures of outside barbarians in exchange for our own produce. But as the tea, silk, and porcelain which the Celestial Empire produces are absolute necessities to European nations and to yourselves, we have permitted, as a signal mark of favour, that foreign merchants should be established at Canton, so that your wants might be supplied and your country thus participate in our beneficence . . . I do not forget the lonely remoteness of your island, cut off from the world by intervening wastes of sea . . .

Defeated on the diplomatic front, Britain turned to drugs. Desperate to finance their growing trade deficit, they started selling opium – grown in colonial India – on China's black market. And when Chinese authorities clamped down on this illicit trade, as any sovereign country has the right to do, the British retaliated with a military invasion.

Thus began the Opium Wars, fought by the British between 1839 and 1842, and by an Anglo-French alliance from 1856 to 1860. China, unprepared for naval combat, was brutally defeated. But Britain and France refused to relent until China agreed to abolish restrictions on European access and hand large chunks of territory over to European control. The treaties that followed granted sweeping trade privileges to Europe but conceded nothing to China in return. According to these 'unequal treaties', as they came to be called, Europeans could sell their manufactured goods on China's markets while protecting their own markets against Chinese competitors. The consequences were devastating. China's share of the world economy dwindled from 35 per cent before the Opium Wars to an all-time low of just 7 per cent. What is more, China's loss of control over its grain markets led in part to the famines that China suffered during the same droughts that hit India. And, as in India, 30 million people in China perished needlessly of starvation during the late 19th century, after having been integrated into the London-centred world economy.

*

Today, British apologists defend colonialism in India and intervention in China on the basis that it brought 'development' to these regions. But the evidence we have suggests exactly the opposite story. It was the colonial period of forced market integration that inaugurated the 'development gap' between Britain and Asia. In the middle of the 18th century, the average standard of living in Europe was a little bit lower than in Asia. Even as late as 1800, per capita income in China was ahead of Western Europe, and per capita income for Asia as a whole was better than that of Europe as a whole. Literacy rates in China were higher than in European countries, including among women, and birth rates were lower. In the south of India – and in other Indian regions – workers enjoyed higher incomes than their British counterparts in the 18th century, and lived much more secure lives. Indian artisans enjoyed a better diet than the average European, and their unemployment rates tended to be lower because they had more robust rights.

During the colonial period in India, there was no increase in per capita income from the time the East India Company took power in 1757 to the time of national independence in 1947. In fact, during the last half of the 19th century – the heyday of British intervention – income in India *declined* by more than 50 per cent. And it was not just incomes that collapsed. From 1872 to 1921, the average life expectancy of Indians fell by 20 per cent. In other words, the subcontinent was effectively de-developed.

While India and China watched their share of global GDP

diminish, Europeans increased their own share from 20 to 60 per cent during the colonial period. Europe didn't develop the colonies. The colonies developed Europe.

Africa: Europe's Pressure Valve

As European countries industrialised, they began to compete with each other for the raw materials they needed for their factories and also for new markets in which to sell their products. This generated immense pressure to expand into still uncolonised parts of the world. And when a financial crisis sunk Europe into a prolonged depression during the last decades of the 19th century, this pressure intensified: with their economies contracting, European states desperately needed profitable new outlets where they could invest their surplus capital.

At the same time, Europe was facing a crisis of growing social unrest. In Britain, the mass impoverishment created in the early days of the Industrial Revolution threatened to destabilise the country, and social tensions seemed certain to erupt into class war. Britain's ruling class realised that the colonial project promised a way of temporarily relieving some of these tensions without requiring them to relinquish any of their power. Instead of rolling back enclosure or increasing workers' wages, they hoped to find a pressure valve somewhere beyond their borders. These words from Cecil Rhodes, Britain's most famous colonialist, give us a window into the spirit of the times:

> I was in the East End of London (a working-class quarter) yesterday and attended a meeting of the unemployed. I listened to the wild speeches, which were just a cry for 'bread! bread!' and on my way home I pondered over the scene and I became more than ever convinced of the importance of imperialism . . . My cherished idea is a solution for the social problem, i.e., in order to save the 40,000,000 inhabitants of the United Kingdom from a bloody civil war, we colonial statesmen must

acquire new lands to settle the surplus population, to provide new markets for the goods produced in the factories and mines. The Empire, as I have always said, is a bread and butter question. If you want to avoid civil war, you must become imperialists.

Africa became the primary focus of this next wave of imperialism. Except for coastal trading posts, the continent had been largely ignored by Europe. Britain controlled the Cape Colony in the far south and France controlled Algeria in the north, but Africa's vast interior remained one of the few regions on the planet that had not yet been roped into the Europe-centred world system. Indeed, the interior was almost completely unknown to Europeans at the time. Once explorers like David Livingstone and Henry Stanley began to chart Africa's great navigable rivers and reveal the extent of the continent's vast resources, the scramble for new territories was under way.

It wasn't long before European states were caught up in heated conflict with one another over their putative colonial domains. The Congo Basin became an early flashpoint, with Belgium, Portugal, France and Britain staking rival claims to the same region. To prevent such conflict escalating, European statesmen agreed to adopt a common policy on Africa that would minimise misunderstandings. In 1884 they gathered for a series of meetings known as the Berlin Conference, during which they drew borders across the continent, set guidelines about which powers could lay claim to which regions, and established rules for what counted as effective occupation of a territory.

The Berlin Conference added considerable impetus to the scramble for Africa. In 1870, only 10 per cent of Africa was under the control of Europeans; by 1914 they had extended their reach across 90 per cent of the continent. Britain controlled a huge swathe of land stretching all the way from the Cape to Cairo, plus Nigeria and a few outposts along the north-west coast. France controlled most of West Africa, Madagascar and part of the equatorial region.

Germany took Namibia, Tanzania and Cameroon, while the Portuguese laid claim to Angola and Mozambique, and Belgium ended up with the Congo. Once the dust had settled, only Ethiopia and Liberia remained independent.

It would require far too many pages to discuss the history of Africa's colonisation here. But one can get a sense of the form it took by looking at two key examples: the Congo and South Africa. The Congo is interesting for our purposes because it exemplifies the sheer violence that Europeans inflicted on African communities in their frantic rush to extract resources, while the South African case illustrates the long-term strategies of planned dispossession and enclosure that forced whole populations into the capitalist market as cheap, exploitable labour.

King Leopold II of Belgium was one of the first Europeans to make a serious grab for African resources in the late 19th century. Indeed, it was his early intervention that triggered the rest of Europe to follow suit. His company, the International African Association, equipped with a private military and backed by the Belgian government, established control over a region of the central African Congo that was eighty times larger than Belgium itself. Leopold justified this enormous acquisition to the international community by claiming that he was pursuing humanitarian and philanthropic work – 'development' by other names. The Berlin Conference bought his line, and ratified his rule over the region. But behind the smokescreen of development, Leopold transformed the Congo into a source of raw materials – first extracting ivory and then, when automobile production took off in the 1890s, rubber. Rubber extraction was a labour-intensive business, however, and to get enough workers Leopold enslaved much of the native population and forced them to collect rubber. If they failed to reach their quotas, they would have their hands chopped off – the very same tactic that Columbus had used to get gold from the Arawaks. Crucially, the automobile industry – the showpiece of the West's early-20th-century industrialism – depended on colonial violence. But it wasn't just rubber. Leopold also assumed total control over the Congolese economy, decreeing that Africans could only sell their products to the state, while the state in turn controlled all prices and incomes.

Ten million Congolese perished under Leopold's brutal regime – roughly half the country's population. Many of them died at the hands of direct Belgian aggression, but others died because colonial rule destroyed local economies and dislocated indigenous communities, causing widespread dispossession and starvation, along with an increase in fatal tropical diseases. As for the wealth from all the ivory and rubber, it was used in Belgium to fund beautiful stately architecture, public works, arches, parks and impressive railway stations – all the markers of development that adorn Brussels today, the bejewelled headquarters of the European Union.

Further south, the process unfolded according to a very different logic. As Dutch and British settlers spread throughout South Africa during the 1800s, they faced a continual conundrum: it was impossible to find enough labour to work on their farms and, later, in their gold and diamond mines. The African population was quite content with its subsistence lifestyle: under traditional tenure arrangements, most people had access to land on which to graze their cattle and grow food for their families. They didn't see why they should leave their homes for back-breaking labour on plantations and in mines. Nobody was offering wages high enough to induce such a dramatic shift. The colonisers quickly learned that the only way to get Africans into the labour market was to force them – by destroying their existing subsistence arrangements. Hunger would leave them no choice.

Successive colonial administrations introduced policies designed to do exactly that. As early as 1857, they began forcing Africans to pay taxes, which compelled African households to send family members to the mines and plantations for work. Those who didn't pay taxes were punished – so there was always the threat of violence lurking in the background. On top of this, they began to systematically push Africans off their land in a process that mimicked the enclosure movement in England. The Natives Land

Act of 1913 restricted African land ownership to a series of 'native reserves' or 'homelands' that totalled only 10 per cent of the country's area. The division was brutally enforced: Africans were gradually and systematically forced off their land and into the reserves. And because the reserves were on marginal, unproductive land inadequate to support the population, Africans had no choice but to migrate to European areas for wage work.

To make matters worse, a series of 'pass laws' prevented African workers from settling their families in white areas. European colonisers justified this as part of their strategy of racial segregation, but the real benefit was that it allowed them to pay African workers extremely low wages. Here's how it worked. If workers were to settle in European areas with their families, then wages would have to be high enough to meet the needs not only of the workers themselves, but also of their spouses and children. What is more, employers and the state would have to contribute to the Africans' social care needs, like health and retirement. These are the normal costs of maintaining and reproducing labour. But by keeping families confined to the reserves, employers were able to pay 'bachelor wages' to African workers – just enough for the workers to live on, but certainly not enough to support their families. The shortfall would be covered by subsistence farming in the reserves. And the costs of caring for sick and ageing workers would be borne in the reserves as well, thus sparing European employers and the state considerable expense.

It wasn't just the reserve system that kept African labour so cheap, however. Labour unions were banned, a so-called 'colour bar' prevented blacks from accessing better-paid jobs and new rounds of dispossession kicked more people into the labour market and applied downward pressure on wages. It was an ingenious scheme, from the point of view of the colonisers. European firms – including mining giants like De Beers and Anglo American – were able to squeeze record profits out of this highly exploitable workforce. South Africa is a land rich in fertile soil, mineral resources and human labour power. But the vast majority of Africans have been excluded from this abundance. Today, more than 50 per cent of the black population lives in absolute poverty, while the mines and plantations remain monopolised by a handful of white-owned (mostly British) conglomerates.

Fallout in the Sacrifice Zone

From the late 15th to the early 20th centuries, European powers considered their colonies to be a sacrifice zone for the sake of their own development. No loss of human life, no amount of suffering, no degree of degradation was too much so long as the economic interests of colonial companies and states were served. The inequity was justified by dehumanising those with black and brown skin – by repeatedly asserting that they were not quite as human as white people, and that therefore their suffering did not matter.

Colonialism took a heavy toll on the economies of Asia and Africa. Between 1870 and 1913, per capita income in Asia (excluding Japan) grew at only 0.4 per cent per year. In Africa, per capita income growth was only 0.6 per cent per year. Economists regard such low growth rates as a sign of serious crisis. By contrast, incomes in Western Europe grew at 1.3 per cent per year during this period, and in the US at 1.8 per cent per year – three to four times the rate of the colonised world. This differential in income growth rates was a major driver of global inequality. At the end of this period, Europe owned somewhere between one-third and one-half of the domestic capital of Asia and Africa, and more than three-quarters of their industrial capital.

The story in Latin America unfolded somewhat differently. Three centuries of European colonialism came to an end in the early 19th century with revolutions led by liberators such as Simón Bolívar, who, after a long period of struggle against the Spanish Crown, won independence for Venezuela in 1821, Ecuador in 1822, Peru in 1824 and Bolivia in 1825. But these and other independent nations that emerged in the wake of decolonisation tended to be controlled by autocratic local elites who were quite happy to

maintain the economic arrangements that their European counterparts had imposed. And in any case, independence was in name
only: at exactly the same time as European powers were pulling out
of Latin America, the US established the Monroe Doctrine of 1823.
The US was concerned that European powers might try to recolon-
ise Latin America, and the Monroe Doctrine stated that any such
attempt would be regarded as aggression against the United States
itself. Far from being a benevolent gesture in support of the region's
newly independent countries, the real purpose of the Monroe
Doctrine was to protect US interests in the region. This agenda
became particularly clear when President Theodore Roosevelt
added the Roosevelt Corollary in 1904, which was used to justify
military intervention against any Latin American country that
refused to cooperate with US economic interests. The idea was to
keep Latin America open to US companies, as a source of resources
and agricultural goods as well as an outlet for US manufactures –
the same strategy that Britain had pursued in India and China.

This was not just an abstract assertion of power. It was a
uniquely American brand of colonialism – a form of indirect economic rule that consciously distinguished itself from the more
direct interventions of imperial Europe. It was colonialism of a
special type. The Roosevelt Corollary was invoked to justify more
than a dozen US interventions during the early 20th century,
including multiple invasions and occupations of Cuba, Mexico,
Honduras, Colombia, Nicaragua, Haiti, the Dominican Republic
and Puerto Rico.

These are known now as the Banana Wars, as in many cases
the invasions were designed to guarantee abundant land and cheap
labour for American fruit companies. For instance, US marines
invaded Honduras seven times between 1903 and 1925 in order to
contain progressive political parties and install puppet leaders who
would serve the interests of American banana producers. Cuba is
another example: the US occupied Cuba on and off from 1906 to
1934, mostly to secure the interests of American sugar companies.
But there were other issues at stake too. When the US invaded

Colombia in 1903 it was in order to secure control over Panama, to clear the way for the US to dig the Panama Canal. Nicaragua was occupied from 1912 to 1933 largely in order to prevent the Nicaraguan government – or any other nation – from building its own alternative canal. Another key issue was debt. When the Dominican Republic threatened to default on its debts to American creditors, the US invaded and seized control of its ports, channelling the country's customs revenues directly into American coffers. The occupation lasted from 1916 to 1924, at the end of which the US installed a military dictatorship to rule in its interests.

*

It is tempting to see this as just a list of crimes, but it is much more than that. These snippets of history hint at the contours of a world economic system that was designed over hundreds of years to enrich a small portion of humanity at the expense of the vast majority. By the early part of the 20th century, this new order was complete, designed so that the core of the system – Europe and the United States – could siphon cheap raw materials from the periphery and then sell manufactured products back to them while protecting themselves from competition by erecting disproportionately high tariffs.

The system had two built-in features that generated increasing inequalities between the West and the rest. The first was that the terms of trade of developing economies deteriorated over time. In other words, the prices of their primary commodity exports gradually decreased relative to the prices of the manufactured goods they imported. This meant that they had to spend more to get less, which translated into an outward net transfer of wealth. The second was that the wages that workers in developing countries were paid for the goods they traded remained much lower than in the West, even when corrected for productivity and purchasing power, so the South was undercompensated for the value they shipped abroad. Together, these two patterns lie at the heart of what economists call 'unequal exchange' between the core and the periphery. By the end of the colonial period, the periphery was losing $22 billion each year as a result of unequal exchange, which is equivalent to $161 billion in 2015 dollars. That is twice the amount of aid and investment that the periphery was receiving each year during the same period. This arrangement became a major driver of global inequality. In 1820, at the dawn of the second wave of imperialism, the income gap between the richest country and the poorest country was only 3 to 1. By the end of colonialism in the middle of the 19th century, the gap was 35 to 1.

In most undergraduate economics courses, students are taught that the differences between the economies of poor and rich countries can be explained by the laws of comparative advantage and supply and demand. The standard theory holds that prices and wages are set automatically by the market depending on each country's factors of production. Poor countries have a natural abundance of labour, so their wages are low and therefore their comparative advantage lies in labour-intensive production (first mining and agriculture and later also light manufacturing). Rich countries have a natural abundance of capital, so their wages will be higher and they will specialise in capital-intensive production of higher-order commodities. In orthodox economic theory, this is regarded as the natural order of things.

But as soon as we bring history back into the picture, this theory starts to fall apart. Why do poor countries have a comparative abundance of labour in the first place? Because of hundreds of years of colonial rule, under which subsistence economies were destroyed and millions of people were displaced and forced into the labour market, driving unemployment up and wages down. The fact that slavery was used up through the 19th century further contributed to downward pressure on wages, as workers had to compete with free labour. And why do poor countries have a comparative deficit of capital in the first place? Partly because they were plundered of precious metals, and partly because their colonisers forcibly destroyed local industries so that they would have no choice but to consume Western exports. Orthodox economic theory presupposes international inequalities as if they have always existed, but the historical record is clear that they were purposefully created. As the Uruguayan journalist Eduardo Galeano put it, 'The colonial economy was built in terms of – and at the service of – the European market.'

Four

From Colonialism to the Coup

How many ways can you clone an empire?
Shailja Patel, 'How Ambi Became Paisley'

While colonialism was an economic and humanitarian disaster for global South countries, it yielded tremendous windfall wealth for Europe and, later, the United States. But this new wealth was not evenly distributed; it was captured almost entirely by a small yet powerful elite. Between 1870 and 1910, the richest segments of society became richer by leaps and bounds, reaching historically high levels on the eve of the First World War. In 1910, the richest 1 per cent in the United States claimed 45 per cent of the nation's wealth, while in Europe they claimed nearly 65 per cent of total wealth. Zoom out a bit and the numbers are even more staggering: in the US the richest 10 per cent claimed more than 80 per cent of the nation's wealth; in Europe, it was as much as 90 per cent. Such levels of inequality would be almost impossible to imagine were we not once again approaching similar extremes today.

The First World War put a brief damper on things, slowing

economic growth and eroding the wealth of the richest. But before long the party was back on track. After the Treaty of Versailles was signed in 1919, the victors plundered Germany for reparations, and France and Britain got to divvy up the former Ottoman Empire, significantly expanding their colonial reach. The factories of war were retooled to produce for mass consumption, and returning soldiers poured into the workforce. The following decade became known as the Roaring Twenties, a period of renewed wealth and glamour – although again, predominantly for the elite.

But it didn't last long. The party came crashing to an end when Wall Street collapsed in 1929 and triggered the Great Depression. The crash itself, known as Black Tuesday, was the result of heated market speculation that drove prices up into an enormous bubble. The frenzy was bolstered by the confidence people had in the markets during the economic boom of the 1920s, but it was helped along by unscrupulous stockbrokers who allowed investors to buy stocks on credit with very little down payment, to the point where the whole system was shot through with toxic debt. Aided by easy money, investors bought more and more stocks, driving prices higher and higher and leading, paradoxically, to even more stock purchases. But of course eventually the bubble popped, as all bubbles must, and the financial system – unable to cover all its bad debts – collapsed. The economy ground to a halt, and confidence in the market dropped to record lows.

But there was a bright side to the crisis. From the wreckage of the old economic order a series of powerful new ideas emerged – ideas that would change the course of history. These ideas took hold not only in the West, but also across the global South. Once Europe withdrew from Africa and Asia, and as democratic movements swept through Latin America, overthrowing autocratic governments and US imperialism, the fortunes of the South began to change. From the 1950s to the 1970s, a new movement emerged across much of the postcolonial world, driven by the ideals of economic independence and a fairer distribution of the world's wealth. And it worked. Incomes rose, living standards improved, and the gap between rich and poor countries began to narrow for the first time since 1492. It was nothing short of a development miracle. But not everyone was pleased with this turn of fate. Indeed, those whose rhetoric most celebrated international development as an abstract idea turned out to be its most violent enemies in practice.

A New Deal in the West

When the Great Depression hit the Western world, it threw established economic ideas into turmoil. At the time, most economists believed that markets were self-stabilising. In the United States, President Hoover was convinced that the solution to the Depression was to restore investors' confidence by cutting government spending to balance the books. Others held that wages should be slashed to encourage businesses to hire. In theory, such measures were supposed to jolt the economy back to life. But they turned out to have the opposite effect and, against all predictions, deepened the Depression. Companies worried that there was no point in producing, even if it was very cheap to do so, since there was no one to buy their products.

As the Depression continued into the 1930s and the economy failed to recover, conventional views began to crumble and new economic theories emerged from the rubble. The problem, people began to realise, had to do with the internal contradictions of capitalism itself. Capitalists seek to maximise their profits by increasing productivity and decreasing the costs of production. The easiest way to decrease the costs of production, of course, is to push down workers' wages. But if this process is left unchecked, eventually wages get so low that workers cannot afford to buy the products they produce. Demand goes down, and the market becomes glutted with excess goods with no one to buy them. Goods quickly lose their value, businesses stop producing and the economy slows down. This is what happens when capitalism is left to its own devices: it generates such extreme inequality that the whole system simply seizes up.

It was the British economist John Maynard Keynes – musta-chioed member of London's famous Bohemian scene – who brought this critique to prominence. In light of his findings, he proposed a very different way of dealing with the Depression. He argued that governments should not cut spending and wages, but instead do exactly the opposite: increase government spending, open up the money supply and encourage higher wages. These measures, he said, would get people buying again, stimulate aggre-gate demand and therefore boost the economy back to life: what we might call 'demand side' economics.

When Franklin Delano Roosevelt came to power in the United States in 1933, he began to do precisely that. His New Deal – a vast programme of government-funded projects, such as New York's Lincoln Tunnel and Montana's Fort Peck Dam – put armies of unemployed Americans to work with good wages. Massive gov-ernment spending had what Keynes called a 'multiplier effect': by transforming government money into workers' wages, workers gain consumer power that creates new opportunities for private businesses that spring up where the cash is plentiful, like trees around an oasis. When the Second World War gained pace it proved the point: government spending on factory production for the war effort had the same effect, boosting employment (the US reached full employment during the war), increasing wages and stimulating demand. Economic growth soared and – with higher wages for the poor and higher taxes on the rich – inequality was dramatically reduced.

Those were heady days. The edifices of laissez-faire capitalism were collapsing all around, and Keynes and his followers were emboldened to argue for a whole new approach to economics. The democratic state should regulate the market and harness its powers towards desired social ends, securing economic stability and improv-ing living standards. The market should be made to serve society, not the other way round. This new system relied on a class compromise between capital and labour: the state would guarantee strong rights and good wages in exchange for a docile, productive workforce that would have sufficient money to consume mass-produced goods, thereby keeping the economy stable and growing.

As part of the New Deal, the United States also implemented a universal Social Security programme, provided affordable housing and, with the GI Bill, handed out large university tuition subsidies for veterans. In Britain, a growing union movement – propelled largely by coal miners – brought to power Clement Atlee's Labour Party, which rolled out the National Health Service, free education, public housing, rent controls and a comprehensive social security system, as well as nationalising the mines and the railways. Many politicians on the right were willing to go along with it, hoping that granting the working class a fairer deal would stave off the social discontent they feared might spark a Soviet-style revolution. They also hoped it might prevent the rise of fascism, which had attracted Germans beleaguered by their severe economic crisis. By ensuring stability and welfare across the industrialised world, Keynesian principles were designed to prevent another world war.

In 1944, the Bretton Woods institutions were created with this goal in mind. The World Bank would finance reconstruction and development across war-torn Europe, and the IMF would finance state spending in countries experiencing economic slumps, to ensure that low demand in one nation wouldn't trigger a crisis across the region.

Keynesian policies created the conditions for high rates of economic growth through the 1950s and 1960s – growth that was relatively equitably shared across classes. It was a success story like none other. Of course, the system wasn't perfect: there were many who were left out. Middle-class women, for example, remained largely confined to the home and dependent on male wages and salaries. Black people were denied fair labour contracts and access to decent schooling and housing – particularly in the United States, where the Civil Rights Movement had not yet won basic legal equality for African Americans. Gay people were routinely persecuted and marginalised. In short, the Keynesian compromise in the West worked mostly for people who conformed to a particular norm – white, male and straight. It depended to some extent on cheap labour from women and minorities, and of course was financed in large part by surplus wealth siphoned from the rest of the world through the old colonial pipelines.

A Miracle in the South

The rise of Keynesianism coincided precisely with the last decades of European colonialism. In fact, it was partly due to the influence of Keynesian ideology – with its focus on fairness and welfare – that the colonial project began to seem untenable and gradually unravelled. The progressive political parties that began to take control in Europe after the Second World War had little appetite for colonialism as it conflicted with the growing discourse on equality, national sovereignty and human rights. Indeed, the Universal Declaration of Human Rights was adopted by the United Nations a few years after the war ended. Europe's colonial subjects, who had committed immense resources and millions of troops essential to the success of the war effort, wondered why they too shouldn't benefit from this new regime and receive equal rights alongside Europeans.

Anti-colonial thinkers like Mahatma Gandhi and Marcus Garvey had been sowing the idea of independence for a number of decades, and in the middle of the century it began to bear fruit. After waves of powerful civil disobedience, the British finally withdrew from India in 1947. France retreated from Syria and Lebanon, and a revolution in Egypt put an end to British occupation in 1952. Five years later, Ghana won independence and set off a wave of decolonisation across British Africa. By 1960, France had begun to withdraw from its colonies in West Africa. And Latin America was given breathing room for the first time when US president Franklin Roosevelt implemented the Good Neighbor policy, which committed them to respecting the sovereignty of Latin American nations. The policy suspended the long history of US intervention that had beleaguered the region under the Monroe Doctrine and opened up the possibility for democratic revolutions to gain traction and overthrow US-backed puppet regimes.

For the first time, global South countries were free to determine their own economic policies. And seeing how well Keynesian economics was working in Europe and the United States, they were quick to adopt its basic principles: state-led development, plenty of social spending and decent wages for workers. And they added one crucial piece to the Keynesian consensus: a desire to build their economies for their own national good, rather than solely for the benefit of external powers.

This was the era of 'developmentalism'. Latin America's Southern Cone – Chile, Argentina, Uruguay and parts of Brazil – became an early success story. The epicentre of the developmentalist movement was the United Nations Economic Commission for Latin America, based in Chile. Founded in 1948, the Commission was headed by the progressive Argentinian economist Raúl Prebisch, one of the thinkers who developed the theory of dependency and unequal exchange. Prebisch argued that underdevelopment and global inequality were the result of the way that colonialism had organised the world system, limiting the countries of the global South to exporting primary commodities and preventing them from building competitive industries. And because the value of primary commodity exports was constantly declining relative to the manufactured goods they imported from the West, they were continually losing ground.

Drawing on Prebisch's ideas, Latin American governments began to roll out 'import substitution' strategies – a bold attempt to industrialise and produce the very commodities they had been made to import from the West at such great expense. They wanted to free themselves from dependency on Western powers. In Argentina, for example, President Juan Perón's administration (1946–55) invested heavily in infrastructure, nationalised oil resources and

built the country's capacity for heavy industry. It also made substantial investments in public education, healthcare, social security
and housing – a programme spearheaded by the president's wife,
the reformer Eva Perón. To this day, the Peróns are celebrated for
their largely successful efforts to eradicate poverty, support workers and build Argentina's middle class.

Developmentalism was also taking hold elsewhere in the global
South. In much of Africa it appeared in the guise of African socialism, a philosophy that regarded the sharing of economic resources
as an important expression of 'traditional' African values. The
principles of African socialism guided the social justice efforts of
countries like Ghana under Kwame Nkrumah and Tanzania under
Julius Nyerere. In North Africa and the Middle East, developmentalism took the form of Arab nationalism, as exemplified by leaders
such as Egypt's Gamal Abdel Nasser and the Baathist parties of
Iraq and Syria. In India it took hold under Prime Minister Jawahar-
lal Nehru and his successors. East Asia was busy doing something
similar, using infant industry subsidies to build strong businesses
in a protected economy, grooming them to the point where they
were capable of competing and succeeding against their Western
counterparts. All of these strategies relied on relatively high trade
tariffs on foreign goods, restrictions on foreign capital flows and
limits on foreign ownership of national assets. Land reform was
often a central part of the package. And in many cases, governments sought to nationalise natural resources and key industries in
order to ensure that their citizens benefited from them as much as
possible.

These developmentalist policies mimicked the very same
measures that the United States and Europe used to such good
effect during their own periods of economic consolidation. And
they worked equally well in the global South, delivering high per
capita income growth rates of 3.2 per cent during the 1960s and
1970s – double or triple what the West achieved during the Industrial Revolution, and more than six times the growth rate under
colonial rule. It was a postcolonial miracle. And the new wealth

was more equitably shared than before: in Latin America, for example, the gap between the richest fifth and poorest fifth of the population shrank by 22 per cent. Developmentalism also had an impressive impact on human welfare. At the end of colonialism, life expectancy in the global South was a mere forty years. By the early 1980s it had shot up to sixty – the fastest period of improvement in history. The same is true of literacy, infant mortality and other key human development indicators, which experienced their fastest rate of improvement through the mid-1970s.

What is more, the income gap between rich countries and the regions of the global South where developmentalism was most thoroughly applied began to narrow for the first time. In 1960, the average income in the United States was 13.6 times higher than in East Asia. By the end of the 1970s the ratio was down to 10.1, having shrunk by 26 per cent. During the same period, the per capita income ratio between the US and Latin America shrank by 11 per cent, and for the Middle East and North Africa by 23 per cent. The South was steadily closing the divide.

In addition to building their own national economies, global South countries were reaching out to one another for support. In 1955, newly independent African and Asian states gathered in Bandung, Indonesia, to share ideas, build ties of economic cooperation and commit themselves to resisting all forms of colonialism and neocolonialism by Western powers. They saw themselves as developing a third way, defending their interests against the power of both the United States and the USSR and refusing to take sides in the Cold War. In 1961 they met again, this time in Belgrade, to form the Non-Aligned Movement. Led initially by Nehru, Nasser, Nkrumah, President Tito of Yugoslavia and Indonesia's first independent president, Sukarno, the NAM would come to include nearly every country of the global South and became a powerful force for peace, sovereignty, non-intervention, anti-racism and economic justice. Three years later, they formed the G77 to advance their interests and vision at the United Nations, and founded the United Nations Conference on Trade and Development (UNCTAD), which would develop the principles for a fairer global economy.

The South was rising, and leading the way to a better world for the planet's majority.

*

One might think that Europe and the United States would be thrilled to watch this success unfold; after all, the new policies that global South countries were rolling out – tariffs, nationalisation, land reform, capital controls – were bringing about real development, and Western governments, in the spirit of Truman, claimed to be in favour of development.

But they were not amused. Western states had become accustomed to having easy access to cheap labour, raw materials and consumer markets in global South countries, and the rise of developmentalism was beginning to restrict this access. Import substitution policies meant that Western exporters of consumer goods had to pay high tariffs to sell their products to global South markets. Sometimes they found that their products were blocked at customs altogether by nationalist governments intent on protecting local industries. In many cases, Western investors who wanted to operate in global South countries were denied entry. When they were allowed in, they often had to pay higher taxes on their incomes, and capital controls meant they had to pay higher fees if they wanted to repatriate their profits. A growing trade union movement and new constitutional rights meant they had to pay higher wages to the workers they hired. In some countries, they felt stymied by price controls that governments had imposed in order to keep basic goods affordable. In others – and this was their most serious concern – they feared that their land and assets might be nationalised.

In other words, the developmentalist revolution – and the South's growing political power – was eroding the foundations of the world system that Europe and the United States had come to rely on.

The Age of the Coup

The governments and corporations of the Western powers were not willing to let this continue; they needed some kind of counter-revolution in order to regain the access to resources and markets they had previously enjoyed. But there was no resisting the ideas that had been unleashed by Keynesianism, and no stifling the surging passion for economic independence in the South. In some cases they were able to negotiate favourable conditions for foreign direct investment through hard bargaining, winning concessions on taxes and capital controls, for example. But in others this proved to be impossible and they resorted to more aggressive measures in the hope of putting an end to developmentalism altogether.

When President Dwight Eisenhower took office in the United States in 1953, he took a decisive stand against developmentalism, which he regarded as a threat to the commercial interests of America's multinational companies. He hired two people into his administration who shared his views: John Foster Dulles, who became the US secretary of state, and his brother, Allen Dulles, who became head of the CIA. The Dulles brothers had both worked previously at the law firm Sullivan and Cromwell, where they represented large companies including J. P. Morgan, the Cuban Sugar Cane Corporation and the United Fruit Company – some of the very companies that felt they stood to lose out from developmentalism. But the Eisenhower administration knew that it would be difficult to justify attacking a movement that was so obviously rooted in the principles of equality, justice and independence. He had to find a way to get the American public onside. He did it in the end by drawing heavily on Cold War rhetoric: he painted developmentalism as the first step on the road to communism, and by connecting developmentalist governments to the USSR he was able to tar them in the minds of American citizens.

Iran became the first target of Eisenhower's backlash. Iran's democratically elected leader, Mohammad Mossadegh, had become a stalwart of the developmentalist movement. Tall, dignified and

109

Paris-educated, Mossadegh had risen to popularity in his country as a progressive politician. As prime minister, he introduced unemployment compensation and benefits for sick and injured workers. He abolished forced agricultural labour. He raised taxes on the rich in order to fund rural development projects. And, most famously, he sought to renegotiate ownership of the country's oil reserves, which at that point were controlled by the British-owned Anglo-Iranian Oil Company, now BP. When the company refused to cooperate with an audit of its accounts, the Iranian Parliament voted unanimously to nationalise the company's assets.

This move further boosted Mossadegh's popularity at home. But it outraged the British government, which quickly turned to the United States for assistance. The option of military intervention was on the table, but they worried that it might provoke the USSR into coming to Iran's aid and set off a proxy war. So they worked covertly through a secret project called Operation Ajax, which was led by CIA agent Kermit Roosevelt (the grandson of Theodore Roosevelt, the man who established the Roosevelt Corollary to the Monroe Doctrine and paved the way for US intervention abroad). It was a clever plan. First, they bribed politicians to whip up anti-government sentiment and paid demonstrators to take to the streets to create the false impression that Mossadegh was unpopular. Then they convinced the military to depose Mossadegh and hand power over to the Shah of Iran, Mohammad Reza Pahlavi. It worked: the coup in August 1953 toppled Mossadegh and the Shah assumed power as an absolute monarch alongside a military government. He governed Iran for the next twenty-six years, most of that time with US support and with policies that were friendly to Western oil companies – just as in Saudi Arabia, the West's other main client state in the region. Mossadegh, for his part, spent the rest of his life under house arrest.

Operation Ajax was one of the first US operations to overthrow a foreign government, but it was certainly not the last. The following year, in 1954, the Dulles brothers really hit their stride.

Guatemala was ruled from 1931 by Jorge Ubico, a military

dictator who enjoyed the support of the US government in return for handing over to the American-owned United Fruit Company huge tracts of highly fertile land, much of it stolen from indigenous Mayan peasants. After many years of enduring Ubico's brutal rule, a popular revolution deposed him and paved the way for the country's first democratic elections, which brought Juan José Arévalo to power in 1945. Arévalo, a professor of philosophy, was the opposite of his predecessor: while Ubico ruled Guatemala in the interests of the elite, Arévalo saw the poor as his main priority. He introduced a number of pro-poor policies, including new minimum wage laws, as a way of reversing the mass impoverishment that the Ubico regime had produced during the land grabs. After his six-year term, which was marked by unprecedented political freedom and stability, Arévalo stepped down to allow for new elections, which brought one of his ministers, Jacobo Árbenz, to power.

Árbenz – known for his Swiss ancestry and nicknamed the Big Blonde – continued the progressive policies of his predecessor, adding a new land reform programme called the Agrarian Reform Act. At the time, fewer than 3 per cent of Guatemalans owned 70 per cent of the land. Árbenz's plan was to nationalise large tracts of unused private land and redistribute it to landless peasants who had been victims of debt slavery during the Ubico years, to allow them to farm their way out of starvation. Incidentally, some 450,000 acres of the earmarked land belonged to the United Fruit Company. Despite being offered full compensation, the company refused to cooperate. Instead, they lobbied the US government to overthrow Árbenz and whipped up public support in the US using Cold War rhetoric, painting Árbenz as a Russian stooge and Guatemala as a Soviet satellite. The CIA, under the direction of Dulles – who, together with his brother, was on the payroll of United Fruit for thirty-eight years – was happy to comply. Under Operation PBSUCCESS, they bombed the capital, toppled Árbenz and installed the military dictator Carlos Castillo Armas in his place, putting an end to ten hopeful years of democracy in Guatemala. The new government quickly deregulated foreign investment, reversed the policies of the Árbenz era, and proceeded to imprison thousands of the regime's critics. Guatemala was ruled by a series of military dictatorships – all with US support – until 1996. During that time, the regime continued to force indigenous Mayans off their land, and Guatemala came to have one of the highest poverty rates in the Western hemisphere. When opposition arose, it was brutally suppressed: some 200,000 Mayans were killed for resisting the land grabs.

The invasion of Guatemala marked the end of Franklin Roosevelt's Good Neighbor policy of non-intervention in Latin America, after only twenty years of peace. In doing so, Eisenhower effectively restored the Monroe Doctrine and revived America's habit of violently projecting power across the region.

Brazil, too, was hit with a coup supported by the United States. After assuming the presidency in 1961, João Goulart – a former football player and national hero – began to roll out his signature Basic Reforms plan. He aimed to extend voting rights to illiterate people, deliver adult education to the poor, tax any profits that multinational companies attempted to transfer abroad and redistribute non-productive landholdings larger than 600 hectares. These reforms were a gift to Brazil's poor, but the elite were not pleased. Nor were US multinational companies. In 1962, the Brazilian government nationalised the country's failing telephone provider, a subsidiary of the American-owned ITT Corporation. ITT's CEO, Harold Geneen, happened to be friends with the director of the CIA at the time and lodged a complaint – not so much because he cared about the subsidiary, but because he worried that ITT's interests elsewhere in Latin America might eventually be affected by governments mimicking Goulart's policies. President Kennedy demurred. But shortly after Lyndon Johnson took office, the CIA took action, with the help of Britain. In 1964, in an operation called Brother Sam, the US assisted a military coup that deposed Goulart and installed a junta that would rule for twenty-one years. The new regime was overtly friendly to Western corporate interests and deregulated foreign investment. This rapid

market liberalisation reversed the gains against poverty that Goulart had won and restored the profit levels of American and European companies. In response to growing citizen discontent, the
junta suspended democratic freedoms and openly tortured and
assassinated political dissidents.

We could rehearse many more examples of Western-backed
interventions in Latin America. In 1953, Britain overthrew the
world's first democratically elected Marxist president in Guyana.
In 1961, the US attempted to overthrow the revolutionary government in Cuba, with the failed Bay of Pigs invasion. In 1965, President Johnson ordered the invasion of the Dominican Republic in
order to quash a popular rebellion against the military junta. Similarly, in El Salvador the US armed and supported a violent military
government through the 1980s against a popular revolution, tacitly
approving its use of death squads, torture and mass displacement
of civilians. In Nicaragua, the US provided illegal financial and
military support to a right-wing insurgency known as the
Contras throughout the 1980s, in the hope of overthrowing the
democratically elected government of Daniel Ortega, a politician
known for his commitment to developmentalism and social democracy. The US also supported right-wing dictatorships at various
times in Bolivia, Ecuador, Haiti, Paraguay, Honduras, Venezuela
and Panama. The tactical support for many of these operations
came from the School of the Americas. Located on a US military
base in Georgia, it has long been crucial to training the assassins
and dictators dispatched across Latin America to serve US interests in the region, and is still operating today as the Western Hemisphere Institute for Security Cooperation.

*

Latin America was not the only region where the US sought to
quell developmentalism. A year after the US-backed coup in Brazil,
similar – but even more devastating – events unfolded in Indonesia. After gaining independence from Dutch rule, the leader of

113

Indonesia's nationalist struggle, Sukarno, son of a primary-school teacher, assumed the presidency and rolled out classic developmentalist policies. He protected the economy from cheap foreign imports, redistributed wealth to the poor and evicted the IMF and the World Bank. Western powers resented Sukarno for these policies, and for the key role he played in mobilising the Non-Aligned Movement. So when he began to nationalise American and European assets, such as oil and rubber facilities, they took the opportunity to intervene.

When the CIA made it clear that they would back a coup, General Suharto – who was upset with President Sukarno for supporting policies that undermined the military's power – offered to lead it. In 1965, with the aid of weapons and intelligence from the United States, Suharto hunted down and killed between 500,000 and 1 million of Sukarno's supporters in one of the worst mass murders of the 20th century. By 1967, Sukarno's base had been either eliminated or intimidated into submission, and Suharto took control of the country. His military regime – which ruled until 1998 – was open to Western corporate interests. *Time* magazine famously described the political transformation of the 1960s as 'The West's best news for years in Asia'. Suharto's regime relied for its economic policies on a group of Indonesian economists who had been trained at the University of California, Berkeley, with funding from the Ford Foundation. Known as the Berkeley Mafia, they worked closely with Suharto to liberalise the economy and eliminate the last vestiges of developmentalism in the country.

In Africa, Ghana was the country to watch. In 1957, Ghana became one of the first countries in Africa to win independence, and the liberation leader Kwame Nkrumah became its first elected president. The continent's leading developmentalist thinker, Nkrumah built up Ghana's manufacturing capacity and significantly reduced the country's dependence on European imports; he nationalised the mines and regulated foreign corporations; he rolled out free healthcare and education; and he put people to work building infrastructure in rural areas. Nkrumah also became a leading voice for the liberation of the rest of Africa, and articulated a Pan-Africanist vision for uniting the continent in economic and political cooperation, abolishing once and for all the artificial divisions that colonial powers had inscribed and manipulated for their own benefit. But his vision was not limited to Africa. Like Sukarno, he was a founding member of the Non-Aligned Movement and – having watched the Western-backed coups unfold in the 1950s and early 1960s – became a fierce critic of continuing Western intervention in global South affairs. His iconic 1965 book, *Neo-Colonialism: The Last Stage of Imperialism*, put this critique into powerful prose and gave voice to the frustrations of people across the South.

All of this made Nkrumah an immediate target. Britain and the United States began plotting his removal as early as 1961. And in 1966 it happened: while Nkrumah was out of the country on a state visit, a CIA-backed coup toppled his government and installed a military junta to rule in its place. The junta brought the IMF and the World Bank in to manage the economy, privatised the country's assets, cut down barriers to foreign corporations and forced Ghana back into its previous role as exporter of raw materials. Nkrumah, for his part, lived the rest of his life in exile in Conakry, Guinea. He never returned home.

A number of other African countries experimented with the developmentalist revolution – mostly north of the Sahara – but many never got the opportunity, Western intervention was so swift. Patrice Lumumba, the young Pan-Africanist who was elected the Congo's first post-independence leader in 1960, was in office for only two months before being assassinated in a violent a coup orchestrated by Belgium and the US, on the direct orders of President Eisenhower. The US feared Lumumba would loosen their grip on the Congo's vast mineral resources, including the uranium they relied on for their nuclear programme and the cobalt they needed for their jet engines. Lumumba was shot, chopped to pieces and burned to ashes in a barrel. In his place, Western governments installed the military officer Mobutu Sese Seko, one of the world's most notorious dictators, who went on to command the country for nearly forty years with the support of aid from the US, France and Belgium, most of which he siphoned into his own offshore accounts. During Mobutu's long reign, per capita income in the Congo, which he renamed Zaire, declined at an average of 2.2 per cent each year – an extraordinary collapse. The Congolese experienced poverty on a scale even worse than they had known under Belgian colonial rule.

In Uganda, the independence leader Milton Obote became the nation's first elected prime minister in 1962. He was not the most savoury of characters, to be sure: as his tenure in office wore on he became increasingly paranoid, violent and authoritarian. But in the end he did begin to take decisive steps towards developmentalist policy. In 1969, the parliament authorised his 'Common Man's Charter', which stated: 'We hereby commit ourselves to create in Uganda conditions of full security, justice, equality, liberty, and welfare for all sons and daughters of the Republic. We reject exploitation of material and human resources for the benefit of a few [and resolve to] fight relentlessly against poverty, ignorance, disease, colonialism, neocolonialism, and apartheid. We must move in accordance with the principles of democracy; political power must be vested in the majority of the people and not the minority.' Britain, Uganda's former coloniser, was not pleased by this shift to the left, particularly when Obote's government moved to partially nationalise some of the country's major private corporations, including a number of well-known British banks. Britain intervened – with Israeli support – to topple the Obote government in 1971, and paved the way for their preferred replacement: Idi Amin, a former officer of the British Colonial Army. Amin suspended the constitution, announced military rule, forcibly expelled the Asian population and, according to evidence compiled by Amnesty International, proceeded to murder more than 500,000 of his detractors.

Portugal continued to cling to its African colonies until as late as 1975, well after the rest of the global South won its independence. They assisted in the assassination of Amílcar Cabral, the liberation leader of Guinea-Bissau and Cape Verde, depriving Africa of one of its best-known intellectuals. In Angola, they waged a long war against independence leader Agostinho Neto, an accomplished poet and devoted social reformer. When Neto sought assistance from the US for his struggle against Portuguese colonial rule, the US refused, as they were more interested in retaining their access to Angolan oil under the colonial government. When Angola finally won its independence and Neto became president, the US feared that Neto, a developmentalist, would nationalise the oil reserves, so they threw substantial support behind his opponent, the brutal rebel leader Jonas Savimbi, fuelling a civil war that would last until 2002 and leave Angola in ruins.

And then there was South Africa. Both the United States and Britain actively supported the apartheid regime all the way through the 1980s, for they feared that if Nelson Mandela and the African National Congress ever came to power they would nationalise the country's enormous deposits of gold, diamonds and platinum, which American and British companies controlled.

But no Western power intervened in postcolonial Africa as much as France. After Francophone Africa won formal independence in 1960, France worried it would lose control over the region's resources to the nationalist movements. François Mitterrand, minister of the interior at the time, famously confessed in a rare moment of honesty that 'Without Africa, France will have no history in the 21st century.' To prevent this outcome, President Charles de Gaulle and his successors intervened covertly to install puppet leaders – ridiculed in France as 'black governors' – in newly independent African nations. Known as Françafrique, this agenda was spearheaded by a secret cell headed by Jacques Foccart, chief adviser on African affairs, and funded by Elf Aquitaine, the French state-owned oil company (now Total). They rigged Cameroon's first elections and hand-picked the president, Ahmadou Ahidjo, after poisoning his main opponent. France kept Ahidjo in power for twenty-two years in return for backing French interests. They also picked Gabon's first president, Léon M'ba, and when he died installed the dictatorship of Omar Bongo, whom they supported for forty-two years in exchange for direct access to the country's oil, which has long been a major source of French wealth. In Côte d'Ivoire, France kept their man Félix Houphouët-Boigny in power from 1960 to 1993.

Many other African states have been wrapped up in the scandal of Françafrique, including Nigeria, Guinea, Niger, Congo Brazzaville, the Central African Republic and, most importantly, Burkina Faso, one of the few African countries that did successfully implement a developmentalist programme. The full scale of this vast network of political corruption and coups did not become clear until 1994, when French magistrate Eva Joly exposed it during her landmark investigation of Elf Aquitaine – what the *Guardian* called 'the biggest fraud inquiry in Europe since the Second World War'. But this did not stop France from continuing to intervene in African affairs. As recently as 2009, France is said by some to have supported rigged elections in Gabon to ensure that Bongo's son came to power after his father's death, guaranteeing France's continued access to the country's resources.

This legacy complicates some commonly held assumptions about African politics. In the Western imagination, Africa is stereotyped as a continent plagued by corrupt dictators, with the supposition being that Africans are perhaps too 'primitive' to appreciate the virtues of Western-style democracy. But the truth is that ever since the end of colonialism, Africans have been actively prevented from establishing democracies. The legacy of strongman rule in Africa is largely a Western invention, not an indigenous proclivity. Western powers have thwarted countless attempts at real independence, which casts a rather ironic light on the West's historical image as a beacon of democracy and popular sovereignty.

Meanwhile, Back in America

It was not only abroad that the Western elite found their interests blocked by the growing Keynesian consensus. The extension of Keynesian policies across the West led to higher growth rates,

RICHEST 0.1% SHARE IN NATIONAL INCOME

Source: Thomas Piketty's data on www.quandl.com

poverty reduction and improved social well-being. But it had its enemies. The elite who had gained so much during the Gilded Age and
the Roaring Twenties suffered a serious hit to their wealth as a result
of these policies. In the United States, the share of national income
going to the richest 1 per cent was cut in half, to 8 per cent. It was even
worse for the richest 0.1 per cent. The share of national income going
to this cohort reached historic lows in the 1960s and 1970s.

Part of this had to do with the higher taxes levied on the upper
classes; in the United States, the top marginal tax rate hovered
around 90 per cent during the 1940s and 1950s. (Today, politicians
like to claim that higher taxes will slow down the economy, yet historical data shows that the US enjoyed some of its highest rates of
growth during the period of 90 per cent tax.) But it also had to do
with higher wages commanded by workers who were increasingly
empowered – through unions – to bargain for a fairer share of

profits. During the 1940s and 1950s, around 35 per cent of workers in the United States were unionised – higher than ever before.

The elite – those whose wealth was eroded by higher taxes and higher wages – were desperate for a solution, and they found it in the ideas of Friedrich Hayek and Milton Friedman. Friedman was an American economist born to immigrant parents from Eastern Europe who ran a textile sweatshop in New Jersey. His father was vehemently against unions and state regulations – anything that might compromise his business profits – and Friedman grew to share his views. Since the 1930s, Friedman had openly called for the destruction of the New Deal, particularly its price- and wage-fixing mechanisms. His chief inspiration was Hayek, the Austrian-born economist at the London School of Economics who had become known for his 1944 book *The Road to Serfdom*, in which he argued that any intervention in the economy would inevitably lead to the kind of totalitarianism that characterised fascist Germany and Communist Russia. But there was virtually no audience for these views at the time. Everyone was Keynesian, and the memory of the Great Depression meant that people were reluctant to return to the dangerous days of laissez-faire capitalism. Nonetheless, the two men continued to propagate their ideas, hoping they would eventually take hold. In 1947, they formed the Mont Pèlerin Society along with others who shared their ideology. It was a club of free-market economists, named for its location in the elite Swiss resort town, established to push these ideas as urgently as possible into the public sphere.

By 1950, both Hayek and Friedman had accepted posts in the economics department at the University of Chicago, which soon became a hub for the liberal revival in economics. Friedman, as head of the department, pursued his ideas with a kind of activist fervour. He believed in the vision of a totally pure market, and held that the economy should be returned to its 'natural' state, prior to what he saw as the distortions of human intervention. Once freed of such distortions, his thinking went, the market – left to its own devices – would function smoothly and perfectly, distributing

wealth and goods in the most efficient manner possible. Friedman sought to achieve a sort of utopian perfection, a universe playing out according to simple, logical economic models, where everyone acting in their own self-interest would yield the maximum benefit for all. For Friedman, economic problems like high inflation or unemployment were signs that the market was not truly free, that some form of artificial interference needed to be removed.

What made Friedman's ideas so powerful was that he insisted that the free market was not only in accordance with the economic laws of nature, but also with the values of democracy and freedom. He worked to establish strong connections in the public imagination between the ideas of market freedom and individual liberty. We should all be free to express our own desires in the market, he claimed; indeed, he regarded this as the very essence of democratic participation. These views eventually became the basis for his 1962 book, *Capitalism and Freedom*. This version of freedom was to compete with the Keynesian idea of freedom, in which real freedom lay in freedom from want, which in turn required placing constraints on elite accumulation. For Friedman and Hayek, any such constraint was a sort of evil – a flaw that marred the perfection of an otherwise beautiful system and eroded the very possibility of freedom. The theory was compelling for its sheer elegance.

For Friedman and his followers, their great enemy was not only Keynesianism in the United States, but also social democrats in Europe and the developmentalists in the global South. They saw all of these systems as contaminated forms of capitalism that needed to be purified. There was price-fixing to make basic goods more affordable. There were minimum wage laws to protect workers from exploitation. Certain services – like education and healthcare – were kept out of the market altogether to ensure universal access. These policies were improving people's lives, but Friedman claimed that they were doing hidden harm by disrupting the equilibrium of the market. Price controls, subsidies and minimum wage laws should all be abandoned, and the state should sell off any services that corporations could run at a profit, including education,

healthcare, pensions and national parks. Governments should cut back social spending so as not to interfere with the labour market. Taxes should be at a flat rate. And corporations should be free to sell their products anywhere in the world. If implemented, he claimed, these policies would lead to unprecedented growth and prosperity.

This economic ideology came to be known as neoliberalism. It is 'neo' in the sense that it revived classical market liberalism from the death it had suffered after the Great Depression, but it also added a few new elements. The notion that market freedom is tantamount to individual liberty was a new and distinctive feature of the ideology – and became central to its political success in the West. And neoliberalism abandoned any pretence to neutrality in favour of a more politically charged agenda: it was against subsidies and protections for the working class and regulations that supported unions, but was quite comfortable with subsidies and protections for the rich and regulations that supported large corporations.

During the 1970s, neoliberal ideas were celebrated by the upper classes and the corporate world, who were thrilled to have an academic mouthpiece – in the form of Friedman and the University of Chicago – to lend their economic agenda an aura of legitimacy. Before long, the Chicago School was flush with corporate donations. There was only one problem: there was no way that ordinary citizens were going to buy into it, since Keynesianism had delivered them such monumental gains. It was not possible to acquire the political capital necessary to make these radical changes in the US or Europe.

But it *was* possible to test these theories abroad, in the meantime.

The Chile Experiment

During the 1950s and 1960s, the United States had become particularly concerned about Chile. As the home of the UN's Economic Commission for Latin America and figures like Raúl Prebisch, Chile had become the centre of developmentalist thinking in Latin

America. The US feared that these ideas would spread across the rest of the continent.

To counter this tendency, the US government launched Project Chile in 1956. The goal was to resist developmentalism by training Chilean economics students – around 100 of them – in the principles of neoliberal theory at the University of Chicago. A decade later, the programme was expanded to include students from across the continent, and eventually led to the formation of the Center for Latin American Economic Studies at Chicago. It was ideological warfare. The idea was to train students to scorn social safety nets, trade barriers, infant industry protection, price controls, public services and many of the other policies being promoted by progressive Latin American economists at the time. Juan Gabriel Valdés, a Chilean minister during the 1990s, has described this operation as 'a striking example of an organized transfer of ideology from the United States to a country within its direct sphere of influence'. Interestingly, this project was conceived under the Point Four programme inaugurated by Truman, and was conducted by the US International Cooperation Administration (which would later become USAID), with funding from the Ford Foundation. In other words, it was one of America's first official 'international development' programmes.

But despite the millions of dollars that donors like USAID and the Ford Foundation pumped into this project, it was failing miserably. Developmentalism continued to gain pace in Latin America, and many voters wanted yet more nationalisation, land reforms and cooperation among global South countries.

Nowhere was this clearer than in Chile. Developmentalism received a promising boost when voters elected Salvador Allende – a thoughtful, unpretentious doctor with thick-rimmed spectacles who was popular for his progressive views. At the time, much of Chile's population was still mired in extreme poverty, while a small elite controlled most of the country's vast land and wealth. Allende was lifted to power on his promise of a fairer society: better wages, public education, healthcare, housing and fairer rents. His victory was an impressive achievement, given that the CIA and US corporations had attempted to manipulate the outcome of the election in favour of Allende's right-wing opponent, Jorge Alessandri.

Allende's government delivered. He established a minimum wage, reduced the price of bread, rolled out free school meals, expanded low-income housing and extended public transportation to working-class neighbourhoods. He nationalised the copper mines and capped land ownership at 80 hectares (fully compensating all private owners), ending the colonial *latifundia* and redistributing land to peasant farmers.

And it worked. Wages rose, poverty rates declined, school enrolment reached record levels. But the United States was not happy. Allende's nationalisation and land reform programmes appeared to threaten US economic interests; after all, US corporations had $964 million invested in Chile and were earning an average return of 17.4 per cent on it. Allende pledged full compensation for anyone who would lose their property or investments as a result, but this failed to pacify the US, which feared Allende's popularity would trigger a broader turn to the left in Latin America. At the time, 20 per cent of total US foreign investments were tied up in Latin America, and US firms had 5,436 subsidiaries in the region, with significant profits at stake; they didn't want to see the rise of more Allende-style governments among Chile's neighbours.

At first, the United States tried to force Allende to back off his nationalisation programme by applying non-military pressure, doing everything in their power to strangle the Chilean economy. President Richard Nixon famously ordered the CIA director, Richard Helms, to 'make the economy scream'. The US blocked government loans to Chile and encouraged private banks to do the same. They placed a moratorium on Chilean copper imports for six months, thus depleting Chile's foreign currency reserves. And the CIA used *El Mercurio*, a newspaper owned by US multinational ITT, to disseminate anti-Allende propaganda. But all these efforts came to naught: by 1973, Allende was still in power. In fact, his party had *gained* support during those three years. The US felt it had no choice but to shift to a more aggressive stance, and resorted to the tactic they had used in Guatemala and Indonesia – the good old-fashioned coup. It was executed on 11 September 1973, by General Augusto Pinochet with CIA support under the code name Operation Fubelt.

British-made bombers – sent on the order of the CIA – came in low over the rooftops of Santiago and pounded the presidential palace with mortars and missiles. The rooftops and walls exploded in columns of billowing dust and smoke, putting an end to Salvador Allende and the hopes of his people. In the minutes before his death, Allende delivered his last address to the nation: 'My words do not have bitterness but disappointment,' he began. 'I will pay for the loyalty of the people with my life. I am certain that the seeds which we have planted in the good conscience of thousands and thousands of Chileans will not be shrivelled for ever. Workers of my country: I want to thank you for the confidence you deposited in a man who was only an interpreter of great yearnings for justice. I have faith in Chile and its destiny. Other men will overcome this dark and bitter moment when treason seeks to prevail.'

For his efforts, Allende ended up sprawled on a red couch in his office with half his skull blown off. His spectacles lay shattered on the floor. Richard Nixon, in a similar office 5,000 miles away, nodded with approval.

Pinochet's rise to power was swift and brutal. According to declassified CIA documents, after bombing the presidential palace he proceeded to arrest and imprison between 80,000 and 100,000 people who supported Allende's ideas, most of them peasants and workers. Three thousand two hundred people were disappeared or executed, many of them in sports stadiums reconfigured as mass death camps during the early days of the regime. Two hundred thousand fled the country as political refugees.

The coup in Chile was similar in style to earlier US-backed coups, but it had a crucial new element. Instead of simply installing a new leader who would be friendly to US corporate interests, the US sought to totally remake economic policy in line with

125

free-market principles – which was possible only because all opposition had been destroyed. According to a 1975 US Senate Committee investigation: 'CIA collaborators were involved in preparing an initial overall economic plan which has served as the basis for the Junta's most important economic decisions.' The CIA funded a group of Chilean economists – graduates of the University of Chicago known as the Chicago Boys – to advise Pinochet's regime, with the goal of instating the prescriptions laid down by Milton Friedman in *Capitalism and Freedom*. Indeed, Friedman himself was a key adviser to the Pinochet regime.

The results of Friedman's experiments in Chile were devastating. Hyperinflation set in immediately after the coup, hitting as high as 341 per cent. To quell it the Chicago Boys clamped down on the money supply, which caused a recession and sent unemployment to nearly 19 per cent (it had been 3 per cent under Allende). Over the following years, they set about privatising nearly 500 state companies, including banks, and even sold off the public schools and the social security system. They removed tariff barriers until even the manufacturers' association that had backed the coup complained about cheap imports undercutting their businesses. They ended subsidies and price controls, which sent the cost of living soaring. And they halved government spending on social services, while the military received an increase. Even *The Economist* called it 'an orgy of self-mutilation'.

There was some recovery after 1978, buoyed by speculative finance from abroad, but in 1982 the economy crashed hard: hyperinflation struck again, and unemployment reached 35 per cent. Eventually things got so bad that Pinochet was forced to respond by firing many of the Chicago Boys and renationalising many of the privatised companies and banks. In fact, the only reason the economy didn't fall apart completely was because Codelco, the state copper mining company, had never been privatised and continued to supply 85 per cent of the country's revenue. It was not until 1988 that the economy recovered, at which point Friedman and the Chicago Boys finally felt they could declare the experiment a success. But a success for whom? The poverty rate was 41 per cent. Average wages were 14 per cent lower. The minimum wage was 42 per cent lower. And hunger was widespread, with the food intake of the poorest 40 per cent of the population having plunged from 2,000 calories per day to 1,600. Even as late as 1993, GDP per capita was 12 per cent below its pre-coup level. The only people that benefited from the new economic regime were the elite. Banks and foreign investors were having a field day, 'liberated' as they were from regulation. And with the incomes of the richest 10 per cent soaring – with their share of the national pie up by 28 per cent – Chile had become one of the most unequal societies in the world.

*

The people of Chile were not the only victims of this new tactic. The same economic strategy was applied elsewhere in Latin America, also with backing from the United States. The Chicago Boys were key advisers to the Brazilian government in the 1970s as it presided over economic reforms similar to those inflicted on Chile. In Uruguay, a US-backed military junta took power in 1973 and applied Chicago School principles. In Argentina, a US-backed junta seized power in 1976 and did the same: banning strikes, lifting price controls, privatising state companies and using torture to quell any resistance. Real wages declined by 40 per cent, and more than half the population was pushed below the poverty line. The very countries that had once been a beacon of hope for equitable development in the global South had been radically transformed. Arnold Harberger, the economist in charge of the Latin America programme at the University of Chicago, served as an adviser to each of these regimes, and also consulted for Bolivia's military dictatorship.

The point to take from this sordid story is that neoliberal economic policies were so obviously destructive to people's lives that it was very difficult to get them implemented in a democratic government. In most cases, the only way to bring them in was through military dictatorship and a state terror programme that would quash resistance wherever it emerged. In order to aggressively deregulate the economy, you first have to aggressively regulate the political sphere. Total market freedom requires total political unfreedom, even to the extent of mass imprisonment and concentration camps.

Neoliberalism Comes Home

Chile was the first victory in the Chicago-led counter-revolution. But it remained impossible to impose neoliberal policies in the United States and Europe – the Keynesian system was far too popular and, unlike in Chile and other Latin American countries, where democracy had been suspended, voters would quickly reject any attempt to roll it back. Yet this consensus began to change in the 1970s. Keynesianism had delivered high growth rates through the 1950s and 1960s, but by the early 1970s the US and Europe were beginning to face a crisis of 'stagflation' – a combination of high inflation and economic stagnation. Inflation rates soared from about 3 per cent in 1965 to about 12 per cent ten years later. According to standard Keynesian theory, when inflation rises, unemployment should decrease. But this time something strange was happening: unemployment was rising along with inflation. This dealt a serious blow to the credibility of Keynesian ideas, and created a golden opportunity for critics to offer up the alternatives they had been formulating – and testing – behind the scenes.

What set off the crisis of stagflation? Most scholars point to a few key events that happened during the Nixon administration. For one, Nixon was engaged in expansionary monetary policy – in other words, he was effectively printing money. On top of this, government spending on the Vietnam War at the time was spiralling out of control. As international markets worried that the US would not be able to make good on its debts, the dollar began to plummet in value and contributed further to inflation. And while all of this trouble was unfolding, another crisis hit. In 1973, OPEC decided to drive up the price of oil. The price of consumer goods suddenly shot up too, because the energy required to produce and transport them was more expensive. And because production became more expensive, economic growth slowed down and unemployment began to rise. It was a perfect storm.

The crisis of stagflation was the direct consequence of specific historical events. But the neoliberals rejected these explanations. Instead, they insisted that stagflation was a product of Keynesianism – the consequence of onerous taxes on the wealthy, too much economic regulation, labour unions that had become too powerful and wages that were too high. Government intervention, they claimed, had made markets inefficient, distorted prices and made it impossible for economic actors to act rationally. The whole market system was out of whack, and stagflation was the inevitable consequence. Keynesianism had failed, they claimed, and the system needed to be scrapped. In the end, this argument prevailed. Not because it was correct, but because it had more firepower behind it – and when it came to swaying public opinion it helped that Hayek and Friedman had both won the Nobel Memorial Prize in Economics for their ideas along these lines, in 1974 and 1976 respectively. The argument held a great deal of appeal for the wealthy, who were looking for a way to restore their class power, and they were more than happy to step in to support it. The crisis of the 1970s became a perfect excuse to dismantle the social contract of the post-war decades.

The upper class got their fix in the form of the 'Volcker Shock'. Paul Volcker, chairman of the US Federal Reserve, argued that the only way to put an end to inflation was to dramatically raise interest rates, clamping down on the supply of money in order to recuperate its value. During the Reagan administration, Volcker jacked up interest rates from the low single digits to as high as 20 per cent. This caused a massive recession, as it dramatically increased the costs of doing business. As businesses laid off workers, unemployment rates shot to over 10 per cent. This decimated the power of organised labour, which had been the crucial counterbalance to the excesses that had led to the Great Depression. In sum, the Volcker Shock had devastating effects on the working class. It caused wages to collapse, and mortgage defaults tripled. But it cured inflation.

If tight monetarist policy (i.e. targeting low inflation) was the first component of neoliberalism to be put in place in the early 1980s, the second was 'supply-side economics'. Reagan wanted to give more money to the already rich as a way of stimulating economic growth, the assumption being that they would invest their windfall cash in a productive way and generate new wealth that would gradually 'trickle down' to the rest of society. He cut the top marginal tax rate from 70 per cent to 28 per cent, and reduced the maximum capital gains tax to 20 per cent, the lowest since the Great Depression. But Reagan didn't cut taxes for everyone; in order to plug the hole left by tax cuts for the rich, he *raised* payroll taxes on the working class. A third component of Reagan's economic plan was to deregulate the financial sector. Because Volcker considered this policy to be too extreme, Reagan appointed Alan Greenspan to take his place in 1987. Greenspan went about unravelling many of the banking regulations that had been established in the post-war era. He even managed to abolish the Glass–Steagall Act, which had been designed to prevent banks from engaging in the sort of reckless speculation that had triggered the Great Depression.

Margaret Thatcher, who drew inspiration from Milton Friedman, implemented many of these same policies in Britain, at exactly the same time: high interest rates designed to clamp down on inflation, regressive taxation such as the 'poll tax' of 1989, and aggressive financial deregulation. Thatcher was particularly focused on breaking the labour unions, which she regarded as preventing the economy from operating efficiently. She defeated the National Union of Mineworkers in 1985 after a bruising battle, and introduced legislation to curb workers' rights. She also made deep cuts to public spending and – the centrepiece of her economic policy – privatised most of Britain's famous national companies, including British Petroleum, British Airways and Rolls-Royce, along with public utilities including water and electricity.

These policies drove social inequality to unprecedented levels in the US and Britain. Productivity increased steadily while wages stagnated, effectively shifting an increasing proportion of profits from workers to the owners of capital. CEO salaries grew by an average of 400 per cent during the 1990s while workers' wages grew by less than 5 per cent and the US minimum wage *decreased* by more than 9 per cent. The share of national income captured by the top strata of society also increased at an alarming rate. In the US, the portion going to the top 1 per cent more than doubled from 8 per cent in 1980 to 18 per cent today. Britain witnessed a similar jump during this period, with the share claimed by the richest growing from 6.5 per cent to 13 per cent. According to US Census data, the top 5 per cent of American households have seen their incomes increase by 72.7 per cent since 1980, while median household incomes have stagnated and the bottom quintile have seen their incomes *fall* by 7.4 per cent. In other words, the neoliberal counter-revolution restored levels of inequality that had not been seen since before the Great Depression.

So much for the trickle-down effect. As it turns out, making rich people richer doesn't make the rest of us richer. Nor does it stimulate economic growth, which is the sole justification for supply-side economics. In fact, quite the opposite is true: since the onset of neoliberalism, the rich countries of the OECD have seen per capita growth rates *fall* from an average of 3.5 per cent during the 1960s and 1970s down to an average of 2 per cent during the 1980s and 1990s. As these numbers show, neoliberalism has failed as a tool for economic development – but it *has* worked brilliantly as a tool for restoring power to the wealthy elite.

*

The developmentalist policies that were introduced across the global South after the end of colonialism succeeded in reducing inequality and poverty. The movement operated according to a vision that was diametrically opposed to Truman's narrative: it saw

131

inequality and poverty not as natural phenomena, or as a sign of moral failure, but rather as a matter of injustice – a political problem that demanded political solutions. Poor countries didn't want aid from the West, they wanted a fairer global economic system, with the latitude to determine their own economic policies. They refused to be playgrounds for foreign extraction.

We can learn a great deal from the legacy of developmentalism. The solution to mass poverty turns out to be remarkably simple. Poor people don't need charity, they need fair wages for their work, labour unions to defend those wages and state regulation that prevents exploitation. They need decent public services – such as universal healthcare and education – and a progressive taxation system capable of funding them. They need fair access to land and a fair share of natural resource wealth. In other words, real development requires the redistribution of power, which then in most cases naturally precipitates a redistribution of resources. Developmentalist policies were generally brought in by democratically elected governments that had broad popular support, although a few of them – as in Egypt – calcified into authoritarian regimes. But in all cases, developmentalist governments sought to change the rules of national economies to make them fairer for the majority, so that economic systems would serve the interests of the people rather than just the interests of the national elite and foreign corporations.

In short, the fight against poverty and underdevelopment during this period was understood as a *political* battle. It sought to challenge the prevailing distribution of power and resources around the world.

And this is exactly what the West would not tolerate. Not all developmentalist states were subject to retaliation during this period, like India, China, Libya, Algeria, Egypt, Syria, Iraq, Tanzania and a number of East Asian countries. Some of them were either too powerful to cross without igniting open warfare, while others simply didn't pose enough of a threat to Western interests. But in the key cases described above, Western governments intervened on the side of disgruntled national elites in order to roll back developmentalist legislation. Under the banner of the Cold War, pro-poor legislation was demonised in Western media as 'communist', and this designation gave Western governments licence to employ even the most draconian tactics with impunity. Yet few of the global South leaders who were assassinated or deposed during this period identified as communist; for the most part, they were explicitly non-aligned, and championed the third way of a Keynesian mixed economy. Indeed, they were merely mimicking the policies that the US and Europe had used themselves to such great effect. If we dig behind the rhetoric, it becomes clear that Western support for right-wing coups had little to do with Cold War ideology, and certainly nothing to do with promoting democracy (quite the opposite!); the goal, rather, was to defend Western economic interests. The veil of the Cold War has obscured this blunt fact from view.

It is interesting to imagine how states such as Guatemala, Brazil, Iran, Indonesia and the Congo would have developed had they been allowed to continue with their pro-poor policies in peace. It is possible that by now they would have come very close to eradicating poverty, and perhaps even shed their Third World status altogether – as many East Asian countries managed to do. Sadly, they were prevented from taking this path.

*

But there is one point of caution that we should take care to note. Developmentalism was not without its flaws. Rapid economic growth, industrialisation and 'modernisation' came with significant costs. In many cases it meant pushing peasant farmers off the land in order to make way for bigger, more 'efficient' operations. It meant displacing communities in order to build dams. It meant drawing people into the labour force for the first time, making them dependent on wages for survival and roping them into consumer markets. And it had environmental costs, too, such as soil degradation from high-input farming, pollution from power stations and factories, and ecosystem disruption caused by industries like mining and forestry. In 1980, at the end of the developmentalist period, even Raúl Prebisch – one of the movement's founders – had come to recognise these issues: 'We thought that an acceleration in the rate of growth would solve all problems,' he said. 'This was our great mistake.'

In other words, the focus on rapid economic growth sped up the process of commodifying human life and nature that had begun under colonialism. And as under colonialism, in most cases 'traditional' values and lifeways were treated as a barrier to economic growth and social progress, and were often purposefully eradicated. Developmentalism was, after all, a Western model. By adopting the growth-at-all-costs agenda and by looking to the West as the apex of economic achievement, global South countries missed their opportunity to chart an alternative trajectory from the outset – one that would be rooted in care, ecology and sustainability; one that would draw on rather than reject indigenous values; and one that would measure progress by more meaningful indicators than GDP. Instead they jumped on to the very bandwagon that we now recognise has brought us to the brink of climate change and ecological crisis.

PART THREE

The New Colonialism

Five

Debt and the Economics of Planned Misery

There are two ways to conquer and enslave a nation. One is by the sword. The other is by debt.

John Adams

The Western-backed coups of the 1950s and 1960s hobbled progress in a number of key countries, and put an end to some of the developing world's most effective leaders. But despite these setbacks, the global South was still rising. Governments across the region realised that because they controlled most of the natural resources and raw materials that Western powers needed for their industries, they didn't have to accept the shoddy terms of trade that the West offered. Some took steps to improve the prices of their commodity exports by working together in groups. The Organization of Petroleum Exporting Countries (OPEC), for example, gained traction during the 1960s and, much to the dismay of Western powers, proved that they could drive up oil prices. Other groups began to organise around commodities like copper, bananas and bauxite. The possibilities were endless.

137

Emboldened by their growing strength, the countries of the G77 coalesced around a proposal to make the rules of the global economy fairer for the world's majority. They called it the New International Economic Order (NIEO), and in 1973 they got it passed by the General Assembly of the United Nations. The NIEO proposed that developing countries should have the right to regulate multinational corporations; the right to nationalise foreign-owned assets when necessary; the right to protect their economies with tariffs; the right to cooperate with each other to maintain reasonable prices for raw materials; and, most importantly, the freedom to do these things without fear of retaliation or invasion by Western powers. They also believed that access to development finance and technology transfers should come without strings attached, so that Western creditors would not be able to manipulate them.

The adoption of the NIEO at the UN represented the highest achievement of developmentalism – the very summit of Third World political consciousness. It drove right to the deepest causes of global inequality, pointing out that the international economic system was effectively rigged in the interests of Western powers at the expense of virtually everyone else.

Western powers, for their part, were enraged by this movement, and worried about the successes the South was scoring at the United Nations. They realised that in the new era of global democracy – in the halls of the UN General Assembly – they would no longer be able to dominate the world's majority. Their strategy of resisting the rise of the South with coups had worked well enough for a time, but it was a piecemeal effort, and as the 1970s wore on and people became more sensitive to issues of human rights and national sovereignty, Western voters were often reluctant to allow such neocolonial violence to be conducted in their name.

They needed a new plan. In 1975, the leaders of the US, Britain, France, Italy, Japan and West Germany met at Château de Rambouillet in northern France to form the alliance that – with the later addition of Canada – would become the G7. The goal was to counter the rise of developmentalism and the NIEO, and to prevent global South countries from working together to increase the prices of raw materials. Henry Kissinger, the US secretary of state at the time, laid out the new geopolitical strategies that the group would use. He proposed to shift the most important decisions at the UN away from the General Assembly to the Security Council, which the rich nations controlled. Next, he laid out plans to divide the G77 by using aid as an instrument of control. The idea was to create a new group of so-called Least Developed Countries (LDCs) – the poorest and most desperate members of the global South – and offer them aid in exchange for siding with the West against OPEC and the rest of the G77. Aid would be wielded as an intentional strategy to shatter global South unity.

Borrowing from Truman, Kissinger also sought to wield the *narrative* of aid in order to defuse the rising political power of the South, especially at the United Nations. He insisted that the question of global inequality and development should not be approached as a political question but rather as a matter of national responsibility. Rich nations were not responsible for causing the poverty of the global South, he insisted. Quite the opposite – they were prepared to give aid to help poor countries develop. Desperate to avoid any substantive redistribution of power and resources, Kissinger sought to change the narrative about inequality altogether, hoping to convince the LDCs to abandon their demands for global political reform and settle for aid handouts instead.

It is possible that these new strategies might have turned the tables on the South. But the Non-Aligned Movement was a formidable force, and it seems likely that they would have been able to see through Kissinger's plans. We will never know, because only a few years after the G7 gathered at Château de Rambouillet, something happened that changed the course of international history for ever, giving Western powers the decisive upper hand and abruptly reversing the South's rise. In what seemed like the blink of an eye, the US and Europe seized de facto control over the economic destinies of developing countries, conquering them all over again without spilling a single drop of blood. Instead of conquistadors on horses or secret agents in smoke-filled rooms, this time the job was done by bankers and bureaucrats – an army of men in grey suits with briefcases, dealing in nothing more glamorous than loan portfolios.

A Crisis of Debt

This surprising turn of events had been building in the background for a number of years, beginning with drama in the Middle East. In 1967, Israel launched unexpected attacks against Egypt that sparked a regional conflagration known as the Six Day War. During the chaos that ensued, Israel took the opportunity to seize territory from its Arab neighbours, annexing Gaza and the Sinai Peninsula from Egypt, East Jerusalem and the West Bank from Jordan and the Golan Heights from Syria. Outraged by this incursion, the Arab states plotted to recover their land. Six years later, in 1973, they launched a surprise attack of their own against Israel. But things didn't go quite as smoothly as planned. The United States stepped in to support Israel, its main ally in the region, with an immense shipment of military aid. Arab States were upset by this move, as it gave Israel an unexpected advantage. So they retaliated by unleashing the 'oil weapon'. Working with Saudi Arabia and OPEC, they raised the price of oil by 70 per cent, hoping this would force the US to back down. The US was undeterred. In fact, three days later President Nixon asked Congress to deliver an additional $2.2 billion in military aid to Israel. In response, the Arab coalition took an even more extreme step, imposing a total embargo on oil shipments to the US and a partial embargo on shipments to Western Europe. By the end of the embargo in March 1974, the price of oil had risen from $3 per barrel to nearly $12.

The embargo sent a massive shock through the US economy and triggered the crisis of high inflation and low growth that characterised the 1970s. Desperate for a quick solution, Nixon considered invading the Middle East to seize the oil fields, but at the last minute the two sides managed to reach a negotiated settlement. Israel withdrew from the Sinai Peninsula, thus placating Egypt; and Saudi Arabia would ensure that oil prices remained at a level acceptable to the United States in exchange for US military aid that would help the House of Saud hold off their domestic political enemies. But there was another, more important dimension to the settlement. As a result of the oil price increases, OPEC states suddenly found themselves awash with excess cash worth more than $450 billion. The only problem was that they didn't know what to do with all the money. Because there was nowhere to invest it internally, Saudi Arabia and other OPEC nations decided to circulate or 'recycle' the money through Wall Street banks, probably to some extent under the pressure of US compulsion, as part of the negotiated settlement.

So $450 billion of petrodollars poured into US banks in a very short period of time. But the banks, too, faced the problem of what to do with it all. Western economies were stagnating, so domestic investments were not a profitable option. Scrambling for a different plan, they decided to invest the money abroad in the form of loans to global South countries. What began as a fringe idea quickly turned into a booming business. Many global South countries, having emerged from the rubble of colonialism just two decades prior, were hungry for capital to build up their economies and to fuel import-substitution industrialisation, which was taking off across the region. On top of this, after 1973 they also needed additional finance to cover the higher costs of oil. In short, they were eager to borrow.

The banks considered these loans to be a safe investment. They assumed that governments would be very unlikely to default. 'Countries don't go bust,' as Citibank CEO Walter Wriston was fond of saying. This made good sense at the time – especially given that developmentalism was working and global South economies were soaring; no one thought they would have any difficulty repaying debts. So banks like Citibank, Chase, Deutsche Bank and others sent representatives jetting all around the global South to convince governments to take out big loans. They called this 'go-go banking', or 'loan pushing'. Many of these loans were legitimate, of course. But in the midst of all the excitement, some banks got carried away. Loan pushers were trained to invent inflated projections of how beneficial the loans would be, manipulating statistics to convince governments to borrow even if they knew full well that they would never be able to repay. Pushers often focused specifically on dictatorships, since – given the absence of democratic accountability – they were much more likely to accept these risky loans, which they could very easily use to line their own pockets, either by stealing the money directly from public accounts or by channelling it through the government and into their own contracting businesses. In this sense, the dictatorships that the US government helped install during the 1950s and 1960s – as in Guatemala, Chile and the Congo – suddenly proved useful in a new way.

It was basically a global sub-prime market. For loan pushers, what counted was not the quality of the loans, but their quantity. For each loan they sold, they made a handsome kickback in the form of so-called 'participation fees': for example, a loan of $100 million with a participation fee of just 1.5 per cent would land them a quick bonus of $1.5 million. These 'juicers' created a strong incentive to get as many loans out the door as possible, without giving much thought to whether the recipients would ever be able to pay them back. These kinds of incentives are known to be problematic, since they induce predatory lending behaviours that generate toxic debts at high risk of default.

Debt levels in the global South skyrocketed – particularly in Latin America, which was the focus of most of the lending. And the situation was made even worse in 1979, when the Iranian Revolution led to a second oil price hike that forced developing countries to borrow yet more to finance their energy needs. By 1982, total debt stocks had quadrupled, from $400 billion in 1970 to more than $1.6 trillion twelve years later. In many countries, debt levels reached well over 50 per cent of GDP. If the loans had been used to build productive capacity, this might have been all right. But because they were used largely to cover rising oil prices, the prospect of future repayment began to seem a pipe dream. To make matters worse, the terms of trade between global South countries and their Western counterparts were continuing to deteriorate; their raw material exports were worth less and less compared to the manufactured products they had to buy from abroad, so any income they might have used to repay debt was quickly diminishing. And the recession in the West meant there was less demand for their exports in the first place. It was a crisis waiting to happen.

The banks, meanwhile, were having a field day. Through the miracle of compound interest, they were raking in enormous profits – more than $100 billion per year by 1980. There was only one problem. The loans were denominated in US dollars, and the interest rates were variable. This meant that any significant rise in US interest rates would mean the interest rates on the loans would rise too, possibly pushing vulnerable poor countries into default. And that's exactly what happened in 1981, when US Federal Reserve Chairman Paul Volcker jacked interest rates up as high as 21 per cent. Poor countries found that they simply could not repay their loans at such high rates. In 1982, Mexico took the inevitable step and defaulted on part of its $80 billion debt. This move spurred other heavily indebted countries – such as Brazil and Argentina – to do the same, and set off what became known as the Third World Debt Crisis.

Remote-Control Power

From the perspective of the bankers, the Third World Debt Crisis was a complete catastrophe. According to basic free-market theory, when a borrower defaults on a loan, the loss should be shouldered by the lender; after all, it was their risk to begin with. But Wall Street had so much invested in Third World debt they knew that they would be unable to absorb the losses, and would almost certainly collapse. They refused to let this happen. They set about

143

convincing the US government to bail them out, claiming that if they collapsed then the whole financial system would crash, credit markets would dry up and the global economy would spiral into recession.

And that is exactly what they got. The US government stepped in to bail out the banks by forcing Mexico and other countries to repay their loans. They did this by repurposing the International Monetary Fund. The IMF was originally designed to use its own money to lend to countries with balance of payments problems, so that they could keep government spending up and therefore avoid another depression. It was John Maynard Keynes's plan for making sure that the economy of the industrialised world stayed afloat during hard times. But now the G7 was going to use the IMF for a different purpose entirely: to force global South countries to *stop* government spending and use their money instead to repay loans to Western banks. In other words, the IMF came to act as a global debt enforcer – the equivalent of the bailiff who comes to repossess your car, only much more powerful. This radical shift in the mission of the IMF was only possible because during this period IMF leaders – such as managing director Jacques de Larosière – systematically purged the institution of people who supported the original Keynesian philosophy and replaced them with figures more amenable to neoliberal ideology.

This is how the plan was supposed to work: the IMF would help developing countries finance their debt on the condition that they would agree to a series of 'structural adjustment programmes'. Structural adjustment programmes, or SAPs, included two basic mechanisms for debt repayment. First, developing countries had to redirect all their existing cash flows and assets towards debt service. They had to cut spending on public services like healthcare and education and on subsidies for things like farming, food and infant industries; they also had to privatise public assets by selling off state companies like telecoms and railways. In other words, they had to reverse their developmentalist reforms. The savings gleaned from spending cuts and the proceeds of privatisation would then be funnelled back to Wall Street to repay debts. In other words, public assets and social spending retroactively became collateral in the repayment of foreign loans – an arrangement that was, of course, never agreed at the time the loans were signed. Global South countries were made to pay for the banks' risky practices with billions – even trillions – of dollars taken from ordinary people. This amounted to an enormous transfer of wealth from the public coffers of impoverished global South countries to the richest banks in the West.

The second mechanism was slightly less direct. Countries that were subject to structural adjustment programmes were forced to radically deregulate their economies. They had to cut trade tariffs, open their markets to foreign competitors, abolish capital controls, abandon price controls and curb regulations on labour and the environment in order to 'attract foreign direct investment' and make their economies more 'efficient'. The claim was that these free-market reforms would increase the rate of economic growth and therefore enable quicker debt repayment. As the bankers put it, countries would be able to 'grow their way out of debt'. Debtor countries were also forced to orient their economies towards exports, to get more hard currency to repay their loans. This meant abandoning the import-substitution programmes they had used to such good effect during the developmentalist era. In addition, structural adjustment programmes required debtors to keep inflation low – a kind of monetary austerity – because the bankers feared they would use inflation to depreciate the value of their debt. This was a big blow to global South countries, not only because it prevented them from inflating away their debt, but also because it barred them from using monetary expansion to spur growth and create employment.

So SAPs introduced a three-part cocktail: austerity, privatisation and liberalisation. These principles were applied across the board, not just in Mexico, Argentina, Brazil and India – the first victims of structural adjustment – but in every country that was placed under the control of the IMF, regardless of their local economic conditions or the particular needs of their people. It was a one-size-fits-all blueprint, handed down from above by Washington-based technocrats – the central planners of an emerging global economic order that claimed, ironically, to detest central planning.

The promise was that these policies would alleviate the debt crisis and prevent it from recurring. But this was a very subtle sleight of hand – a kind of ruse. The structural adjustment reforms themselves had nothing to do with the real causes of the crisis. The real causes of the crisis were *exogenous*: they had to do with exorbitant interest rates and declining terms of trade, over which global South countries had no control. But the IMF had no intention of tackling these problems, for to do so would require challenging the interests of Western governments and their commercial banks. Instead, the IMF acted as though the problem was *endogenous*, as though it had to do with problems in the local economy. So the IMF pushed domestic economic reforms *as if* they were a response to the crisis when in fact they were not. The crisis was simply an excuse for rolling out an economic agenda that Washington had long been seeking to impose.

*

From the 1950s through the 1970s, Western powers had struggled to prevent the rise of developmentalism in the South. What they failed to accomplish through piecemeal coups and covert intervention, the debt crisis did for them in one fell swoop.

The SAPs pushed the very same policies that the Chicago School had tested out in Chile, but instead of being imposed through violence, they were imposed by leveraging debt. Debt became a powerful mechanism for pushing neoliberalism around the world, and for rolling back the developmentalist agenda Washington found so threatening – more powerful, even, than the coups that had been used in the past, and without the embarrassing inconvenience of dictators and torture chambers. The brilliance of structural adjustment is that it *seemed* as though it was voluntary – as though global South countries *chose* to accept the programmes in order to get out from under their debt. In reality, however, they were not voluntary at all.

Behind this veneer of legitimacy, Western creditors proceeded to assume de facto control over economic policy in developing countries, overriding national sovereignty. Power over economic decisions was shifted from national parliaments and elected representatives to technocrats in Washington and bankers in New York and London. It operated as a new kind of coup. But this time the coup was invisible, and most citizens would never know it happened; they would continue to believe that their elected representatives held power, when in fact power – at least over certain key portfolios, such as macroeconomic strategy – had been shifted abroad, to the core of the world system. In this way, Western hegemony was able to mask itself behind the façade of national governments that otherwise appeared to carry on as normal.

Only two decades after global South countries gained their independence from colonialism, structural adjustment brought about the end of meaningful national economic sovereignty. Economic independence, once the dream of popular movements across the global South, quickly became an illusion.

*

The IMF was not alone in its efforts. Beginning in the 1980s, the World Bank began to require structural adjustment as a basic condition for its loans. If countries needed loans to finance development projects – power plants, irrigation systems, etc. – they had to agree to the very same conditions that the IMF had prescribed as a remedy for over-indebtedness, even if they themselves were not over-indebted. Lacking other options for finance, developing countries had no choice but to accept these conditions.

The genius of the World Bank's conditional lending was that it was virtually risk-free for the creditors. The World Bank sells bonds on Wall Street, allowing commercial banks and private investors to buy global South debt. These 'innovative debt products', as the Bank calls them, are simultaneously safe (usually AAA rated) as well as high yielding, with returns of up to 15 per cent. How is the Bank able to deliver such large and secure returns? Because it wields direct power over its debtors. Through structural adjustment conditions, the Bank can force debtors to channel all their available resources towards repaying the loans, requiring them to cut spending else-where and raise new funds by selling off their assets. It's a foolproof strategy. And it comes with the added benefit of prising open the receiving country's market to foreign investors.

This model of lending would never fly in normal commercial banking. Imagine you walk into Barclays to get a loan for a new business. Now imagine that they will lend to you only if you agree to give them complete control over your household, so that if your interest payments don't come in fast enough, they can garnish your wages, liquidate your house and force your children to get jobs. Imagine, further, that you are not allowed to declare bankruptcy under any circumstances; if you can't repay your loan you have to sell everything you own, stop feeding your children, stop buying whatever medicines you might need to stay healthy and channel all that money to the bank. Such an arrangement would never fly. We would never allow it. And yet such invasive conditions are routine when it comes to development loans.

An Adjusted World

The IMF and the World Bank promised the world that structural adjustment would improve economic growth and reduce poverty. But it ended up doing exactly the opposite. Instead of *helping* poor countries, as they were supposedly designed to do, SAPs basically destroyed them, reversing all the gains they had made during the developmentalist period. During the 1960s and 1970s, global South countries enjoyed an average per capita income growth rate of 3.2 per cent. But during the era of structural adjustment – through the 1980s and 1990s – income growth rates plunged to 0.7 per cent. Progress in development was stopped in its tracks. Liberalisation did not help global South countries grow their way out of debt. Instead, the money for debt repayment had to be gained from more direct forms of appropriation: austerity and privatisation.

In Latin America, income rose rapidly during the developmentalism of the 1960s and 1970s, and then suddenly collapsed after 1980. The region went into a long period of stagnation during structural adjustment, recovering its pre-crisis income levels only in the mid-1990s. In sub-Saharan Africa things were even worse. During the 1960s and 1970s, per capita income in sub-Saharan Africa grew at a rate of 1.6 per cent – modest, but still higher than Europe during the Industrial Revolution. Yet during the 1980s and 1990s, when structural adjustment was forcibly applied to the continent, per capita income *fell* at a rate of 0.7 per cent per year. The GNP of the average African country *shrank* by around 10 per cent, and the number of Africans living in extreme poverty more than doubled.

Robert Pollin, an economist at the University of Massachusetts, calculates that developing countries lost roughly $480 billion per year in potential GDP during the 1980s and 1990s as a result of structural adjustment. To get a feeling for how much this is, total annual aid disbursements during the same period amounted to less than $100 billion per year. In other words, losses due to structural adjustment outstripped gains from aid by a factor of five. It would be difficult to overestimate the scale of human suffering – and the loss of economic potential – that these numbers represent. Indeed, structural adjustment turned out to be the greatest single cause of impoverishment in the 20th century: the number of people living on less than $5 per day increased by more than 1 billion during the 1980s and 1990s.

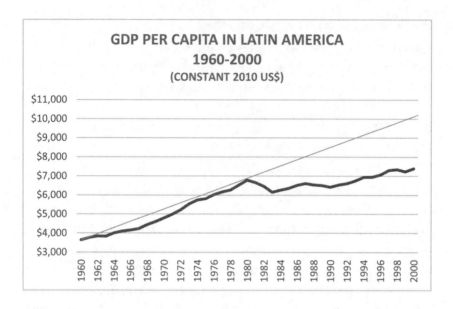

The grey line in the graph indicates hypothetical income had the 1960–1980 trend continued. Source: World Development Indicators

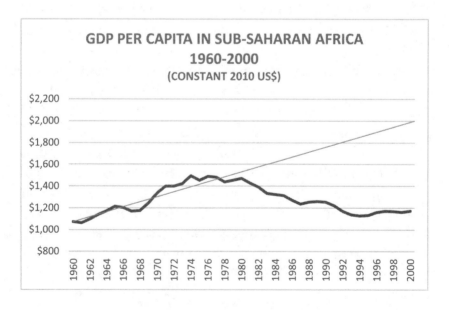

The grey line in the graph indicates hypothetical income had the 1960–1980 trend continued. Source: World Development Indicators

We can get a better sense for how devastating structural adjustment was by zooming in on particular regions, countries and cities. Take Africa, for instance, which suffered a total of thirty-one structural adjustment programmes during the 1980s and 1990s. In Dar es Salaam, public expenditure per person was cut by 10 per cent per year during the 1980s. In Khartoum, 1.1 million people were added to the ranks of the poor, many of whom had lost their public-sector jobs during spending cuts. A structural adjustment programme imposed in Harare in 1981 raised the cost of living by 45 per cent in a single year; 100,000 people ended up hospitalised due to malnutrition. In Côte d'Ivoire, the 'Tiger of West Africa', poverty doubled in a single year, between 1987 and 1988, as a result of a structural adjustment programme. In Nigeria, the poverty rate rose from 28 per cent in 1980 to an astonishing 66 per cent by 1996. In Algeria, the government was made to privatise 230 firms and fire 130,000 state workers. Poverty rates rose from 15 per cent in 1988 to 23 per cent in 1995.

In Latin America, the urban poverty rate rose by 50 per cent between 1980 and 1986 as small farmers were undercut by cheap imports and forced to leave their homes and land in the countryside and move to the cities to eke out a precarious living. According to UN statistics, the overall poverty rate increased from 40 per cent in 1980 to a staggering 62 per cent in 1993. By the end of the 1990s, the standard of living for most people in nearly every Latin American country was lower than it was in the 1970s. We can see this process of impoverishment reflected in cuts to workers' wages: from 1985 to 1995, both average and minimum wage rates fell 40 per cent in most countries. In Brazil, wages fell by 67 per cent, and in Colombia by 84 per cent. At the same time, unemployment rates shot up. In Ecuador, for example, unemployment doubled during the 1980s. In Peru, structural adjustment cut formal employment from 60 per cent of the urban workforce to 11 per cent in just three years during the 1980s. As the formal economy contracted, many people were forced to scratch out a living in the informal sector. In Mexico, informal employment nearly doubled between 1980 and 1987.

As wages and employment collapsed, the share of wages in national incomes fell – a sign of growing national inequality. In Latin America in 1980, wages represented around 40 per cent of the national income, but by 1996 the share of wages had declined to 32 per cent. In some countries it was even worse:

TABLE 2   Share of wages in national income.

	1970	1980	1989
Argentina	40.9	31.5	24.9
Chile	47.7	43.4	19.0
Ecuador	34.4	34.8	16.0
Mexico	37.5	39.0	28.4
Peru	40.0	32.8	25.5

Source: Adapted from Petras and Veltemeyer, 'Age of reverse aid'

When wages fall as a proportion of national income, as we see here, it means there is a shift of income from wage-earners to capital-holders. In other words, the rich get richer while the poor get poorer. We can also see this happening at the level of specific cities. In Buenos Aires in 1984, the richest 10 per cent of the population were ten times richer than the poorest 10 per cent. By the end of the decade, they were twenty-three times richer. In Rio, inequality rose from a Gini index of 58 in 1981 to 67 in 1989. At the end of it all, Latin America had become one of the most unequal regions in the world.

It was too much to bear. In the face of rising unemployment, rising food prices and declining wages, people took to the streets. 'IMF riots', as they were called, swept across the global South in waves – a first wave in 1983–85, and a second that began in 1989 and lasted for a number of years. One of the biggest hit Caracas in 1989, when riots erupted against IMF-mandated increases in fuel prices and transportation fares. Before long a full-blown insurrection was under way. Four hundred people were killed during the crackdown that followed. That same year, protests in Lagos against the IMF led to the murder of fifty students in three days. By 1992, some 146 IMF riots had played out in thirty-nine countries subjected to structural adjustment. But there was more to come. In 1993, 500,000 protestors in India marched against the IMF and World Bank's agricultural policies, marking the largest public demonstration in history at that point.

But the protests had little effect. The ultimate targets of rioters' discontent were suited men shuffling loan papers in Washington, where the IMF and the World Bank headquarters sit side by side just off Pennsylvania Avenue, a short walk from the White House and Capitol Hill. They were remote and unreachable, insulated from the cries of the displaced farmers and workers in the streets, invulnerable to any political pressure from below. And that was precisely how it was meant to work.

*

Why did structural adjustment have such a negative effect on growth and incomes? With the benefit of hindsight, the answer is relatively easy. Forcing governments to repay their debts at exorbitant interest rates – and forcing them to take out new loans in order to cover the old ones – meant that many countries ended up spending large proportions of their national budgets on debt service. Cutting spending on social services meant that hospitals and clinics fell apart, and investment in education fell to the point where it became impossible to produce the skills necessary for development. Cutting subsidies meant that farmers no longer had access to affordable inputs like seeds and equipment, that families spent increasing proportions of their income on food, and that infant industries no longer received the support they needed to become competitive on the global stage. Privatisation meant that key public services were run at a profit, which raised prices out of reach of the poor. Reducing trade tariffs meant that customs revenues collapsed, while foreign goods and competitors flooded in and undercut local producers, driving them out of business. Liberalising the financial sector meant that investors could pull their money out at the drop of a hat, which left finance dangerously unstable and unpredictable.

In short, structural adjustment reversed the very policies that global South governments needed for development and poverty eradication, and which they had used to such great effect in the past. It was de-development imposed in the name of development.

We shouldn't be surprised that structural adjustment yielded these results, for there is a flagrant double standard at play. Western policymakers told developing countries that they had to liberalise their economies in order to grow, but that's exactly what the West did *not* do during its own period of economic consolidation. Every one of today's rich countries developed its economy through protectionist measures. In fact, until recently, the United States and Britain were the two most aggressively protectionist countries in the world: they built their economic power using government subsidies, trade tariffs, restricted patents – everything that the neoliberal playbook denounces today. Structural adjustment allowed the West to 'kick away the ladder' they had used to climb the heights of development, ensuring that no one else would be able to follow. The development narrative has it wrong. It is not that poor countries have been unable to climb the development ladder; it is that they have been specifically precluded from doing so.

There were, however, some global South countries that did *not* implement across-the-board free-market principles and, not surprisingly, they managed to develop reasonably well – like Turkey, China and the East Asian Tigers.

*

How could the IMF and the World Bank get away with imposing structural adjustment when it clearly wasn't working – indeed, when it was actively causing harm? Why could nobody stop them? One key reason is that the World Bank and the IMF enjoy special 'immunity' status. In the United States, they claim this status under the International Organizations Immunity Act of 1945, which was intended to grant diplomats and international organisations like the Red Cross and the United Nations immunity from lawsuits in their host countries so that they can get on with their work without interference. Most countries in the world have similar laws. The IMF and the World Bank are covered by these laws even though they are very unlike other international organisations; after all, they actively determine economic policy in global South countries. By virtue of this arrangement, no one can sue them – even when their policies cause tremendous damage. As a result, they have no incentive to be careful when manipulating the macroeconomic policy of other countries, because there are no consequences for them if they screw up. All of the risk belongs to the debtor country, which is denied any means of recourse or compensation in the case of disaster. Many have tried to sue the IMF and the World Bank for damages. All have failed.

But there's a second reason that the IMF and the World Bank have been able to power through with structural adjustment programmes despite their dismal record, and it has to do with how these two institutions are governed. Voting power in both is apportioned according to each member nation's share of financial ownership, just as in corporations. Major decisions require 85 per cent of the vote. Not incidentally, the United States holds about 16 per cent of the shares in both institutions, and therefore wields de facto veto power. The next largest shareholders are France, Germany, Japan and the UK – all members of the G7. Middle- and low-income countries, which together constitute some 85 per cent of the world's population, have only about 40 per cent of the vote. In other words, even if every single country in the global South united in disagreement against an IMF and World Bank policy, they wouldn't be able to block it. And of course it doesn't help that the leaders of these institutions are not elected, but are appointed by the US and Europe: according to an unspoken agreement, the president of the World Bank is always an American, while the president of the IMF is always European.

This minority (and white) control over global decision-making – not only through the World Bank and the IMF but also through the UN Security Council – functions as a form of 'global apartheid'. There have long been calls by global South countries to democratise the World Bank and the IMF, but for decades they were ignored. A reform package was finally introduced in 2010, but it turned out to be little more than window dressing: only 3 per cent of voting power shifted from rich countries to poor countries (about half of that going to China), and the US retained its veto.

A number of World Bank and IMF insiders have defected from these organisations and set out to expose what they see as their misdeeds. Joseph Stiglitz, chief economist of the World Bank from 1997 to 2000, has written books highly critical of the institution. William Easterly worked as a senior adviser to the Bank's Macroeconomics and Growth Division before resigning, and has since become a trenchant critic of structural adjustment. But perhaps none have captured attention like Davison Budhoo, the IMF senior economist whose job it was to implement structural adjustment programmes in Latin America and Africa during the 1980s. In 1988, Budhoo, a native of Grenada, resigned with a lengthy letter addressed to his former employer, IMF managing director Michel Camdessus. He wrote:

> Today I resigned from the staff of the International Monetary Fund after over twelve years, and after 1,000 days of official Fund work in the field, hawking your medicine and your bag of tricks to governments and to people in Latin America and the Caribbean and Africa. To me resignation is a priceless liberation, for with it I have taken the first big step to that place where I may hope to wash my hands of what in my mind's eye is the blood of millions of poor and starving people. Mr Camdessus, the blood is so much, you know, it runs in rivers. It dries up too; it cakes all over me; sometimes I feel

that there is not enough soap in the whole world to cleanse me from the things that I did do in your name and in the names of your predecessors, and under your official seal.

When the failure of structural adjustment programmes became too apparent to ignore, and as pressure from social movements mounted against them, the IMF and the World Bank ostensibly backed down. At the end of the 1990s, they made a show of replacing structural adjustment programmes with 'Poverty Reduction Strategy Papers'. The new PRSPs were supposed to bring in more local ownership of structural adjustment, and require countries to focus on poverty reduction as a condition for receiving loans. But it was little more than a PR exercise, for the underlying policies remain almost exactly the same – the only substantive difference is that they allow a bit more room for social spending.

Capital's Iron Law

In the lobby of the World Bank headquarters in Washington DC, one prominent wall bears the words 'Our dream is a world free of poverty' – the slogan reproduced next to the logo on all of the Bank's major publications. The formal mission of the IMF, for its part, is to reduce economic instability. If the Bank is so committed to reducing poverty, and the IMF so committed to reducing economic instability, then how do we explain the fact that they continue to pursue policies that appear to *increase* poverty and economic instability? Some critics argue that these institutions are just a bit too overzealous about free markets and don't fully realise that their policies can be so destructive. Once they understand the consequences of their policies they will change course, the thinking goes. But there is another possible explanation, namely that these institutions continue with their policies because *they are not failing at their actual objectives.*

In the early 1980s, the G7's goal was to use the World Bank and

157

the IMF to cripple the South's economic revolution and re-establish Western access to its resources and markets. On this point, they certainly didn't fail. But there was another, deeper purpose that the World Bank and the IMF served, and that was to save Western capitalism itself. We know that from time to time capitalism bumps up against limits to the creation of new profits. There is the market saturation limit, for instance: when consumers have more than they need, buying slows down and businesses can't turn over as many products. There is the ecological depletion limit: when natural resources run low, the cost of essential inputs begins to rise. And there is the class conflict limit: as workers bargain for higher wages, the cost of labour becomes more expensive; and if you deny their demands, or indeed if you try to push wages down to increase your profits, you risk sparking social instability. All of this makes it increasingly difficult for firms to extract big profits.

When capitalism hits these limits, investors find themselves with fewer options for investing their capital, since nothing gives an acceptably high return. They can't just put it into savings because interest rates on savings accounts are typically lower than inflation, and that means losing money. This is what economists call a crisis of over-accumulation. In a crisis of over-accumulation, capital begins to lose its value – and according to the driving logic of capitalism, *this cannot be allowed to happen.* In order for capitalism to carry on, crises of over-accumulation *have* to be solved; someone needs to step in to provide a way to mop up the excess capital, to funnel it into some kind of profitable investment. It is an iron law.

There are a number of ways to solve a crisis of over-accumulation. One is with a 'temporal fix'. Capital can be invested in long-term projects like infrastructure, education and research that will improve the future productivity of capital. This is what happened in the United States with the New Deal and after the Second World War: the government mopped up huge amounts of over-accumulated capital by investing in roads and bridges and dams, putting people to work with good wages, and sending more than 2.2 million citizens to university on the GI Bill – all of which paid off handsomely a decade down the line. This kind of temporal fix works well, but because it requires wealth redistribution – and because the benefits come only after a lag – it is not very popular with the capitalist class.

There are also quicker, often more draconian fixes available. You can drive down the price of oil – a constant foreign policy objective of the United States – which makes the costs of production cheaper. Or you can release new labour into the market or make existing labour cheaper, such as with the entry of women into the workforce in the latter half of the 20th century and the successful attempts by President Ronald Reagan in the 1980s to weaken the power of trade unions. Another option is to create new markets in sectors that are normally protected from market forces, such as with the privatisation of the railways in Britain and ongoing attempts to dismantle the country's National Health Service. Yet another option is to create new markets for investing in debt, such as the student loan industry in the United States, or to encourage consumers to spend beyond their means with credit cards. Capitalists tend to prefer such fixes because they offer faster returns – particularly for companies that are under legal pressure to maximise shareholder value. But some of these fixes – such as privatisation, wage reductions and wars for oil – can be difficult to achieve because they often inspire impassioned political resistance. Think of how citizens across the US and Europe mobilised to protest the invasion of Iraq in 2003, for instance; or consider the long-standing campaign in the UK to defend the public health system, for which Britons regularly take to the streets.

To avoid having to confront domestic resistance, which can be politically costly, policymakers might solve a crisis of over-accumulation by resorting to a 'spatial fix' – in other words, by opening up new consumer markets, labour markets and investment markets abroad.

This is where the World Bank and the IMF have come in handy. When the West's economy stagnated in the late 1970s, they offered a spatial fix by creating opportunities for investment in the sovereign debt of foreign countries, with high returns that were basically guaranteed. To get a sense of the scale of this investment opportunity, consider the fact that the Bank sold around $58 billion of AAA-rated sovereign-debt bonds on Wall Street in 2015. That's a substantial market. On top of this, the large-scale development projects funded by World Bank loans required recipients to hire American contractors to carry out the work and to purchase equipment and materials from American businesses rather than local ones, even though this can be up to 30 per cent more expensive. Through these 'tied aid' arrangements, the World Bank stimulates demand for American products with every loan. Some studies suggest that American businesses get up to 82 cents in new purchases for each dollar that the US government contributes to the Bank.

In addition to these new investment and business opportunities, the World Bank and the IMF also prised open the markets of foreign countries so that Western multinational firms could access much cheaper labour, thereby restoring their profit levels. In the past, American manufacturers not only had to pay American wages, they also had to bargain with their workers. If workers were unhappy with their compensation or working conditions, they could go on strike and pressure their employers for a better deal. If employers wanted to keep production ticking along, they would have to make concessions to workers' demands – or at least bargain with them in good faith. But as structural adjustment forced open markets across the global South during the 1980s and 1990s, companies – enabled by new transport technologies such as containerised shipping – suddenly had another option open to them: they could just pull up stakes and move to Bangladesh or Mexico, where labour was a fraction of the cost.

In fact, companies found they had the power to scan the globe in search not only of cheaper labour, but of the *cheapest possible* labour. And developing countries, in turn, found that in order to successfully attract foreign investment they had to compete with one another to drive wages down. It became a global 'race to the bottom' towards ever cheaper labour and ever lower standards. The solidarity that marked the rise of the South in the 1960s was suddenly replaced with cutthroat competition. In the countries of the G7, corporations gained the upper hand over their workers at last – at least in industries that were amenable to offshoring, like manufacturing. If their workers become too demanding, they could always threaten to move elsewhere. And workers, for their part, quickly learned that if they wanted to keep their jobs they shouldn't risk speaking up – better to remain quiet and docile. All of this had a powerful disciplining effect on labour – not just in Western countries but around the world.

Because of all of this, structural adjustment turned out to be highly profitable for Western corporations. US investments abroad grew to more than $10 trillion, and income from those investments increased from about 20 per cent of domestic profits in the late 1970s to about 80 per cent by the end of the 1980s. What is more, American companies began to enjoy an increasing rate of return on those investments during the structural adjustment period, up from 5 per cent in 1975 to over 11 per cent in 1990.

Some of this profit came from productive processes in the market – in other words, from the creation of new value in global South countries. But given that structural adjustment destroyed growth rates, we can conclude that much of it came instead from the appropriation of already existing wealth. By requiring debtor countries to privatise public assets, the World Bank and the IMF created opportunities for foreign companies to buy up telecoms, railroads, banks, hospitals, schools and every conceivable public utility at a handsome discount, and then either run them for private gain or strip them down and sell off the parts at a profit. The privatisation of public assets releases a tremendous asset into the market that was previously inaccessible to capital, creating new opportunities for profit. The World Bank alone privatised more than $2 trillion of assets in developing countries between 1984 and 2012. That amounts to an average of $72 billion per year of profitable opportunities for Western investors *in addition* to the $58 billion of high-interest bonds that the Bank sells on Wall Street each year.

While privatisation creates wonderful new opportunities for

investors, it quite often has disastrous consequences for the poor. When utilities are publicly owned, they generally have a mandate to provide service to the whole population. But for privately owned utilities the mandate is to make a profit, so they have no reason to serve those who cannot afford to pay. That's exactly what happened during World Bank privatisations during the 1980s and 1990s. Bolivia provides a powerful example. In the mid-1990s the World Bank pressured the government of Bolivia to privatise the water supply of the city of Cochabamba. The contract went to Bechtel, an American corporation, which raised the price of water by 35 per cent. Unable to afford this most basic resource, in 2000 the people of Cochabamba erupted in protests that became a worldwide symbol of resistance against privatisation. But the World Bank continued to stand by their policy. As late as 2008, a leading Bank official was asked to explain why the Bank supports water privatisation, despite mounting evidence that it hurts the poor. He replied by stating: 'We believe that providing clean water and sanitation services is a real business opportunity.'

It would be impossible to overestimate how important the World Bank and the IMF are to the countries of the G7. Not only did they become the most powerful tool in the fight against developmentalism, they also offered a spatial fix to the crisis of Western capitalism, which was bumping up against its own limits in the late 1970s. By turning poor countries into new frontiers for investment, extraction and accumulation, they allow Western capitalism to surmount its limits and carry on without having to confront its own internal contradictions – at least for the time being. It is not a real solution to the crisis, of course; it's just a way of moving the crisis around geographically. But without it, capitalism in the United States and Europe would have crashed up against market saturation, ecological depletion and class conflict long ago, and may well have collapsed. This is why the World Bank and the IMF are so valued by the US government and Wall Street: they are essential to the continuity of the system.

This helps us make sense of why the World Bank and the IMF have continued to pursue the policies they have. It is not about reducing poverty, despite what their official slogans and marketing materials would have us believe. In fact, the word 'poverty' doesn't appear once in the World Bank's Articles of Agreement. Rather, the statement of purpose in Article 1 clearly delineates the Bank's role as 'to promote private investment' and 'to promote the growth of international trade'. According to these standards, the World Bank has been a resounding success, not a failure. And we shouldn't be surprised. It would be absurd to imagine that a multibillion-dollar institution controlled by Wall Street and the US government would ever be left to 'fail'.

When we look at it through this lens, it makes sense that all of the World Bank's past presidents have been not development experts (as one might expect of an organisation devoted to development and poverty reduction), but rather US army bosses and Wall Street executives – people who have a strategic interest in America's role in the global economic system. Here they are, in order of appearance:

Eugene Meyer, Chairman of the Federal Reserve
John McCloy, US Assistant Secretary of War
Eugene Black, bank executive with Chase
George Woods, bank executive with First Boston
 Corporation
Robert McNamara, US Secretary of Defense and executive
 of Ford Motor Company
Alden Clausen, bank executive with Bank of America
Barber Conable, US Congressman
Lewis Preston, bank executive with J. P. Morgan
James Wolfensohn, corporate lawyer and banker
Paul Wolfowitz, US Deputy Secretary of Defense
Robert Zoellick, Deputy Secretary of State and US Trade
 Representative

The US government's choice of top brass sends a clear message about the Bank's true aims. It wasn't until 2012 that an actual development expert – Jim Yong Kim – was appointed to the top job, in an attempt by President Barack Obama to recuperate the Bank's reputation.

The Inequality Machine

All of this helps us rethink common misconceptions that most people hold about development aid. Official aid in the form of conditional loans has not been designed to promote development in global South countries, but in many cases to *prevent* them from pursuing the policies necessary for development and poverty eradication, while creating new opportunities for investors in rich countries. As we have seen, during the 1980s and 1990s the result was slower economic growth, lower wages, more unemployment, fewer public services and rising poverty. It is true that income growth also slowed in the rich world during this period, as a result of the imposition of neoliberal policies at home. But growth rates still hovered around 2 per cent. In the global South, by contrast, income growth rates collapsed to 0.7 per cent, so the difference between the rates of growth in rich and poor countries grew. The global income gap widened as a result. In 1960, the richest fifth of the world's population earned thirty times more than the poorest fifth, according to the United Nations Human Development Report. By 1995 they earned seventy-four times more.

We can also see the process of increasing inequality in the form of countries' GDP per capita. The graph on the next page illustrates this trend during the era of structural adjustment.

The gap between the per capita income of the United States and that of all developing regions grew significantly during the 1980s and 1990s, after narrowing in most cases during the developmentalist period. In 1980, the per capita income of the US was around twenty-seven times higher than that of sub-Saharan Africa. Twenty years later it was fifty-two times higher – the inequality ratio had

GLOBAL INEQUALITY, 1980-2000
(CHANGE IN GDP PER CAPITA, CONSTANT 2005 US$)

United States · SS Africa · Lat. Am. & Carib. · M. E. & N. Africa · South Asia

Source: World Development Indicators

grown by 91 per cent. The same is true for other developing regions. For Latin America, the inequality ratio grew by 42 per cent, and for the Middle East and North Africa it grew by 38 per cent. South Asia, where structural adjustment was not forcibly applied to the same extent, managed to shrink the inequality ratio during this period by 15 per cent, although the *absolute* gap between the per capita incomes of South Asia and the United States continued to grow.

The race-to-the-bottom effect triggered by structural adjustment and globalisation is one of the main drivers behind this ever-widening gap. In the 1960s developing countries were losing $161 billion (in 2015 dollars) each year through what economists call 'unequal exchange', the difference between the real value of the goods that a developing country exports and the market prices that it gets for those goods. We can think of this as an expression of undervalued labour. If workers in the developing world had been

paid the same as their Western counterparts for the same productivity in the 1960s, they would have earned an additional $161 bil-
lion per year for their exports. This disparity was largely the result
of colonial policy, which had maintained wages at artificially low
levels. But structural adjustment made this system even more inequitable. The German economist Gernot Köhler calculated that
annual losses due to underpaid labour and goods rose by a factor of
sixteen, reaching $2.66 trillion (in 2015 dollars) by 1995, at the height
of the structural adjustment period. In other words, developing
countries would have been earning $2.66 trillion more each year
for their exports if their labour was paid fairly on the world market.
The best way to think of this is as a hidden transfer of value from
the global South to the North – a transfer that, in 1995, amounted
to thirty-two times the aid budget, and outstripped total flows
from the OECD by a factor of thirteen.

But another major driving force behind the growing inequality
gap is the debt system itself. Not only because it paved the way for
structural adjustment, but also because of the plain fact of debt service, which constitutes a river of wealth that flows from the periphery of the world system to the core. During the first decade of
structural adjustment, the South sent out an average of $125 billion
each year in interest payments on external debt. This flow stayed
roughly steady through the next two decades, but has shot up to an
average of $175 billion annually in recent years. Altogether, since
the debt crisis began in 1980, the South has handed over a total of
$4.2 trillion in interest payments to foreign creditors, mostly in the
North. If we include payments on principal, we see that developing
countries made total debt service payments of $238 billion per year
during the 1980s, rising dramatically through the 1990s to $440 bil-
lion per year in 2000, and then to more than $732 billion per year
by 2013. Altogether, during the whole period since 1980, the South
has made debt service payments totalling $13 trillion. The graph on
the next page illustrates the scale of these payments.

This is a problem because these outflows drain away vital
resources that might otherwise be spent on eradicating poverty.

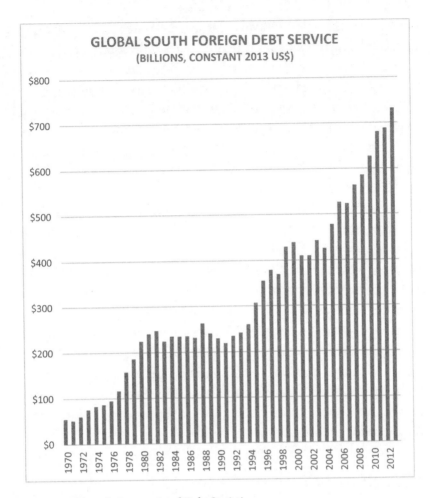

GLOBAL SOUTH FOREIGN DEBT SERVICE
(BILLIONS, CONSTANT 2013 US$)

Source: World Bank, International Debt Statistics

Lebanon, for instance, spends 52 per cent of its budget on debt service, and only 23 per cent on health and education combined.

Indeed, the amount that the global South spends collectively on debt service each year vastly outstrips the amount that the UN tells us is necessary to eradicate poverty entirely; you could cancel all debt payments and cancel global poverty in the same swoop, if you could muster the political will.

A key reason for the growing size of the debt burden has to do with the nature of compound interest. Consider this thought experiment. If you start with $1 trillion dollars in debt, compounded at an interest rate of 10 per cent per year it will become $117 trillion in fifty years and $13.78 quadrillion in 100 years. The multiplier of compound interest is powerful almost beyond our imagination. Between 1973 and 1993, global South debt grew from $100 billion to $1.5 trillion. Of the $1.5 trillion, only $400 billion was actually borrowed money. The rest was piled up simply as a result of compound interest. So despite the monumental effort that developing countries make to repay their loans, they are only chipping away at an ever-growing mountain of compound interest and not even beginning to touch the principal that lies beneath, which threatens to persist for ever.

One final point to bear in mind. Despite the imposition of dozens of structural adjustment programmes across the global South – which, remember, were *intended to reduce debt* – debt stocks have not reduced much at all. In fact, they have increased. External debt as a percentage of gross national income in the global South was 25 per cent in 1980, when the debt crisis struck. At the end of the first decade of structural adjustment, it was up to 38 per cent. By the end of the second decade, it was 39 per cent. In other words, structural adjustment failed even on its own putative terms. The 'remedy' prescribed for the debt crisis beginning in the 1980s made the disease worse.

The Hidden Power of Debt

Whenever I explain the history of structural adjustment in lectures and talks, I am always asked the same question: why would global South countries agree to this? Why didn't they just default on their loans instead of submitting to remote-control power by Washington?

Technically, they could have. Defaulting on the debt would have liberated the global South from the stranglehold of the international banks, forcing the banks to absorb the fallout from their risky lending. But in reality this was not an option, for there was always the threat of US military invasion if countries decided to default. Having witnessed the experiences of Iran, Guatemala, the

Congo and Chile, the governments of global South countries knew that to threaten Washington's economic interests – or, indeed, even the interests of powerful US banks – was to invite the possibility of a US-backed coup. This threat was always very real. The developing world had no choice but to play by Washington's rules.

This brutal fact crystallised very clearly in the story of Thomas Sankara, which came to serve as a kind of cautionary tale. When he became president of Burkina Faso in the 1980s, Sankara – a thirty-three-year-old known for his warm smile and trendy beret – made the debt issue one of his main concerns. Affectionately known as Africa's Che, he is remembered for a speech he delivered at Addis Ababa in 1987 at the headquarters of the Organization of African Unity, to a room packed full of heads of state and government ministers from across the continent. The audience was gripped by the words of the young man who stood so bravely before them. He said things they would never dare to say. Some exchanged glances of shocked disbelief, others looked worried, half expecting him to be shot mid-sentence. His passion rippled through the room, and when he finished the audience erupted in thunderous applause. One could almost feel a revolution stirring.

Sankara had thrown down a gauntlet at the feet of the president of France, his region's former colonial power. He challenged the postcolonial order by striking at its very core: debt. 'Debt must be seen from the standpoint of its origins,' Sankara said. 'And the origins of debt lie in colonialism. Our creditors are those who had colonised us before. They managed us then and they manage us now. But we did not ask for this debt,' he continued. 'And therefore we will not repay it. Debt is neocolonialism. It is a cleverly managed reconquest of Africa. Each one of us becomes a financial slave. We are told to repay. We are told it is a moral issue. But it is not.' And then he delivered the clincher: 'The debt cannot be repaid. If we don't repay, the lenders will not die. That is for sure. But if we do repay, we will die. That is also for sure.' Sankara was considered dangerous not only because he threatened to default on Burkina Faso's debt, but because he was spreading that idea across the continent. He was on the verge of galvanising a continent-wide debt-resistance movement – and from the perspective of Western creditors, it had to be stopped. Three months after his speech, Sankara was assassinated in a coup widely believed to have been backed by France, which brought Blaise Compaoré to power – a dictator who ruled for twenty-seven years.

The use of violence to enforce debt payments in the global South has a very long history. When Venezuela refused to pay its foreign debts in 1902, Britain, Germany and France responded by sending navy gunboats to blockade the country's ports. In 1916, the US invaded the Dominican Republic and seized control of the country's customs agency to enforce debt repayment – a seizure that lasted for twenty-five years. The coup against Sankara is only the most recent example.

Of course, if a number of developing countries were to default at the same time, as part of a united front, they might have a better chance. But this would require global South leaders – and their political elites – to be unified and proactive about the issue, and many of them have good reasons to turn a blind eye: after all, they benefit personally from new loans, plummeting wages and close relationships with Western powers, and they can always avoid the impact of a debt crisis by stowing their personal wealth offshore. In any case, now that structural adjustment has run its course, default is no longer really an option. Global South countries are now totally dependent on foreign investment for survival. Default would mean being frozen out of the global financial system, and this would spell immediate economic collapse. Consider Greece in 2015: when the left-wing Syriza party came to power they planned to default on the country's debts, but the threat of losing foreign investment – and the recession that would follow – frightened them into submission.

*

Unlike Thomas Sankara, I have never been assassinated for talking against debt; I'm just an academic, not a head of state. But I do find that people get very passionate about the issue. When I teach my students about the history of debt in the global South, even the more progressive ones will insist that the debts should be repaid. After all, the thinking goes, they took out the loans in the first place – so aren't they *obligated* to repay? I retort by pointing out that many of the initial loans were taken out by unelected dictators, or that the principal has already been paid off three or four times over, or that the economic policies imposed by the lenders failed so it makes sense that they should absorb the loss.

But none of this convinces. The feeling that debts have to be repaid is so deeply entrenched in our culture that it is almost impossible to dislodge. It is not just an economic claim, it is a highly *moral* one. It's about giving people what they are due. It's about accepting one's responsibilities. It's about fulfilling one's obligations. Refusing to pay a debt seems like reneging on a promise – it's just *wrong*. And this is why debt is so powerful. The anthropologist David Graeber puts it nicely when he says, 'There's no better way to justify relations founded on violence, to make such relations seem moral, than by reframing them in the language of debt – above all, because it immediately makes it seem that it's the victim who's doing something wrong.'There have been some efforts to challenge the framing around debt, and to call it what it is. In the early 1990s, a coalition of academics and NGOs formed the Jubilee 2000 campaign, which was later joined by churches and celebrities and grew powerful enough to exert significant pressure on Western politicians to drop $90 billion of debt owed by the world's poorest nations. In response to popular pressure, the IMF instituted a debt-relief programme for Highly Indebted Poor Countries (HIPCs) in 1996, and the Paris and London clubs soon promised debt relief for middle-income countries. In 2005, the IMF responded to yet further pressure during the G8 summit in Gleneagles and expanded debt relief through the Multilateral Debt Reduction Initiative.

It sounds nice. But there's a catch. In all of these cases, debt relief is tied to stringent conditions that require countries to liberalise and privatise their economies – in other words, debt relief has become a mechanism to impose further structural adjustment. As economist Jeffrey Sachs put it, it was 'belt-tightening for people who cannot afford belts'.

*

If you've ever found yourself wondering what is responsible for global poverty today, this is your answer. And yet because the institutions that have overseen this destruction enjoy legal immunity, they will never be held to account.

But the impact of neoliberalism has been manifest not only on flows of money. It has also altered flows of power. One of the key tenets of development is that it is supposed to enhance people's control over their own lives and fates, and ultimately promote human freedom. The World Bank itself defines development as promoting 'economic and political freedom', and 'freedom of choice'. This claim is very familiar to us. Yet the history outlined above suggests the opposite. Interventions by the World Bank and the IMF in the name of development have shifted political power away from democratically elected decision-making bodies and placed it in the hands of remote, unelected bureaucrats. Economic and political freedom has been attacked, ironically, in the name of economic and political freedom. Structural adjustment is a powerful manifestation of this paradox, but it has also been perpetrated in other, more insidious ways.

Six

Free Trade and the Rise of the Virtual Senate

> Only free men can negotiate. Prisoners cannot enter into contracts.
>
> Nelson Mandela

At the same time that structural adjustment was being imposed across the global South, cracking open markets and clearing the way for Western exports and multinational companies, there was already something else afoot – yet another tactic with which the South would have to contend. A new organisation was being designed that would govern the emerging world of global commerce. At first glance it seemed banal – the domain of bleary-eyed technocrats sitting behind computer screens in Geneva offices – but this new organisation quickly came to be the most powerful in the world, and today enjoys the prerogative to override the sovereignty of even independent nations. Whoever controls the rules of international trade controls the flow of our planet's vast wealth and resources – and the architects of the World Trade Organization understood this well. But the secret of this new system is that it

173

would not appear tyrannical in the least. On the contrary, it would draw its legitimacy from the very opposite – the idea of freedom – promising the right to engage in that most human of all activities, to truck and barter, without restriction by king or state.

*

As a tactic of extraction, inequitable trade rules are nothing new. Indeed, to understand the hidden power of the modern trade system, we need to depart from our narrative arc for a moment and rewind a little bit – back to the 1770s, when the rebellious settlers of America's East Coast were fighting for their independence from the British Crown. America's rebels understood something about the power of trade that most people fail to grasp today – and it sparked the rage of an entire nation.

At the time, the young United States, like all colonies, was under what is known as an 'unequal treaty' with Britain. America's trade tariffs were decided by London, and fixed at a low rate so as to allow British exporters the right to sell their goods on the American market with ease. The British called this 'free trade', and they pursued it with an almost religious zeal. But there was a double standard at play. The British were imposing low tariffs on America and their other colonies while knowing full well that their own industrial development had depended on exactly the opposite. Ever since the 14th century, and particularly during the 18th century, Britain had aggressively protected its own markets with high tariffs, excluding foreign competitors in order to build up its own industries.

The system was rigged, and the Americans knew it. Indeed, they routinely referred to free trade as a 'conspiracy' through which the British interfered with the American economy. The Americans wanted to have greater control over their own tariffs so that they could protect themselves from British imports and successfully develop their own young industries. And that's exactly what they got once they won the War of American Independence. After independence in 1776, the United States gained the power to formulate their own trade laws. Alexander Hamilton, the first secretary of the Treasury, became the main author of US economic policy in the Washington administration. Hamilton knew from studying the British experience that a country's industries needed protection from foreign competition during the early stages of their development. So that's what the Americans did. They quickly raised trade tariffs, and enacted a kind of import substitution policy – similar to that which they would later deny to Latin America. But they didn't stop there: they also used cartels, subsidies and other forms of state support to build their industrial power, again following in the footsteps of the British. Hamilton explicitly rejected the theories of Adam Smith and other British free-trade figures. He recognised that they were promoting free trade not because it was better for all, but because it benefited their own economic interests. Hamilton knew that for young economies like that of the United States, strong protectionism and solid state support were the only path to real industrial development.

Between the 1860s and the 1930s, the United States was the most heavily protected economy in the world. The model worked marvellously well, and the US quickly became the world's dominant industrial power. Britain, for its part, had to compensate for its loss of the American market by pushing free trade elsewhere in the world, forcing it onto China through the Opium Wars and on their colonies in South Asia and Africa by executive fiat. The global South lost their economic independence because the Americans had gained it. Meanwhile, every other Western country followed the American System, as it was called by that time, line by line. During the first decades of the 20th century, protectionism was the norm across the industrialised world.

But then the Great Depression hit, followed by the Second World War. In the wake of the war, when Western powers gathered at the Bretton Woods Conference in New Hampshire to decide how to prevent such a catastrophe from recurring, they set up the General Agreement on Tariffs and Trade (GATT). John Maynard

Keynes, the key figure at the conference, argued that the rise of protectionism across the industrialised world had contributed to low aggregate demand: people weren't buying enough stuff because prices were too high, and the economy ground to a halt. For Keynes, excess protectionism was a primary driver of the Great Depression – a depression that had caused such misery in Germany and Japan, for example, that it had eventually given rise to the fascist politics that led to the war. Keynes believed that demand could be revived by carefully relaxing trade tariffs. This would allow prices to fall, people would start consuming again and the economy would be jolted back to life. The goal of the GATT was to reduce tariffs across the board through collective bargaining among industrialised countries. The system was designed to be beneficial to all, in the spirit of unity and solidarity, so the rules were not rigidly applied: member states could negotiate to avoid policies that would cause their economies significant harm.

In other words, the GATT began its life as an ostensibly benevolent institution, set on maintaining economic stability and peace. Just like the original IMF and the World Bank, which were founded during the same conference, it was rooted in Keynesian principles and committed to a kind of collective good.

During the 1980s, however, as neoliberal ideology was ascending across the Western world, this system took a dramatic turn. As the markets of developing countries were being forced open, there was an opportunity for the GATT to expand its remit beyond the already industrialised countries and embrace the South as well. Towards this end, GATT members met in the Uruguayan city of Punta del Este to decide what this new institution would look like. Unlike previous meetings, this time the agenda was led by neoliberal economists and policymakers from the United States who had a very different vision from the one Keynes espoused – one focused less on solidarity and more on economic realpolitik. When the talks concluded in 1995, the World Trade Organization was born. The WTO was a completely different animal from the GATT. Instead of seeking to maintain economic stability and cooperation, it was designed to open up the world to capital flows from rich countries, especially the United States, Western Europe and Japan. And in place of the flexibility of the GATT, it would be an all-or-nothing deal, or a 'single undertaking': countries had to sign on to the whole package of WTO rules, or be frozen out of the world economy.

While accession to the WTO was technically optional, developing countries didn't really have much of a choice. After fifteen years of structural adjustment, their economies had been reorganised towards exports. They now depended on access to Western markets for their survival. Joining the WTO would facilitate such access, but in return they would have to reduce their tariffs, stop subsidising their own industries, deregulate capital flows and allow foreign corporations to operate domestically without prejudice – in other words, exactly the opposite of what they knew they needed for meaningful industrial development. Whereas structural adjustment imposed free-market policies on developing countries one by one, the WTO extended and standardised the neoliberal system across the global South in one fell swoop. Most countries had no choice but to comply.

Poor Theory, Poor Countries

If free trade runs counter to the development needs of poor countries, why do most mainstream economists continue to advocate it?

One reason is that the *theory* of free trade is so remarkably compelling. The keystone of modern free-trade theory comes from David Ricardo, the early-19th-century British economist. Ricardo argued that the global economy would operate most efficiently and productively if every country specialised in producing the goods in which they have a comparative advantage over other countries, given their particular set of technologies. If Portugal is better at producing wine and England is better at producing cloth, it doesn't make any sense for England to waste its time producing wine – it should just focus on cloth and import the wine from Portugal. The more modern version of the theory – known as the Heckscher–Ohlin–Samuelson theory – shifts the comparison from relative endowments of technology to relative endowments of 'factors of production'. It argues that in order to achieve maximum efficiency in the global economy, countries that have an abundance of cheap labour should specialise in labour-intensive goods, while countries that have an abundance of capital should specialise in capital-intensive goods. According to the theory, the only way to ensure this happens is to remove any 'distortions' in the trade system, such as subsidies and tariffs. Once exposed to the tough reality of market competition, industries will sink or swim depending on their relative competitiveness, and each country will naturally gravitate towards the things they're relatively better at. This will lead to increased trade, income and consumption across the board.

The Heckscher–Ohlin–Samuelson model sounds so reasonable, on the face of it. It seems so obviously correct. But it has the insidious effect of naturalising global inequalities. The model assumes that each country has a *natural* endowment of factors of production. In other words, it wants us to believe that rich countries have a natural abundance of capital relative to poor countries, which have a natural abundance of cheap labour, as though this arrangement has always been the case – as if it was written in the stars or handed down by the gods. But of course it is not written in the stars. We have to ask: why is labour so cheap in poor countries in the first place? And why is capital so abundant in rich countries?

In a famous 1848 speech, a well-known German economist made a barbed critique of free-trade theory – and of European imperialism – with the following words:

We are told that free trade would create an international division of labour, and thereby give to each country the production which is in most harmony with its natural advantage. You believe, perhaps, gentlemen, that the production of coffee and sugar is the natural destiny of the West Indies. Two centuries ago, nature, which does not trouble herself about commerce, had planted neither sugar-cane nor coffee trees there.

The economist was Karl Marx. And his point was that the relative endowments of capital and labour are the product of historical and political processes – they are *man-made*, not natural. Rich countries have expensive labour because of a long history of unions and strong labour laws, and have abundant capital because of long-standing tariff protections that allowed them to develop their industries. Poor countries, on the other hand, have cheap labour and no capital because of a long history of colonisation, dispossession, unequal treaties and structural adjustment. Comparative advantage isn't given, it is created. To suggest that the global South should focus on exporting raw material while the North should focus on capital-intensive industry is the equivalent of saying that black people are just *naturally* better at working in the cotton fields while white people are just *naturally* better at being overseers, and that investing in educating a black person to become anything other than a common labourer is a 'distortion' that runs against their natural abilities. It takes an inequitable social relationship and gives it the aura of the natural, of the unquestionable.

The Heckscher–Ohlin–Samuelson theory runs straight against the evidence of history. As we have seen again and again, a country's factor endowments can be quite easily changed with the right policies. Making strategic use of tariffs and subsidies, global South countries could have built national industries and increased their capital endowments – indeed, that is exactly what they began to do after they gained independence during the 1950s and 1960s, before structural adjustment. But this kind of industrial strategy requires careful planning and government intervention, which is something that free-traders are vehemently against, for it interferes with the 'natural' order of things.

*

Based on the theory of comparative advantage, free-trade advocates lead us to believe that trade liberalisation will ultimately boost economic development in poor countries.

179

But while it may be true that free trade increases efficiency in some abstract, mathematical sense, and perhaps even boosts consumption in the short term, it is not a meaningful strategy for long-term economic development. In fact, the theory itself never pretends to make this claim – it is merely a fancy bit of rhetoric that gets wheeled out by people who stand to benefit from it. In order for real economic development to occur, poor countries need to build their capacity for capital-intensive industry. This means intentionally insulating their industries from global competition until they are fully prepared to compete on the open market – just as Britain and the United States did during their own periods of economic development, along with every one of today's rich countries. It's surprising, and perhaps even offensive, then, that rich countries have now turned around and denied this strategy to poor countries. They insist that poor countries should be liberalised as quickly as possible in order to expose them to competition, so that they will have an incentive to develop their most competitive industries in order to survive. Protection, they say, only induces laziness and complacency.

The Cambridge economist Ha-Joon Chang likes to illustrate the problems of this theory by using the example of his very young son, Jin-Gyu. If Jin-Gyu is going to have a chance at becoming something great and succeeding in the world, then he will need many years of parental protection and investment to make sure he stays healthy, attends a good school and has plenty of time to focus on his studies before being let loose into the world to make it on his own. But what if we were to apply the logic of free trade to the Chang family? We might say that little Jin-Gyu lives in an economic bubble, his parents subsidise his idle existence and he is protected from the harsh realities of competition. What he needs is to have the subsidies cut off, get a job and make a living for himself – this will force him to become productive and efficient. 'But,' Chang argues, 'if I drive Jin-Gyu into the labour market at the age of six, he may become a savvy shoeshine boy or even a prosperous hawker, but he will never become a brain surgeon or a nuclear physicist – that would require at least another dozen years of my protection and investment.'

'Likewise,' Chang says, 'industries in developing countries will not survive if they are exposed to international competition too early. They need time to improve their capabilities by mastering advanced technologies and building effective organizations. This is the essence of infant industry protection.' Infant industry protection – at least for a certain period of time – is the only way that poor countries have a shot at becoming anything more than the national equivalent of a shoeshine boy.

*

The stated goal of the World Trade Organization is to create a 'level playing field' among trading partners. Each member has to play by the same rules – the same low tariffs and the same ban on subsidies. But in reality the idea of a level playing field is something of an illusion. When rich countries step onto the playing field they do so with industries that are immensely powerful and competitive – precisely because they spent their formative years of development under heavy protection. Poor countries, for their part, step onto the playing field with industries that have never had the benefit of protection and therefore have no hope of competing with their counterparts in rich countries. It may be a level playing field, but what good is a level playing field in a match between schoolchildren and a Premier League team? The rules are the same for both sides, but that doesn't mean the game is equitable. The young industries of poorer countries are sure to collapse in the face of more powerful competition from the North, and will be forced to fall back once again on exporting raw materials or agricultural goods with little value added. Certainly not a recipe for development.

Even if we assume that the game is in fact equitable, if we look more closely it becomes clear that the 'level playing field' is actually not very level at all: the rules are unfair even by the WTO's own standards. Theoretically, the WTO requires every country to reduce their tariffs and subsidies to the same level, but in reality these cuts are applied selectively in favour of rich countries. Under the WTO, poor countries are required to stop subsidising their industrial goods, to prevent them from competing 'unfairly' with rich-country exports. As a result, many have no choice but to give up any hope of industrialisation and focus instead on agriculture. But through the US Farm Bill and the European Common Agricultural Policy, rich countries subsidise their own agricultural goods to the tune of $374 billion per year, then dump them on global markets for less than the cost of production, undercutting producers across the global South and driving down their market share. This flagrant double standard undermines the agricultural sector in poor countries, which is *supposed* to be their field of comparative advantage. It's subsidies for the rich, and free trade for the poor.

In other words, because of the selective application of the WTO's rules, many poor countries are effectively prevented from developing the one sector that free-trade theory says they should develop. Whether they attempt industrial development or agricultural development, they're blocked both ways. And the WTO's Agreement on Agriculture (AoA) locks these imbalances into international law.

Benin, Burkina Faso, Mali and Chad are all major African cotton producers. A total of 8 million workers are employed in their cotton industry – making it the largest private employer in these countries – and 13 million people rely directly on their incomes. But they find themselves up against a wall. Because of subsidies that the US government hands out to its own cotton producers, the global price of cotton is around 10 per cent lower than it otherwise might be. And that is a 10 per cent loss that these countries – which are some of the poorest in the world – can ill afford. If they are to have any chance at development, they need a fair price for their cotton exports, not one purposefully distorted by the United States. The 'Cotton Four', as they are known, have taken their case to the WTO, pointing out that the US subsidies are illegal under WTO rules. But the US has refused to back down.

Under the WTO, the Cotton Four have the option of taking the US to court (the Disputes Settlement Body) – and the court will probably rule in their favour. But the WTO cannot force the US to change course. Enforcement is left up to the plaintiffs; should they win the case, the Cotton Four would be entitled to place sanctions on the US. But what use are sanctions from a little group of poor countries against the richest and most powerful economy in the world? It is like a fly punishing an elephant: the US wouldn't even notice. Because the power of enforcement is distributed asymmetrically according to market size, there is little reason for rich countries to play by the WTO's rules. They can do whatever they want. But poor countries have no choice. If they decide to break trade rules that harm them, rich countries can impose sanctions that could very well ruin them altogether.

One might imagine that sanctions are too disproportionate to be applied to trade disputes; after all, sanctions are normally used as an act of direct aggression – an instrument of economic war. Perhaps demanding compensation might be a more reasonable approach. And indeed, developing countries have articulated this argument many times, calling for a fairer enforcement mechanism. But rich countries have refused to relinquish their power. Indeed, their insistence on using sanctions gives us a clue as to what is really at stake at the WTO. As long-time WTO negotiator Yash Tandon likes to point out, 'trade is war' – and the war is being waged by the North against the South.

For many poor countries, though, the real pain of trade liberalisation is even more concrete and immediate than all of this – and one doesn't need to ponder free-trade theory to get the point. Simply put, cutting trade tariffs means losing customs revenue. And customs revenue is generally an important source of income for poor countries – sometimes accounting for over 50 per cent of their budget. Poor countries rely on customs revenue because it is easy to collect; personal incomes are often too low to tax and governments often lack the capability to collect other kinds of taxes, such as capital gains taxes, inheritance taxes and so on. Indeed, a study conducted by the IMF itself shows that of all the tax revenue that countries have lost due to trade liberalisation over the past twenty-five years, more than 70 per cent has never been recovered through other forms of taxation. In other words, trade liberalisation directly denies poor countries the very resources they so desperately need to spend on social services and reducing poverty.

The 'Efficiency' of Involuntary Sex Work

I first became aware of the negative effects of trade liberalisation on developing countries when I returned to Swaziland in 2004. During the first few weeks of January 2005, something extraordinary happened. Textile factories began to close up one after the other, and more than 25,000 workers were sacked – most with no prior notice, and many without having received pay for the previous month. For a country as small as Swaziland, where formal sector jobs are almost impossible to come by, this was a devastating blow. How could it have happened? Where did all the factories go? Swazis found themselves at a loss as to how to answer this question. There had been no natural disaster. There had been no economic crisis. There had been no change in government policy. The jobs just vanished, and the industrial parks – once bustling with activity – were left eerily empty.

I, too, was confused. I spent days struggling to figure out what was going on, scouring the newspapers and staying up late to read online by dial-up modem in a run-down Internet café. Eventually the story became clear.

For most of modern history, Western countries protected their domestic textile industries against imports from countries where production costs are far lower. They placed special quotas on imports from East Asian countries such as Korea and Hong Kong, so that not too much cheap clothing would flow in. At the same time, Western countries granted special preferences to very poor countries like Swaziland – like unlimited quotas and duty-free access to Western markets – to help their national textile industries grow, and to encourage other producers to relocate there. The preferences were part of a carefully planned system that used trade rules to promote industrial development where it was needed most, creating jobs in regions of extreme poverty and unemployment. And it worked: Swaziland's textile industry grew rapidly, and a number of Asian firms moved to Swaziland to take advantage of the country's trade preferences. The industry soon became the largest formal employer in the country, with 35,000 workers on its direct payroll by 2004. For Swaziland, it was an economic miracle.

But when the WTO was formed, it placed this system squarely in its sights. Multinational companies argued that the quotas and preferences 'distorted' the market, preventing them from operating in the places where labour was cheapest. And Asian countries argued that it gave unfair advantage to countries like Swaziland. The WTO upheld their argument and, on 1 January 2005, Western countries abolished their quotas on textile imports from East Asia. The landscape of the global textile trade changed literally overnight. It was great news for Asia: textile firms around the world frantically relocated there to take advantage of cheaper labour. But countries like Swaziland, where labour was slightly more expensive, were left in the lurch. Swaziland's factories lost their comparative advantage, and either closed down for good or relocated to East Asia themselves. The textile industry collapsed in record time, and tens of thousands of workers lost their jobs.

A humanitarian catastrophe soon followed. The vast majority of the retrenched workers were women, many of whom had no choice but to turn to sex work to keep afloat. A survey of sex workers in the city of Manzini in 2005 found that most of the women were newcomers who had been fired when the textile factories closed. 'We are not happy with the work we are doing but we have to make a living,' one was quoted as saying; 'the number of people working here is increasing at a high rate, which is evidence that people are desperate for money and there are no jobs.' As one might imagine, this only added to Swaziland's already crippling HIV/AIDS crisis. Indeed, much of the disease burden that Swaziland bears today can be attributed to the spike in women's unemployment after 2005.

For me, this was a kind of epiphany – one of the most important realisations of my life. I was working with World Vision in the development sector at the time, doing home-based care with AIDS patients and setting up little income-generating schemes here and there, honestly trying to help assuage the suffering of my fellow Swazis in whatever ways I could. I was shocked to realise that the fate of Swaziland's poor hinged on decisions made by technocrats in Geneva. With the flick of a pen, new rules – written in the name of free trade – crushed the already fragile lives of my country's people. All of us at World Vision felt helpless against this remote and faceless force.

*

What do free-trade theorists have to say about such catastrophes? Well, they assume that the labour and capital 'released' from uncompetitive industries due to liberalisation will quickly be re-allocated to other industries that align more closely with the country's comparative advantage. This is the assumption of 'perfect factor mobility'. But, as with many economic assumptions, reality almost never plays out according to theory. Workers who lose their jobs in one industry usually lack the skills necessary to quickly take up jobs elsewhere, and end up either languishing in unemployment or taking on very low-skilled, poorly paid work. The only way to ensure that some kind of productive transition takes place is to provide substantial unemployment benefits and training programmes – something that poor countries can rarely afford. Indeed, under structural adjustment programmes they are often denied the right to spend on this kind of social assistance.

As for capital mobility: the theory states that the capital from one dying industry will shift automatically to other, more competitive ones. But if capital is fixed, in the form of a machine, for example, it is usually too specialised to be used in another industry, so it sits languishing until someone sells it off – like the shuttered factories that stand like empty giants on the outskirts of Manzini. And if the capital is liquid, there's no guarantee that it will stay in the country when it could just as easily move abroad. Indeed, that's what happened in Swaziland when textile investors packed up and moved to East Asia. The mobility of liquid capital is *too* perfect, while that of labour and fixed capital is not perfect enough.

So the theory just doesn't square with reality. In fact, in order for this theory to make any sense at all, we would have to conclude that the involuntary movement of thousands of Swazi textile workers into the sex trade is an efficient and desirable outcome, on the basis of comparative advantage. Of course, while Swaziland suffers in this scenario, East Asia wins – and free-trade advocates in the WTO are always quick to point that out. Given the history of the South, this is a sad truth to swallow. The 1950s and 1960s saw valiant attempts by global South leaders to unite in solidarity and mutual assistance through the Non-Aligned Movement and the G77, but structural adjustment and the WTO have unravelled these efforts, pitting one poor country against another. It is a strategy as old as colonialism itself. Divide and conquer.

How to Profit from a Plague

Much of the pain that developing countries suffer under the global free-trade regime actually has nothing to do with free trade at all. One of the WTO's agreements, the Trade-Related Aspects of Intellectual Property Rights (or TRIPS), focuses on copyright and patent rules. One might think that trade would be enhanced by *lowering* patent standards: making it easier for countries to share technology is surely a good way to spur technological development and make trade more efficient. It would increase productivity, innovation and exchange. But TRIPS is designed to do exactly the opposite. The point of TRIPS is to *raise* patent standards and enshrine them in international law – and this is being conducted, ironically, under the banner of liberalisation. It is a contradiction in terms.

Towards the end of the 19th century, the global average length of a patent was about thirteen years. By 1975, before the period of liberalisation, it was around seventeen years. Under TRIPS, however, rich countries have succeeded in imposing a new twenty-year standard. This is great for individuals and companies that own patents, because it means that they get to sit back and extract rent from them for a much longer period. But it has a devastating effect on poor countries. Because patent licensing fees can be so expensive, many poor countries are unable to afford the knowledge and technologies that they need for basic development, like computer programs, agricultural implements and medicines. As a result of TRIPS, developing countries have to pay an additional $60 billion per year in licensing fees to multinational companies.

This might sound like a technical problem, but it can have devastating consequences for human well-being. The most powerful example of this is, of course, the story of the AIDS crisis.

*

When I was still a small boy, my father diagnosed one of the first cases of HIV in Swaziland. It was 1988. Intrigued, he decided to start testing more widely. The following year, he discovered that 2 per cent of the women in his antenatal clinic were HIV positive – a surprisingly high number. One year later, it was double that, and the next year it doubled again. The virus spread so fast that by the end of the 1990s, nearly 25 per cent of the population was infected. He and my mother watched as the clinics and hospitals where they worked overflowed with emaciated bodies. 'It was horrifying,' my father recalled. 'We quickly ran out of beds, and were forced to care for patients on the floor. It was a total crisis.' I still remember my parents coming home from work late at night, exhausted. Yet for them the worst part about the epidemic was not just the suffering they encountered, but the fact that they were unable to treat it. Not because there were no medicines; there were. The first antiretroviral drugs were approved by the United States government in 1987, the year before my father diagnosed his first case. But they were priced at around $15,000 per yearly course – way out of reach for all but the very richest.

The prices were so high because the drugs were locked under a powerful new patent system imposed by the TRIPS Agreement. In the past, pharmaceutical companies were only allowed to hold patents on the process of *manufacturing* drugs, not on the compounds themselves. This meant that developing countries could produce generic versions of important medicines – and sell them for a fraction of the cost – so long as they were able to find their own methods of manufacturing them. TRIPS put an end to this practice by extending corporate patents down to the level of the molecule itself. During the AIDS crisis, generic firms in India were capable of producing and exporting antiretrovirals for as low as $350 per year, which would have been affordable enough to save millions of dying patients, but the WTO – pressured by the pharmaceutical companies – actively prevented them from doing so. 'It was criminal,' my father tells me. 'I was shocked that the drug companies were willing to let people die so needlessly.'

Eventually, neighbouring South Africa, where the epidemic was just as bad, chose to disobey the WTO's rules and began using generic antiretrovirals, pleading a public health emergency. They insisted no patent was so sacred that millions should have to die to respect it. The United States responded by threatening them with crushing sanctions through the WTO's court – and the world watched in horror at this callous move. But then something happened in the United States that weakened their case. In 2001, a number of Americans died of exposure to anthrax. The US government feared that an epidemic might be on the horizon, possibly triggered by biological weapons. Just in case, they decided to stockpile Cipro, the antibiotic that treats anthrax. But Cipro was under patent by Bayer, making it very expensive to buy. So the US government stepped in and, citing a possible public health emergency, forced Bayer to suspend its patent so that generic versions could be produced.

It quickly became clear to the world that patents were not inviolable after all, even for the United States. And if exceptions could be made after a few Americans fell ill, why couldn't the same exceptions be invoked for the sake of millions of dying Africans?

Still, the United States and the WTO refused to back down. It took two more years of grassroots community organising and strategic advocacy before they finally gave in. It was only in 2003 that developing countries gained the right to manufacture and import generic versions of life-saving drugs to defend against AIDS and other public health emergencies. Unfortunately, by the time this concession was made, the epidemic was already entrenched. Ten million Africans had died of AIDS by then – most of whom would have lived had they had access to affordable medicines.

It's not just AIDS drugs that are at stake. Medicines for malaria, tuberculosis and other drugs essential to saving lives in the global South are also in question. Eighteen million people die each year because of preventable diseases, in large part because they lack access to affordable medicine. How does the pharmaceutical industry justify the exorbitantly high prices of these drugs, if it has nothing to do with the costs of manufacture?

Their main argument, which gets wheeled out whenever patents are in question, is that the income from patents provides an incentive to develop the products in the first place. Plus, the profits can be ploughed back into research and development (R & D) to make new and better drugs. But we know that 84 per cent of research on pharmaceuticals is funded by governments and other public sources, while only 12 per cent comes from the pharmaceutical industry. Most of the scientists who develop these drugs are not industry technicians driven by profit, but academics. In fact, many of the key components of the AIDS drugs were developed in public universities, and then bought and patented by corporations. Pharmaceutical companies complained that the TRIPS exception for public health emergencies allowed privately produced products to be publicly appropriated. But the opposite is true. The products are, for the most part, publicly produced and then privately appropriated through the patent system. As for the argument about reinvesting in R & D: the pharmaceutical industry spends far more of its profits on marketing than on research, which suggests that their commitment to research is questionable at best.

The successful battle for a public health exception to TRIPS marked a tremendous victory against the most draconian principles of free trade. But the victory is by no means secure. Once Big Pharma recognised the threat posed by the generics market in developing countries, they took the battle back to the WTO, where they are now developing what they call TRIPS+. The idea behind TRIPS+ is to extend US-style patent laws to the rest of the world, so that producers in all countries have to obey US patents just as if they were operating in the United States.

The End of Democracy

Those who defend the WTO like to point out that – unlike the IMF and the World Bank – the WTO does not impose its will unilaterally. All it does is provide a forum for collective decision-making and furnishes a mechanism for policing decisions that are made. Technically, this is true. Decisions at the WTO are theoretically made on a consensus basis. But it sounds better than it really is. In the consensus process, bargaining power is ultimately based on market size, so the largest and most powerful economies – like the US, UK, Germany and Japan – almost always get their way. This is why so many of the WTO's trade rules end up being asymmetrical, like the subsidy rules that favour rich countries at the expense of poorer ones. But many key decisions are made before the consensus process ever even begins. G7 negotiators have a long history of convening special 'Green Room' meetings from which most developing countries are excluded – a tactic that allows them to agree on positions before they even enter negotiations. In the past, when representatives from poor countries have attempted to enter these exclusive meetings to demand their rightful place at the table, they have often been forcibly removed by security.

As if their market size and exclusive meetings weren't enough to secure them a strong advantage in the halls of the WTO, rich countries have the additional advantage of being able to afford more staff. They can maintain a permanent contingent of negotiators at the WTO headquarters in Geneva to participate in daily, year-round meetings, and send hundreds of people to the bargaining sessions to advocate their interests. Poorer countries that cannot afford to employ so many highly skilled staff end up with their voices ignored. Indeed, many countries cannot even afford to send staff to meetings where decisions are being made that affect them directly. As a result, international trade rules end up being skewed heavily in favour of rich countries.

Negotiators from the South are not the only ones to recognise the unfairness that is built into the international trade system. So, too, do citizens in the North. Awareness of trade injustice on both sides of the North–South divide propelled the mass protests outside the WTO meetings in Seattle in 1999, which became the symbol of the anti-globalisation movement and set off a wave of similar protests. The pressure from below grew so immense that a second round of WTO negotiations was called to address some of the inequities that protestors had brought to light. But the Doha Development Round – as it came to be known – offered little more than window dressing. Western nations have continued to refuse to back down from their agricultural subsidies and the most damaging provisions of TRIPS. As a result of their intransigence, the talks have stalled since 2008 and show no sign of ever coming back to life.

Given the stalemate at the WTO, rich countries have devised a workaround. Instead of relying on multilateral negotiations, they have resorted to expanding bilateral free-trade agreements instead – trade deals that are negotiated directly between two or more countries without having to go through any kind of centralised international authority.

The first major FTA was the North American Free Trade Agreement between Canada, Mexico and the United States, which came into effect in 1994 and cut most tariff barriers to the flow of goods between the three countries. The agreement was highly controversial and widely resisted by voters in all three countries. In Mexico, hundreds of thousands of farmers took to the streets of the capital with their tractors in protest, fearing that they would be unable to compete with subsidised American corn. They were correct. When NAFTA came into effect, American corn flooded into Mexico and undercut local producers. Some 2 million farmers were driven out of business and forced to leave their land. As if to add insult to injury, much of that newly vacated land was then acquired by foreign firms that consolidated large plantations – a scenario not unlike the process of enclosure described in Chapter 3. And just as with enclosure elsewhere in the world, many of the displaced farmers had no choice but to accept low-wage work in the sweatshops that sprang up near the US border as American corporations, enabled by NAFTA, moved south to take advantage of cheaper labour.

One might think that the subsidised corn from the United States would mean cheaper tortillas in Mexico – the region's staple food. And surely this would be a good thing for the country's poor. But, paradoxically, the opposite happened: because NAFTA deregulated retail prices on food, the cost of tortillas shot up by 279 per cent in the first decade, causing hunger and malnutrition to rise.

It was a dream scenario for US companies: they get new export markets, new access to land, higher retail revenues *and* cheaper labour. Many large Mexican firms benefited too – indeed, that is why the Mexican government agreed to NAFTA in the first place. But ordinary people suffered tremendously. The incomes of Mexican farmworkers have fallen to one-third of their previous levels, real wages across the board are lower and the minimum wage is worth 24 per cent less. Ten years after NAFTA, there were 19 million *more* Mexicans living in poverty than before NAFTA. More than half the population now lives below the poverty line. According to a recent

report in the *New York Times*, 'Twenty-five per cent of the population does not have access to basic food and one-fifth of Mexicans
suffer from malnutrition.' Since NAFTA came into effect, per capita
income growth has been only 1.2 per cent on average – less than half
what it was during the decades before NAFTA.

American workers ended up suffering as well. NAFTA led
directly to the displacement of 682,900 US jobs by 2010, most of
which were high-paying, unionised manufacturing jobs. NAFTA
proved to be a powerful force for breaking the remaining power of
organised labour in the United States, and contributed directly to
wage stagnation.

*

NAFTA had a devastating impact on the living standards of many
ordinary Mexicans and Americans. But its power would extend far
beyond the borders of either nation. Buried deep in the agreement's
text, a new idea had been inserted in Chapter 11 that would come to
shake the principles of democracy and national sovereignty around
the world.

For investors, one of the risks of operating in a foreign land is
that your host government might decide to nationalise your assets.
During the developmentalist period, global South governments
often resorted to this tactic in their attempts to reclaim wealth
from foreign control, nationalising land and even businesses
owned by Western companies. When this happened to, say, American companies, their only recourse was to persuade the US government to retaliate by sending a blockade or staging a coup – which,
as we know, they did on many occasions. It was a messy business,
and politically risky: no government really wants to be seen invading another country for the sake of corporate interests. So in 1965
they came up with a way to work such disputes out in the orderly
environs of a court: the International Centre for Settlement of
Investment Disputes (ICSID), which would be overseen by the
World Bank. The idea was that in cases of expropriation, states

would be obligated to compensate investors at a fair value for their property. Each dispute would be worked out by three arbitrators – one picked by each side, and a third agreed upon by both.

By the end of the 1980s, most of the world's countries were plugged into the international arbitration system. Some, including almost all of Latin America, were forced into it against their will under structural adjustment programmes. But despite early suspicions, even they found that the system worked pretty well. After all, it had the effect of slowing down the onslaught of Western-backed coups, which was a welcome change.

But when NAFTA came online, the arbitration system took on a disturbing twist. Investors started to file suits not only in cases of expropriation, but also to push back against environmental and social regulations that they claimed reduced their profits – or even, bizarrely, their 'expected future profits'. There have been a number of cases like this brought under NAFTA's Chapter 11. One famous early case involved Metalclad, a US corporation that was operating a hazardous waste landfill in Mexico under permits issued by the Mexican federal and state authorities. When the local municipal government concluded that the landfill was polluting the local water supply and threatening the health of nearby residents, they closed it down and declared the area a protected environment. In response, Metalclad sued, claiming the decision amounted to an 'expropriation' of the company's land and facilities. Mexico was forced to pay $15.6 million in damages. In another case, the US-based company Dow AgroSciences sued the government of Canada for banning the use of its pesticides on the basis that they might cause cancer in humans.

All of these cases follow the same pattern: corporations sue the state for domestic laws that limit their 'expected future profits', even when the laws are meant to protect human rights, public health or the environment.

It is worth pausing to consider the implications of this. Normally, states enjoy what is known as 'sovereign immunity' status, which means they cannot be sued. But this principle is suspended in cases of investor–state disputes. 'Investor protection' effectively grants corporations the power to circumvent the normal justice system and strike down the laws of sovereign nations. In other words, corporations are empowered to regulate democratic states, rather than the other way around. This is a frontal assault on the ideas of sovereignty and democracy, and one that is being conducted, ironically, once again under the banner of freedom. Even when lawsuits are not filed, the mere threat of them can make elected lawmakers think twice before enacting new regulations.

What is perhaps most troubling about these new investor–state dispute mechanisms, though, is that they are intrinsically imbalanced. Investors have the right to sue states, but states do not have a corresponding right to sue foreign investors. The most a state can hope to win out of a settlement is the nullification of the suit; a state cannot claim damages from foreign corporations. In other words, the system grants special new powers and freedoms to undemocratic corporations while eroding those of sovereign, democratic states.

There is a fascinating irony at play when it comes to the use of sovereign immunity in these cases. Remember, the World Bank and the IMF invoke sovereign immunity in order to protect themselves from lawsuits by the states and citizens who have suffered so much damage at their hands, even though these institutions have no legitimate claim to sovereignty. To this day, no one has successfully challenged this immunity. It is remarkable, then, that sovereign immunity is *upheld* to protect private, undemocratic institutions like the World Bank and the IMF from lawsuits by *public* entities, while it is *suspended* so that democratic states, which have a legitimate claim to sovereignty, can be sued by *private* entities. It is not just a contradiction – it is an inversion of the legal order.

To make matters worse, the dispute hearings themselves are undemocratic. They are conducted in secret tribunals that have none of the checks, balances and transparencies that characterise normal public courts. The judges in these hearings are corporate lawyers from private firms, not public appointees. The citizens and communities that are negatively affected by the investors are not represented in the hearings. And yet, despite all this, the decisions have the power to override the laws of parliaments and the rulings of national courts. One arbitrator from Spain has famously expressed his shock at these arrangements in haunting terms: 'When I wake up at night and think about arbitration, it never ceases to amaze me that sovereign states have agreed to investment arbitration at all . . . Three private individuals are entrusted with the power to review, without any restriction or appeal procedure, all actions of the government, all decisions of the courts, and all laws and regulations emanating from parliament.'

NAFTA has served as a blueprint for similar FTAs elsewhere around the world, and there are now dozens of them. CAFTA (Central American Free Trade Agreement), for example, was passed in 2005, and also includes an investor–state arbitration mechanism that has been brought into use on a number of occasions. In El Salvador, citizens recently voted to ban a gold mine planned by Pacific Rim, a Canadian corporation, because it threatened to destroy part of the country's river system. Pacific Rim is now suing El Salvador for $315 million of potential lost profits. The US–Peru FTA has recently been used by the American company Doe Run to sue the Peruvian government after the government lifted the company's operating license for failing to remediate pollution at a smelter it was operating in La Oroya. The suit was also apparently part of the company's attempt to avoid claims brought on behalf of children and others allegedly poisoned by the smelter's operations. While the company has not prevailed in this claim, the whole ordeal gives an indication of the *Alice in Wonderland* nature of investor–state disputes.

There have been a total of more than 500 investor–state disputes filed at the ICSID, and the number is rising fast. During the 1990s there were fewer than ten cases per year. In 2012 there were fifty-nine, up from fifty-one the previous year. The highest award issued so far has been $2.3 billion (later reduced to $980 million) to the American oil company Occidental Petroleum after Ecuador annulled the company's oil concession, maintaining that proper government consent had not been obtained. Fortunately, this system is finally coming under attack at high levels. Alfred de Zayas, a UN special rapporteur, recently slammed investor–state dispute settlement provisions as a threat to human rights and a violation of international law. In the United States, more than 100 law professors have signed a letter to Congress pointing out that such provisions pose a threat to national sovereignty and the rule of law.

*

The chorus of critique is growing, but it is an uphill battle. As this book goes to press, there are two new FTAs under negotiation: the Transatlantic Trade and Investment Partnership (TTIP), which will govern trade between the US and the European Union, and the Trans-Pacific Partnership (TPP), which will extend NAFTA down into South America and out across the Pacific Ocean. These deals go much further than earlier ones, which seem almost quaint by comparison. The primary aim of the TTIP, for instance, is not to reduce trade tariffs, as these are already at minimal levels, but rather to reduce any 'barriers' to corporate profit maximisation: labour laws, digital privacy laws, environmental protections, food safety standards and financial regulations. The TTIP could make it illegal for governments to stop commercial banks from engaging in securities trading, which was one of the main causes of the 2008 financial crisis. It will also prevent governments from limiting the size of banks, and will prohibit the proposed Robin Hood tax on financial transactions – two measures that are considered essential to preventing another financial crisis. And perhaps most worryingly of all, it will restrict governments from limiting the extraction and consumption of fossil fuels. If it is passed, elected politicians will find themselves stripped of the power to defend the interests of their people and the planet against economic crisis and climate change.

What is also worrying is that we only know about these provisions because of whistle-blowers who have leaked draft chapters of the TTIP to the public. The rest of the agreement remains shrouded in secrecy. Only the negotiators – which include 605 corporate representatives – have full access. The same applies to the TPP. After a number of draft chapters were leaked, the full text was finally published at the end of 2015 – and the results are worse than many expected. The TPP will allow corporations to strike down regulations on food safety, health and the environment, roll back Wall Street reforms and seriously curtail Internet freedoms (it includes much of the text of SOPA, a controversial bill rejected by the US Congress after heavy pressure from civil society). It will also extend the duration of monopoly patents – even for life-saving medicines and seeds.

These treaties amount to something like a corporate coup d'état on an international scale. They create an avenue for extraterritorial legislation that bypasses national parliaments and any form of democratic discussion, pouring scorn on the idea of elected government. In this sense, the ideology of 'free trade' overplays its own hand and exposes itself as farce. The FTAs make it clear that free trade was never meant to be about freedom in the first place. Indeed, the very things that *do* promote real human freedoms – such as the rights of workers to organise, equal access to decent public services and safeguards for a healthy environment – are cast as somehow anti-democratic, or even totalitarian. These freedoms are reframed as 'red tape' or as 'barriers', even when, as is almost always the case, they have been won by popular grassroots movements exercising democratic franchise. In this sense, democracy itself is targeted, bizarrely, as anti-democratic, inasmuch as it grants voters control over the economic policies that affect their lives.

A Virtual Senate

Under the banner of free trade, the world has been redesigned to facilitate the rapid flow of goods. We can see it happening in real time – our ports grow larger and cargo ships chug across the seas in ever greater numbers, stacked high with containers carrying everything from toothbrushes to pomegranates. Finding anything made or even grown locally is often rare to the point of being special. The global flow of goods is an intimate part of our everyday lives. But there is another flow that liberalisation has unleashed, one that is much less known, for it is almost impossible to see: money. If the flow of goods has eroded democratic sovereignty around the world, the flow of money takes this process to another level altogether.

The Bretton Woods system originally designed by Keynes was intended to grant states the power to control the flow of capital across their borders. In other words, states could decide the terms by which foreign investors were allowed to send capital in to set up businesses or buy up shares of local companies. And if those investors wanted to pull their money out, they had to go through a rigorous application process. This was considered crucial to protecting economic stability. When an economy takes a downturn for some reason, an investor's first impulse is to pull their money out and send it somewhere safer. When this happens on a large scale, it drains the economy of much-needed capital, and only makes the problem worse. Slight downturns can become full-blown crises when investors flee en masse. Keynes's system allowed countries to impose 'capital controls' that prevented this from happening.

But free-trade reforms have gradually dismantled these capital controls, and investors and lenders have gained the ability to send massive amounts of capital around the world at lightning speed, putting money in and pulling it out wherever and whenever they please. For poor economies with not much capital base, this poses a serious danger, for even a little bit of unexpected capital flight can spin the economy into crisis. But it also has a more insidious effect. Abolishing capital controls has transferred an enormous amount of power to international investors. Think about it: if you are an investor – and assuming all you care about is profit – you're going to channel your money into countries with what are euphemistically referred to as 'business-friendly' measures like low wages, low taxes, cheap resources, and so on. If you happen to be invested in a country whose government suddenly decides to increase wages and taxes, or decides to regulate waste and pollution, thus reducing your profit margin, then you will quickly pull your money out and send it somewhere else. In the past it wasn't so easy. You would have had to explain yourself to the government, and pay fees to get your money out. But these days there are few if any barriers.

This means that investors can effectively conduct moment-by-moment referendums on decisions made by voters or governments around the world, bestowing their favour on countries that facilitate profit maximisation while punishing those that prioritise other concerns, like decent wages or a healthy environment, by pulling their capital. And when investors decide to punish, it hurts – for poor countries that rely on foreign investment just to stay afloat, quick outflows of capital can be devastating. In this sense, investors operate as a kind of virtual senate. Sitting in their high-rise offices in places like London, New York, Frankfurt and Hong Kong, they are the ones who ultimately decide on economic policy in countries around the world. Voters dare not cross them.

Of course, it can be difficult for investors to keep track of what's going on in terms of economic policy in all the countries around the world. The *Wall Street Journal* and the *Financial Times* can only cover business news in so many countries. Fortunately for investors, they have another option. The World Bank publishes a handy pamphlet known as the *Doing Business* report – a controversial document that ranks the world's countries every year based on the 'ease of doing business' in them. For the most part, the fewer regulations a country has, the higher they score. Investors and CEOs use the rankings to decide where to move their money or headquarter their businesses for maximum profit. There's even an iPhone app that jet-setting capitalists can use to redirect their investments on the fly. A new minimum wage law was just passed in Haiti? Better move your sweatshop to Cambodia! Higher taxes on the rich in South Africa? Time to sell your stocks and invest in

Ireland instead! By providing a panopticon of knowledge about regulatory policies all over the world, the *Doing Business* rankings give investors an incredible amount of power. Countries are forced to respond by cutting regulations to make themselves more attractive to the barons of global capital. A special online 'reform simulator' shows how each country can improve their ranking by, say, slashing corporate taxes or legalising land grabs. The *Doing Business* report has become the World Bank's most influential publication, and drove more than 500 substantive policy changes around the world between 2003 and 2013.

The *Doing Business* rankings are based on ten different indicators, most of which rest on a bizarre black-and-white morality: regulation is bad, deregulation is good. Take the 'employing workers' indicator, for example. According to this measure, countries are scored down for having laws that require minimum wages, paid vacation and overtime rates. They also get docked for requiring employers to pay severance packages to retrenched workers. According to *Doing Business*, all of this counts as 'red tape' that needs to be abolished.

When critics pointed out that this stance runs against the basic labour rights enshrined in the UN's International Labour Organization conventions, the World Bank backed down and removed the indicator from the ranking system. But many equally troubling indicators are still in use. The 'paying taxes' indicator punishes countries for having corporate income taxes, property taxes, dividend taxes and even the financial transaction taxes that are so vital to preventing another financial crisis. They are also punished for requiring employers to pay taxes for services like roads and waste collection; apparently *Doing Business* doesn't stop to ask how states would provide these services without taxes, or how companies could perform in their absence.

Then there's the 'getting credit' indicator. It sounds fair enough – businesses need access to credit, after all – but the name is misleading. It's not really about how easy it is to get credit, but about how easy it is for lenders to recover debts. If countries have bankruptcy laws that, say, protect students who default on their loans, they get punished in the rankings. Countries are rewarded when they make it easier to seize the assets of debtors, even though this removes risk from lenders and can lead to dangerously inflated debt markets. There is also the 'protecting investors' indicator, which pushes towards stronger 'shareholder value' laws. These laws prevent companies from doing anything that might compromise short-term profits, such as paying higher wages or giving back to the community. And the 'registering property' indicator pressures countries to cut regulations on buying land, adding fuel to the wildfire of corporate land grabs currently spreading across the developing world.

The disturbing thing about these indicators is that they have no sense of balance. They don't just want lower minimum wages, they encourage countries to abolish minimum wages entirely; they don't require more modest taxation, they press for zero taxation; they don't ask for more streamlined trade, they want to cut out all tariffs; they don't demand fewer regulations on land, they want total freedom of purchase. Countries are rewarded for pushing to these extremes. There is no recognition that some regulations might actually be important to a fair society, or indeed for a stable economy. But the *Doing Business* indicators are not actually against regulations as such; they are only against regulations that don't directly promote corporate interests. Regulations that protect creditors and investors – and empower them to grab land and avoid taxes – are considered good.

The *Doing Business* rankings reduce economic policy to the shallow metrics of private gain. According to this flagship initiative of the World Bank – which is supposedly devoted to creating a world without poverty – nothing matters aside from corporate profit. The well-being of the people, the health of the land, the fairness of the society – none of these count in the brave new world of free trade. Countries are compelled to ignore the interests of their own citizens in the global competition to bolster corporate power. And here's what may be the most disturbing element of all: the rankings not only inform investors' decisions, they also determine the flow of development aid, as some aid agencies give preferential support to countries that make progress in the rankings. Forget measures of health, happiness and democracy. Forget gains in wages and employment. In the end, what counts most is the 'ease of doing business'.

If you're curious enough to look into the methodology behind the *Doing Business* rankings, you'll find that it's not very robust at all. An official review of the report, ordered by World Bank President Jim Kim and completed in June 2013, raised a list of concerns, including that the methodology has not been peer reviewed. Indeed, it appears to be based largely on the papers of two economists, Simeon Djankov and Andrei Shleifer, both of whom are well-known neoliberal ideologues. Why should we heed the pronouncements of these men? And who gave the World Bank the power to rank countries according to the narrow criteria of 'doing business'? An increasing number of civil-society groups are raising these questions, and the official review even recommends abandoning the use of aggregate rankings within the report altogether.

The rise of the virtual senate represents an important innovation in the history of neoliberalism. In the past, neoliberalism was imposed around the world by external powers. But the virtual senate enjoys the power to get countries to impose neoliberalism *on themselves*, simply by controlling the flow of capital. If a country wants to secure the capital they need for development – or even for survival – they have to kowtow to the wishes of the virtual senate: cut wages, cut taxes, slash regulations. Before the gods of foreign investment, the world is hostage.

*

People commonly think of neoliberalism as an ideology that promotes totally free markets, where the state retreats from the scene and abandons all interventionist policies. But if we step back a bit, it becomes clear that the extension of neoliberalism has entailed powerful new forms of state intervention. The creation of a global 'free market' required not only violent coups and dictatorships backed by Western governments, but also the invention of a totalising global bureaucracy – the World Bank, the IMF, the WTO and bilateral free-trade agreements – with reams of new laws, backed up by the military power of the United States. In other words, an unprecedented expansion of state power was necessary to force countries around the world to liberalise their markets against their will. As the global South has known ever since the Opium Wars in 1842, when British gunboats invaded China in order to knock down China's trade barriers, free trade has never actually been about freedom. On the contrary, as we have seen, free trade has a tendency to gradually undermine national sovereignty and electoral democracy.

What would the world look like if this dimension of free trade was taken to its logical conclusion? We don't have to use our imaginations to guess. All we have to do is take a look at the miniature free-trade utopias – called 'free-trade zones' – that already exist around the world. Most free-trade zones are bounded by barbed-wire fences and walls, and are often patrolled by private security forces. In many cases, elected politicians and national law-enforcement agencies are not allowed to pass through their gates. Within these enclaves, normal laws – labour laws, safety standards, customs duties, taxes and even the basic constitutional rights of citizens – do not apply. These are zones of exception where capital can operate almost unhindered by any form of regulation. The concept took off in the late 1990s, and today there are more than 4,300 such zones in nearly 150 countries. The rationale behind these schemes is that they attract much-needed foreign investment and provide much-needed employment. But the investment is notoriously fleeting, rarely improves anything beyond the borders of the zone, and the near-zero tax rates yield little benefit to the public. As for the jobs that such zones provide: unions are often illegal, wages tend to be lower than the national minimum (as low as 10 cents an hour), workers are commonly expected to put in fourteen-hour days, and they can usually be sacked without compensation.

Free-trade zones are only enclaves, of course. But they offer us a rather horrifying glimpse of what the world might become if the logic of free trade is extended unchecked.

Seven

Plunder in the 21st Century

Coups, structural adjustment, free trade and investor dispute tribunals are all ways that rich countries and powerful corporations have sought to secure their economic interests on the world stage. In a broad sense, each of these tactics has emerged to more or less replace – or at least overshadow – the ones that came before. But it's not quite that clean-cut.

Coups, for example, still remain a live tactic into the 21st century – especially in Latin America. In 2002, the United States tacitly supported a coup attempt against the democratically elected government of Hugo Chávez in Venezuela, and in 2004 helped topple Haiti's progressive president Jean-Bertrand Aristide. In 2009, the elected leader of Honduras, Manuel Zelaya, was deposed in a military coup that was countenanced by the US State Department. There have also been more overt interventions. The US-led invasion of Iraq in 2003 was largely about securing access to oil and defence contracts, as well as preventing Iraq from selling oil in euros instead of dollars. As for the NATO air strikes on Libya in 2011, diplomatic cables released through WikiLeaks reveal that it had to do in part with France's concerns about Libya's attempts to create a Pan-African currency as an alternative to the French-controlled CFA franc. Assassinations are still in the playbook, too. Honduran indigenous activist Berta Cáceres was assassinated in 2016 by US-trained forces, to end her resistance to a dam across the Río Gualcarque.

Third World debt is also re-emerging as a major concern. Because of the collapse in commodity prices following the global financial crisis, global South countries have watched their export revenues plummet – along with their ability to repay their debts. As a result, external debt payments shot up from 6.1 per cent of government revenue in 2013 to 10.8 per cent in 2016. Structural adjustment programmes are still widely used by the World Bank and the IMF to secure debt repayment, in the form of the new Poverty Reduction Strategy Papers. And sometimes creditors take even more extreme steps: when Puerto Rico came to the brink of bankruptcy in 2016, the US Congress responded by assuming executive control over domestic policy decisions through a piece of legislation known as PROMESA, which many denounced as a form of colonisation. And new free-trade agreements are still being negotiated – with investor dispute tribunals intact – as in the Trans-Pacific Partnership.

These old strategies by which powerful actors seek to secure their interests in the global economy still persist. But when it comes to thinking about the relationship between rich and poor countries today, there are three new and much more pressing issues at stake.

The Tax Evaders

If you ever try to suggest that poor countries are poor because they have been disadvantaged by an imbalanced global economy, someone is almost certain to respond by pointing the finger at corruption instead. Poor countries are poor because they are run by corrupt leaders and officials, the argument goes. Corrupt officials make it impossible for businesses to work – and what is

208

more, they steal the resources and wealth that rightly belong to the public, taking food out of the mouths of the hungry. It's no wonder they're poor.

It's not surprising that this argument crops up with such frequency. When Transparency International publishes their highly celebrated Corruption Perceptions Index (CPI) each year, the issue of corruption comes rushing into public consciousness. Development organisations use the opportunity of this annual event to point to corruption as a key driver of underdevelopment in the global South. Until we put an end to corruption and improve governance practices in poor countries, they say, development will never get off the ground. Indeed, this view is supported at the very highest levels. In 2003, the United Nations held the first Convention against Corruption, which asserted that, while corruption exists in all countries, this 'evil phenomenon' is 'most destructive' in the global South, where it is a 'key element in economic underperformance and a major obstacle to poverty alleviation and development'.

It makes good, intuitive sense. After all, the corruption map put out by Transparency International paints a compelling picture. The map depicts most of the global South smeared in the stigmatising red that indicates high levels of corruption. By contrast, rich Western countries, including the United States and the United Kingdom, are painted in happy yellow, suggesting very little corruption at all. This Manichean view fits nicely with our already existing assumptions: cliché images of dictators in Africa, bribery in India and generally unscrupulous bureaucrats and public officials pretty much anywhere outside the Western world. If poor countries are riddled with corruption while rich countries are corruption-free, it seems logical to conclude that corruption is a major driver of poverty. For anyone that isn't aware of the history of colonialism, unequal treaties, structural adjustment and trade rules, this seems as good an explanation as any.

But let's leave aside the structural drivers of global poverty and inequality, and look at the question of corruption on its own terms. There is certainly no denying that corruption is a problem. According to the World Bank, corruption in the forms of bribery and theft by government officials, the main target of the UN Convention, costs developing countries between $20 billion and $40 billion each year. That's a lot of money – and this figure is certainly large enough to warrant our attention as an obstacle to development. But if we broaden our view a little bit and put this figure into perspective, a very different story emerges. As it turns out, this kind of corruption is an extremely small proportion – only about 3 per cent – of the total illicit flows that leak out of the developing world each year. By contrast, the Washington-based Global Financial Integrity (GFI) calculates that up to 65 per cent of total illicit outflows have to do with corruption of a very different sort: commercial tax evasion. And when we look at commercial tax evasion, the neat corruption narrative that Transparency International tells begins to fall apart.

*

'Illicit outflow' is just a fancy name for any illegal movement of money from one country to another. It could be a corrupt official siphoning public funds into a secrecy jurisdiction, or it could be a multinational corporation shifting their money offshore in order to avoid paying taxes. There are lots of reasons that people spirit money across borders. According to GFI, each year up to $1.1 trillion flows illegally out of developing countries and into foreign banks and tax havens. This is an almost unimaginable sum – more than the total amount of foreign direct investment that developing countries receive each year ($858 billion in 2013), and eleven times the amount of official aid they receive ($99.3 billion in 2013). And these outflows have been increasing at a rapid pace over the past decade, growing at about 6.5 per cent per year. Between 2004 and 2013, developing countries lost a total of $7.8 trillion to illicit outflows. It's an enormous problem.

How does this happen? These illicit outflows work through two main channels: hot money and trade misinvoicing.

Hot money is a term used to describe the rapid movement of

capital from one country to another in order to speculate on interest-rate and exchange-rate differences. For example, if the United States looks likely to raise its interest rates, someone with investments in Nigeria might rapidly move their money to the US in the hope of making a quick profit. These rapid, speculative movements of capital are only possible because of the financial deregulation that has been promoted across the developing world over the past few decades by the World Bank, the IMF and free-trade agreements, and they can lead to serious market instability – particularly in small economies. But they also provide an avenue for moving money illegally across borders. In 2013, hot money accounted for 19.4 per cent of total illicit outflows from developing countries, or $211 billion.

Trade misinvoicing, for its part, involves sending money into secret offshore accounts by cheating the trade system. For example, imagine that a South African firm has agreed to buy $1 million of steel from a British firm. The South African firm requests that the British firm send the invoice for $1 million to a tax haven. The tax haven then *reinvoices* the South African firm at more than the agreed value of the goods – say $1.5 million. The South African firm pays the $1.5 million to the tax haven. The tax haven then pays $1 million to the British firm and diverts the rest to an offshore account. As far as the tax authorities in South Africa can tell, the transaction appears legitimate – but the South African firm has successfully spirited $500,000 into an offshore account where it will never be taxed. Tax havens openly advertise their reinvoicing services and offer to assist firms in setting up shell companies to launder money and evade taxes. A quick Google search for 're-invoicing services' turns up dozens of companies located in the Seychelles, Mauritius and so on, ready and willing to help companies secret their money offshore. In 2013, trade misinvoicing accounted for 80.6 per cent of illicit outflows from developing countries, or $879 billion.

Trade misinvoicing is usually used for tax evasion. But it can also serve many other purposes. Sometimes it's used to launder money from criminal activities or to dodge capital controls that countries have put in place to stabilise financial flows. Firms might also use trade misinvoicing to inflate their exports in order to qualify for special tax incentives that governments offer to exporters. But even when the goal is not necessarily tax evasion, the *effect* is the same, for all forms of trade misinvoicing deny governments the opportunity to tax income and wealth.

The researchers at Global Financial Integrity can detect reinvoicing because of the obvious differences between the invoices reported by exporters and importers for the same customs transaction. But this is the *only* form of trade misinvoicing that they are able to detect. There are other forms of misinvoicing that go completely under the radar, such as 'transfer mispricing'.

To understand how transfer mispricing works, we first have to understand normal transfer pricing. Transfer pricing happens when companies sell goods within their own corporate structure, for example if a subsidiary in China sells goods to another subsidiary in Britain. Because of the rapid expansion of corporate monopolies over the past few decades, today at least 60 per cent of world trade takes place *within* multinational corporations, rather than between them. So transfer pricing is not an exceptional practice – it is the norm. And under normal circumstances it is completely legal, as long as subsidiaries report the correct market prices of the goods in question *as if* they were conducting trade with an outside entity, 'at arm's length'. But quite often companies artificially distort transfer prices in order to evade taxes or dodge capital controls; this is when transfer pricing becomes transfer *mispricing*.

Transfer mispricing is remarkably easy. All a company has to do is write out an invoice that falsely reports the cost of an item, and then get their trade partner to write out a similarly false invoice on the other side – in other words, 'same-invoice faking'. Analysts have recorded some flagrant examples of this: a kilogram of toilet paper from China priced at $4,121, a litre of apple juice from Israel priced at $2,052, ballpoint pens from Trinidad priced at $8,500 each. By inflating transfer prices, a company can magically move its money from subsidiaries in high-tax countries to subsidiaries in low-tax countries – often in tax havens. Because this practice is so difficult to detect, no one knows the full scale of the problem. Global Financial Integrity estimates that it probably amounts to outflows that are at least equivalent to the scale of reinvoicing. That means *another* $879 billion flowing out of developing countries each year. And it may even be more than reinvoicing, given that transfer mispricing is so much easier to get away with.

*

The biggest loser in this game is Africa. Already the world's poorest region, sub-Saharan Africa suffers total illicit outflows that amount to 6.1 per cent of its GDP. In fact, Africa loses so much through illicit flows that it is effectively a net creditor to the rest of the world. If we tally up all types of legal and illegal financial flows, including investment, remittances, debt forgiveness and natural resource exports, we see that Africa sends more money to the rest of the world than it receives. The provocative graph below illustrates the sheer scale of the capital that is dripping out of Africa's open veins.

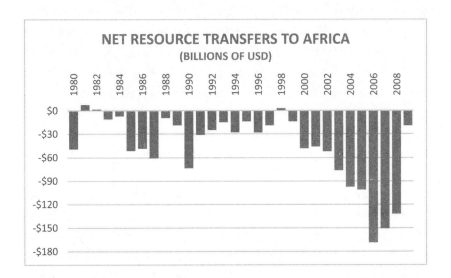

Source: Global Financial Integrity

In total, developing countries may have lost as much as $2 trillion in 2013 through hot money and trade mispricing, or a mind-boggling $14.3 trillion over the past decade. And in case these numbers aren't staggering enough, keep in mind that the misinvoicing figures only reflect trade in goods, not trade in services. GFI is not able to capture misinvoicing for services. We have no idea what the scale of illicit flows might look like in the service sector, but since trade in services counts for 25 per cent of global trade, we can probably bump the figures up by the same proportion.

*

Who is to blame for this state of affairs? Companies that lie on their invoices are guilty of illegal activity, but why is it so easy for them to get away with it? Terms like 'capital flight' and 'illicit outflows' seem to find fault with the victim countries, as though they're just unable to catch the money. But this is misleading. In the past, customs officials in developing countries had the power to prevent misinvoicing. If the prices reported on an invoice diverged suspiciously from the normal market prices of the goods in question – as listed by the Brussels Definition of Value – they could hold up the transaction. This made it virtually impossible for corporations to get away with theft through trade. But the WTO argued that this made trade inefficient. Since at least 1994, customs officials have been required to accept invoiced prices at face value, barring exceptional circumstances. As a result, corporations have free rein to write out their invoices however they please, with little risk of being called out. This is why mispricing has grown at such a rapid rate since the mid-1990s.

Still, none of this theft would be possible without the tax havens. Altogether, there are around fifty to sixty tax havens in the world. They function as tax havens not only because they offer low or zero tax rates, but because they have very little financial regulation and, most importantly, they shroud financial information behind a veil of secrecy. Indeed, the technical term for a tax haven is secrecy jurisdiction. In most cases, banks and corporations operating out of secrecy jurisdictions are not required to disclose anything about where money comes from and where it goes – and in some cases it is actually illegal to disclose such information. Given this, secrecy jurisdictions afford robust protections not just for tax evaders but for all kinds of criminals – including money launderers, arms smugglers and even terrorists.

It is impossible to know how much money is stashed in the world's tax havens, but a lowball estimate in 2010 suggested the figure was at least $21 trillion, and probably closer to $32 trillion – about $9 trillion of which is from poor countries. The money stashed away in tax havens amounts to more than one-sixth of all the world's private wealth. Today, at least 30 per cent of all foreign direct investment flows through tax havens, and about 50 per cent of all trade.

There are three main categories of tax havens. There are tax havens in Europe, like Luxembourg, Switzerland and the Netherlands, which are probably the best known, as well as Belgium, Austria, Monaco and Lichtenstein. Then there are the tax havens in the United States, such as Manhattan, Florida and Delaware, as well as US-linked territories like the Virgin Islands, the Marshall Islands, Liberia and Panama. But by far the biggest and most powerful network of tax havens is organised around Britain – and was crafted by the once powerful British empire. There are the three British Crown dependencies of Jersey, Guernsey and the Isle of Man. Then there are the fourteen British Overseas Territories, which include the Cayman Islands, the British Virgin Islands and Gibraltar. Finally, there are a number of territories that Britain no longer formally controls, but which used to be under its imperial power: Hong Kong, Singapore, the Bahamas, Dubai, Ireland, Vanuatu and Ghana.

Probably the most important central node in this global tax haven system is the City of London. While it may seem confusing, the City of London is not the same thing as London itself. It is a small council within London that houses London's powerful financial sector. The City of London is able to function as a tax haven because it is immune from many of the nation's laws, is free of all parliamentary oversight and – most importantly – is exempt from Freedom of Information rules. It even has its own private police force. As a result of this special status, the City has maintained a number of quaint plutocratic traditions dating back to medieval times, when it was founded. Take its electoral process, for instance. Unlike in normal councils, the franchise in the City of London is not restricted to human beings. Businesses registered within the council's borders are allowed to vote alongside residents. More than 70 per cent of the votes cast during council elections are cast not by humans, but by businesses – mostly corporate banks and financial firms. And the bigger the corporation, the more votes they get, with the largest firms getting seventy-nine votes each. The City even has its own mayor – the Lord Mayor of London, not the better-known Mayor of London – who respects the authority of no one but the monarchy. The Lord Mayor is 'elected' each year by a group of corporations and his sole role (it has been a man every year since 1189) is to promote the interests of the City's banks.

According to the website of the City of London, the Lord Mayor's job is to 'open doors at the highest levels' for business and 'expound the values of liberalisation'. To do this, he has at his disposal a multibillion-pound slush fund for use in lobbying the UK government and governments around the world to bring in laws that are friendly to banks and multinational companies. He's like a one-man structural adjustment team. On top of this, part of the Lord Mayor's mission is to travel abroad in order to build the City's tax haven network. The last incumbent spent 100 days abroad in a single year, and visited more than twenty countries. At the time of writing, the new Lord Mayor was lobbying hard to turn Kenya into a tax haven.

The problem with tax havens is not only that they facilitate the theft of capital, or that they prevent governments from capturing revenues, but also that they induce what analysts call 'tax competition' or 'tax warfare'. Tax havens have set off a kind of global race to the bottom, with countries competing to offer low tax rates to foreign investors in order to attract them in. This constant pressure to reduce taxes makes it very difficult for parliaments and governments to make rational decisions about tax legislation, or to plan their budgets into the future.

Some economists nonetheless believe that the global tax haven system is justifiable according to neoliberal theory: they claim that money should be allowed to move freely around the world in search of the best tax rates. But much about the tax haven system runs directly against the principles of free markets. For example, trade mispricing makes a mockery of the idea of 'market prices': the prices of many of the goods that get shipped around the world have nothing to do with the market at all – they are simply invented out of thin air. The tax haven system also violates the principles of comparative advantage. For one, it provides the equivalent of an unfair subsidy for companies that are rich enough to take advantage of tax evasion services. But more importantly, it means that companies move around the world not to where they can be most efficient, but to where they can find the greatest secrecy or the lowest taxes. The fact that the tiny British Virgin Islands hosts some 850,000 companies (for a population of 25,000) makes the idea of comparative advantage seem quaint.

*

In light of all this, the question of corruption begins to take on a somewhat different hue. Given the role of Britain, the United States and various European countries in facilitating illicit flows by building and maintaining the global tax haven system, and in light of the role that the WTO plays in making it difficult for customs officials to clamp down on mispricing, it seems a bit strange that rich countries appear in corruption-free yellow on the Transparency International map.

One of the problems with TI's methodology is that it measures people's *perceptions* of corruption, rather than corruption itself. People who live in Britain may not normally think of their country as being particularly corrupt, but that may be because corruption is something that they have been taught to associate with countries in the developing world – not with the rich world. In this sense, Transparency International might be helping to create the very perceptions that it seeks to measure.

Corruption in developing countries is cited as a major cause of underdevelopment – and for good reason. But it is important that we expand our conception of corruption to include illicit outflows, anonymous companies, secrecy jurisdictions and so on in order to understand how serious the problem of corruption actually is. Inasmuch as these practices siphon resources out of the global South, they contribute significantly to global poverty and inequality, and yet the mainstream definition of corruption does not encompass them, and they are absent from the UN Convention. Instead, the corruption narrative diverts our attention away from these exogenous problems and places the burden of blame on developing countries themselves.

The Land-Grabbers

In early 2007, something unexpected happened. Reports began to trickle out about rising food prices around the world, and then suddenly, within a matter of weeks, it was a full-blown crisis. Seeing their survival on the line, people took to the streets across much of the global South. In Burkina Faso, food prices soared by 65 per cent, triggering protests and riots in many of the country's major cities. In Cameroon, protests turned violent and led to the deaths of twenty-four people. In Bangladesh, tens of thousands of workers marched in the capital. Mexico, Morocco, Mauritania, Senegal, Côte d'Ivoire and many other countries were hit with similar unrest. In Egypt, the food-price crisis galvanised the mass social discontent that would eventually topple the dictatorship of Hosni Mubarak. By 2008, the IMF had announced that world food prices had increased by 80 per cent in a single year. In a world where more than half the population lives below the poverty line, such an increase in the price of food meant potential starvation for hundreds of millions of people.

For casual Western observers, it was easy to dismiss this crisis as a natural phenomenon – the inevitable result of fluctuating supply and demand in the market. And certainly there was some of this at play. Rising incomes in China were translating into higher demands for meat and milk, and as a result, huge swathes of the world's agricultural fields were being retooled to feed livestock instead of people. In the United States, demand for biofuels meant that one-third of the nation's corn crop was being channelled into ethanol production, with many farmers planting fewer food crops in order to cash in on the biofuel craze. At the same time, climate change had caused droughts in a number of key grain-producing countries, reducing their export volumes; global harvests continued to grow, but not as quickly as before. The rising price of oil – which hit historic highs during this period – might also have had something to do with it, driving up the costs of farming inputs and food transportation. But none of these drivers were significant enough to account for the sheer scale of what was going on.

Beginning in 1991, Goldman Sachs took advantage of new financial deregulations and decided to bundle commodity futures – including food – into a single index. Traders could then speculate on this index and investment funds could link their portfolios to it. It was a new kind of financial derivative, one of many such instruments that were being peddled on Wall Street in those years. For the most part, investors didn't pay it much mind, and the index remained something of a financial backwater for many years. But as the first hints of the sub-prime mortgage crisis began to appear in 2005, nervous investors pulled out of mortgage derivatives and pumped their money instead into commodities, which are supposed to be stable even when the rest of the economy falters. The result was rampant speculation on commodity futures, which affected prices in the real economy. This had a particularly dramatic impact on food prices, which skyrocketed and hit record highs in 2007. In other words, people who were savvy enough to pull out of the housing bubble before it burst ended up inflating another bubble – this time in food.

The crisis didn't stop there. World food prices continued to fluctuate wildly, crashing in 2009 back to pre-crisis levels, and then surging again in 2010 to break yet new records. In 2011, prices were 2.5 times higher than they were in 2004 – a trend aggravated by climate-change-induced weather events that were affecting yields in grain-producing regions of Russia and North America. According to UN sources, in 2011 some 40 million extra people around the world had been plunged into serious hunger.

As if the food-price crisis wasn't bad enough for the world's poor in and of itself, it had a dramatic knock-on effect that no one saw coming. Investors seized the opportunity to buy up millions of acres of land around the world for agricultural production – for both food and biofuels – in order to take advantage of the soaring prices. Many governments got in on the game as well, worried about future social unrest and anxious to secure stable food supplies in a world threatened by climate change. Countries not self-sufficient in food were particularly eager to snatch up farmlands, especially given that a number of big food-producing countries were cutting down on exports in order to ensure they had enough for their own needs.

Many of these purchases were land grabs. A land purchase qualifies as a grab when it entails a transfer of at least 500 acres to be converted from smallholder production, collective use or ecosystem services to commercial activity. Land grabs may provide abstract economic benefit – increasing GDP, for instance – but they often cause environmental damage and human harm: vulnerable people end up displaced from their land and stripped of their access to food and independent livelihoods.

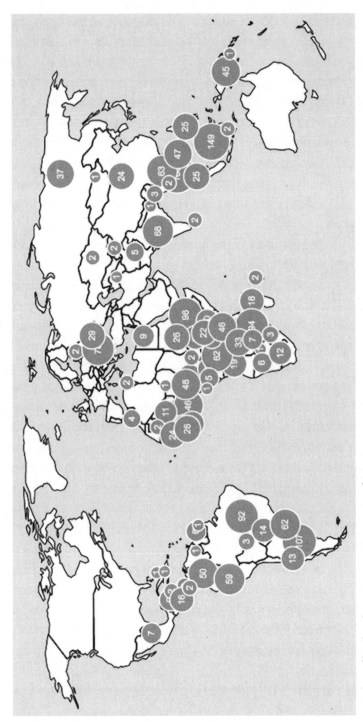

Number of land grabs since 2000. Source: Land Matrix

It is difficult to know exactly how much land has been grabbed in this way, because many of the transactions are conducted in secret, behind closed doors. Early estimates from the World Bank put the figure at 120 million acres during the decade since 2000, while Oxfam claimed land grabs amounted to as much as 560 million acres over the same period, roughly the size of Western Europe. These numbers are difficult to verify, but the latest data from the Land Matrix, which tabulates only confirmed transnational transactions since 2000, reports 162 million acres grabbed in some 1,500 deals that have either already been concluded or are still under negotiation.

While the majority of the land-grabbers are investors from rich countries, and the majority of the target land is in poor countries, the story of land grabs is not a straightforward tale of the North looting the South. Britain is the biggest land-grabber in terms of the number of deals it has executed, and the United States is the biggest in terms of the sheer size of its grabs, but China and India are not too far behind. And about a third of all land grabs involve regional investors. The story is much clearer if we look at it in class terms. The land-grabbers are always rich, regardless of where they are from (after all, the 1 per cent is now a global class), while the people who are displaced from the land are always poor. Indeed, land-grabbers tend to target regions where people do not have formal legal title to their land, and where residents are too poor to mount a serious challenge in the courts. They also tend to favour countries that have poor governance scores, and where local corruption means the deals can be concluded quickly and quietly – a trend that, incidentally, inverts the conventional assumption that good governance attracts foreign investment. South Sudan, for instance, attracted some of the biggest, murkiest land heists shortly after it acquired independence, before it had a government to speak of, and even before proper maps of the new country had been drawn up.

This explains why 66 per cent of the land that was grabbed between 2000 and 2010 was in Africa, accounting for up to 4 per cent of the continent's total land mass. Africa is an ideal target because most communities tend to hold land collectively, without formal titles. Control over specific plots is often reckoned according to customary norms or oral tradition. And much of this land is technically owned by the state – a holdover from the colonial era, when European governments simply appropriated vast swathes of land for themselves through legal writ. This control makes it easy for politicians and bureaucrats in Africa to sell or lease land to foreign investors for a song in return for whatever kickbacks the buyer is willing to extend. In many land-grab cases both sides are party to obvious corruption. As for the actual inhabitants of the land – they end up having to bear the real cost: they lose their homes, their resources, their livelihoods and their communities.

In many ways, this scenario is redolent of the enclosures in England or the clearances immortalised in John Steinbeck's *The Grapes of Wrath*. And more often than not, the countries that are giving away land already suffer from serious hunger problems. In Liberia, 75 per cent of the country's land was in the hands of large investors in 2012, while 24 per cent of Liberian children were malnourished.

Not all land grabs are aimed at improving food security for the grabbers. Astonishingly, sometimes the grabbing is done in the name of improving the plight of the grabbed. As hunger increased in the wake of the food-price crisis, in 2012 the G8 and more than 200 of the world's biggest agribusiness corporations (including Monsanto, Syngenta, Cargill, and later Coca-Cola) launched the New Alliance for Food Security and Nutrition. Their stated goal is to 'lift 50 million people out of poverty over the next 10 years through inclusive and sustained agricultural growth'. But this sugary humanitarian rhetoric is being used to justify the consolidation of land into corporate hands. The project promises agricultural aid and private investment to African countries that agree to change their laws in order to 'facilitate' access to land for foreign firms. Ten countries have signed up, agreeing to cut corporate tax rates, ease export regulations, extend the length of leases and set aside huge chunks of prime agricultural land for agribusinesses. In Côte d'Ivoire, these deals are set to transfer some 1.5 million acres to foreign companies, which, according to a 2013 report by the watchdog group Grain, 'will displace tens of thousands of peasant rice farmers and destroy the livelihoods of thousands of small traders – the very people that the G8 claims will be the "primary beneficiaries" of its New Alliance'.

Land is not the only commons that the Alliance seeks to enclose. Seeds are on the agenda too. An agreement with Mozambique requires that it 'systematically cease distribution of free and unimproved seeds'. Tanzania has been made to pass a new Seed Act that protects corporate patents on biological material. Similar 'reforms' have been foisted on the eight other participating countries.

Food production and biofuel may be the biggest drivers of land grabbing, but there are many other sectors involved as well. In Papua New Guinea, more than a tenth of the country's land was grabbed in a single decade and handed over to foreign logging companies eager to get their saws into the region's famous rainforests. In Cambodia, 5 million acres – or half of the country's total agricultural land – has been handed out to private companies, mostly for sugar production. So many Cambodian peasants have been illegally evicted from the land that the new sugar exports have become known as 'blood sugar'. Across South East Asia, around 1 million acres have been converted from peasant holdings to rubber plantations operated by Chinese companies ready to supply the ravenous market for car tyres in China. And the Land Matrix database shows that dozens of land grabs have been conducted for the sake of tourism. A royal company from Abu Dhabi recently acquired 5.5 million acres of South Sudan's grasslands, which it plans to convert into an upmarket game reserve peppered with five-star hotels.

But perhaps the most disturbing recent trend is that land grabbing is now also being conducted in the name of the most progressive cause of this century: climate change mitigation. In 2005, the United Nations and the World Bank began developing a new strategy for reducing greenhouse gas emissions known as

REDD, or by its rather clumsy full name, Reducing Emissions from Deforestation and forest Degradation. REDD allows companies in rich countries to buy carbon credits to get around their emissions limits, and then uses that money to protect forests in developing countries from being chopped down for commercial purposes. REDD's basic innovation is to recognise that our present economic model assigns value to forests only when the trees are chopped down and turned into commodities; it fails to account for the devastating – and incredibly expensive – *costs* that deforestation produces in the form of climate change. Normally forests serve as important carbon sinks, but when they are destroyed they release vast amounts of carbon into the air; deforestation contributes 20 per cent of total global greenhouse gas emissions. REDD seeks to redress this pricing failure by allowing forest owners to profit from *not* chopping down the trees, recognising that the forest provides an important 'environmental service' to all of humanity and should therefore be assigned an economic value.

This seems like a good step, in theory. But in practice it has had devastating consequences. In many cases, REDD pilot projects have led to the forced eviction of indigenous communities from forests on the basis that their farming practices contribute to deforestation. In Kenya, for instance, the government has cooperated with a World Bank-led REDD scheme by evicting and destroying the homes of the 15,000 indigenous Sengwer people who live in the Embobut Forest. REDD is also incentivising a new wave of land grabs: corporations and states are rushing to buy up forests in developing countries in order to cash in on the payouts, a practice now known as 'carbon colonialism'. Some are taking advantage of loopholes in REDD that actually *permit* deforestation of original forests so long as new forests are planted elsewhere – even if those new forests happen to be plantations. In other words, some of the very companies that are driving deforestation through land grabs are now grabbing yet more land under the guise of offsetting the environmental damage they have caused. Instead of protecting forests from destructive market forces, REDD is rapidly bringing forests *into* the market. And in the end it will lead to zero reduction of carbon emissions at source; after all, the whole idea behind carbon credits is to allow polluters to *avoid* reducing their emissions by buying their way around the rules.

*

While local elites might make handsome profits, the environmental losses that developing countries suffer at the hands of land-grabbers are immense. But there is also a substantial financial loss at stake. In many of these deals, land is sold at fire-sale prices – far below its actual value. Examples from Ethiopia and Peru show that investors end up paying around $0.50 per acre per year, or even as little as $0.30 per acre. Even at conservative estimates, the real value of land on the international market is probably closer to about $600 per acre per year; that's how much global South countries *should* be earning on their land transactions. At this rate, the real value of the land that has been grabbed in the global South since 2000 amounts to about $97 billion. That's just the one-year lease value; the total value would be a year-on-year multiple of this. And of course this figure tells us nothing about the profits that stand to be made off the land in an era of high food prices, soaring demand and dwindling supply.

Some of these deals might be justified by policymakers in target countries on the basis that they will provide tax revenue on corporate income. But given the fact that most of the investors involved are capable of avoiding the tax system altogether, it's unlikely that significant benefits will ever materialise.

The Climate Changers

When Typhoon Haiyan made landfall in South East Asia in November 2013, it was the strongest tropical cyclone ever recorded, clocking wind speeds of up to 200 miles per hour. While much of the region suffered serious damage, the Philippines was the worst hit by far. Even the most calloused, news-hardened observers could not have been left unmoved by the images that circulated around the world that month, depicting destruction on an overwhelming scale. Whole cities and towns were laid to waste; in some not a single structure was left standing. It was the deadliest typhoon to hit the Philippines in modern history, killing at least 6,300 people and leaving another 30,000 injured. As late as 2015, some bodies were still being retrieved from the wreckage, and more than 1,000 remained missing. But the body count is only the tip of the iceberg. A vast humanitarian disaster unfolded in the wake of the typhoon: more than 6 million people were displaced in the Philippines alone, and 1.9 million left homeless, triggering an internal refugee crisis. Aid agencies warned of disease epidemics in the region due to the lack of food, water and medication.

According to the latest report, the total cost of the damage has reached $2.05 billion, making Haiyan the costliest typhoon in the history of the Philippines – more than double the second-costliest storm, Typhoon Bopha, which made landfall only one year prior. This has become a disturbing trend. In fact, the eight costliest typhoons in Philippines history have all occurred since 2008, exacting a total toll of nearly $6 billion.

As it happens, the UN Climate Change Conference was being held in Poland at exactly the same time as Haiyan struck. Yeb Sano, the gentle, soft-spoken delegate from the Philippines, gave an emotional speech that quickly went viral on social media. 'Super Typhoon Haiyan made landfall in my family's home town and the devastation is staggering,' he said. 'I struggle to find words even for the images that we see from the news coverage. I struggle to find words to describe how I feel about the losses and damages we have suffered from this cataclysm. Up to this hour, I agonise while waiting for word as to the fate of my very own relatives.' In a voice choked by tears but bolstered by rage, he continued: 'What my country is going through as a result of this extreme climate event is madness. The climate crisis is madness. I speak for my delegation.

227

But more than that, I speak for the countless people who will no longer be able to speak for themselves after perishing from this storm. We must stop calling events like these natural disasters. [The disaster] is a result of inequity, and the poorest people of the world are at greatest risk because of their vulnerability and decades of maldevelopment, which I must assert is connected to the pursuit of so-called economic growth that dominates the world.'

Sano announced that he would begin a hunger strike until a meaningful climate deal was in sight. He was joined by a number of other delegates and sixty people from the Climate Action Network.

*

Sano's speech illustrated a powerful fact that the rich world has found very difficult to swallow. While the West has been historically responsible for the vast majority of the greenhouse gas emissions that cause climate change, and has benefited tremendously from the industrial use of fossil fuels, the costs of climate change fall disproportionately on poor countries.

From the start of the Industrial Revolution until today, humans have released a total of 588 billion tons of CO_2 into the atmosphere. Rich industrial economies are responsible for about 70 per cent of this, although measurements vary slightly: the number is much higher if you count only industrial emissions, but slightly lower if you include non-industrial emissions, such as from deforestation. Yet, according to data from the Climate Vulnerability Monitor, developed nations bear only 12 per cent of the total costs of climate change. Developing countries, by contrast, have to bear 82 per cent of the total costs, which in 2010 meant $571 billion in losses due to drought, floods, landslides, storms and wildfires. The Monitor predicts that as these costs continue to increase, the share of losses borne by developing countries will increase as well – to 92 per cent by 2030. By then, developing countries will suffer losses amounting to $954 billion per year.

The distribution of climate-change-related deaths is also geographically uneven. Typhoon Haiyan killed 6,300 people – an

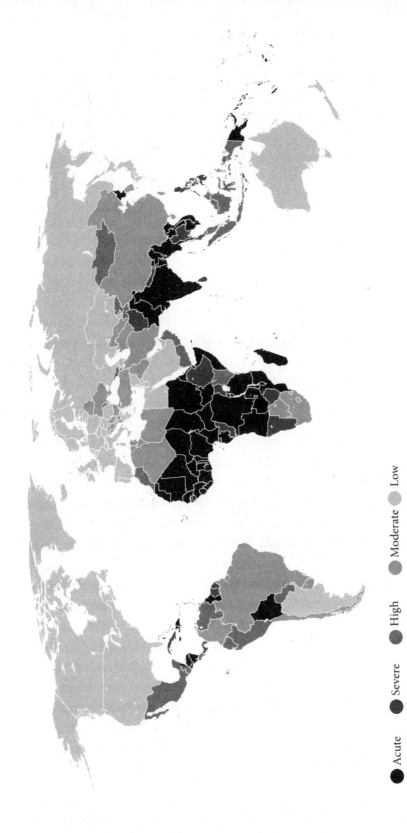

● Acute   ● Severe   ● High   ● Moderate   ● Low

Multi-dimensional vulnerability to climate change.
Source: Climate Vulnerability Monitor, 2012

astonishing number. But this is only a small fraction of the total number of people killed by climate change each year. In 2010 there were 400,000 such deaths, many due to extreme weather events but most due to climate-change-induced hunger and communicable disease. Of these, 98 per cent occurred in developing countries. And, ironically, the vast majority – 83 per cent – occurred in the countries that have the lowest carbon emissions in the world. And it's getting worse. The Climate Vulnerability Monitor predicts that by 2030 climate-related deaths in the developing world will have increased to more than 530,000 per year. Rich countries, by contrast, will witness only 1 per cent of those deaths within their borders.

Emissions patterns are changing, of course. In 2005, developing countries as a group caught up with their richer counterparts in terms of CO_2 emissions – a change for which China is almost exclusively responsible, given its heavy reliance on coal. Indeed, China recently surpassed the USA to become the world's biggest polluter. And Brazil, Indonesia and India have now surpassed Germany and the United Kingdom. Much of this has to do with the fact that globalisation has shifted production to developing countries, and especially to China, effectively outsourcing responsibility for pollution. Still, once corrected for population size the picture looks significantly different. The United States remains the biggest polluter, emitting three times more CO_2 than China on a *per capita* basis. Germany emits almost double what China does, per capita. And India, for its part, emits just a fraction of the world average: each Indian is responsible for only 1.4 tons of CO_2, while the world average is upward of 4.5 tons per person. Africans emit only 0.9 tons per person. And yet the costs of climate change will hit Africa and India the hardest, amounting to 4 per cent and 5 per cent of their GDP, respectively.

Why are the consequences of climate change so unevenly distributed? For one, climate change is causing patterns of rainfall gradually to shift north. As a result, many drought-prone areas of the global South will have even less water than they do now. In developing countries, where agriculture is already precarious and generally conducted on a small, non-industrial scale, even slight changes in precipitation can cause devastating damage. Ironically, the high-yield seeds that have been in use since the Green Revolution in the 1960s are much less resistant to a variable climate than the older heirloom varieties. According to *The Economist*, by 2040 Indian crop yields will decline by up to 9 per cent. In Africa, the growing period could be reduced by 20 per cent. By 2080, agricultural production could fall by as much as 21 per cent across the developing world – all while the demand for food continues to rise. Oxfam predicts that, as a result, world hunger will worsen significantly. The number of people at risk of hunger could increase 20 per cent by 2050 as the availability of calories diminishes across the world.

Disease is another important consideration. In Africa, many cities and towns are built intentionally just above the 'malaria line' – just high enough to escape the reach of malaria-bearing mosquitoes. As the weather warms, mosquitoes are able to move into altitudes that were previously uninhabitable for them. Present estimates suggest that by 2030 an additional 90 million Africans could be exposed to malaria. Similarly, meningitis outbreaks are expected to increase in Africa, as the disease is highly correlated with drought. The recent upsurge in dengue fever and the Zika virus – the latter of which plagued Brazil during the 2016 Olympic Games – are also associated with the changing climate.

These patterns throw the standard narrative of development into question. Rich countries cast themselves as saviours of the world's poor, but this makes little sense given their role in causing climate change. Indeed, the costs of climate change in the developing world amount to many times more than the aid they receive from rich countries.

In the global South, scholars and activists argue that the North owes a 'climate debt' to the South. There have long been calls for compensation, or climate reparations, which would help cover the costs of damage as well as supply the funds necessary to assist developing countries to plan a carbon-free future. In 2014, these calls were underwritten by careful mathematical calculations. Scientists at the Stockholm Environment Institute partnered with Friends of the Earth to devise a fair system for both apportioning responsibility for reducing global emissions to the level required to avoid runaway climate change, and for dividing up the costs of compensation and assistance to developing countries that have been damaged. Their methodology accounts for each country's historical emissions, economic capacities and national poverty burden. According to their calculations, the UK would have to cut its emissions by 75 per cent on 1990 levels and transfer $49 billion to developing countries. The US would have to cut emissions by up to 65 per cent, while paying out $634 billion. Meanwhile, my home country of Swaziland, for example, would be allowed to increase its emissions by 59 per cent in order to provide space for economic growth and poverty reduction, and would receive $80 million in compensation and assistance.

*

Projections of the damage that climate change is likely to cause in the near future are terrifying indeed. But apparently they are not terrifying enough to get the governments of rich countries to take serious action to mitigate their emissions. Scientists tell us that if we want to avoid catastrophic climate change, we can only allow our planet to warm a maximum of 1.5°C above baseline. When the world's governments met in Paris for the COP21 summit in 2015, they agreed to this 1.5°C target. But the text of the agreement indicates that their commitments are little more than lip service. The agreement relies entirely on countries' voluntary pledges, known as Intended Nationally Determined Contributions (INDCs). And unfortunately the sum total of the voluntary pledges that have been made so far fall a good deal short of the target. If all of the pledges are upheld (which is very unlikely, given that they are non-binding), we will still be hurtling towards 2.7 to 3.7°C of warming.

If we want to have a 66 per cent chance of keeping below 1.5°C, we can pump no more than another 205 gigatons of carbon dioxide into the earth's atmosphere between 2015 and the end of the century. This is known as the 'carbon budget'. At our current rate of emissions, we are pumping 40 gigatons of CO_2 into the atmosphere each year, which means the 1.5°C budget will be blown by 2020. To limit ourselves to 205 gigatons of CO_2 will take a monumental effort, given that the world's fossil fuel reserves currently contain more than 2,600 gigatons' worth of CO_2. These are reserves that are known and extractable using today's technologies and in today's economic conditions. In other words, we are presently planning to burn past our global limit by a factor of thirteen – and that's to say nothing of other major causes of carbon emissions, such as livestock, industrial farming, cement production and deforestation. To stay below 1.5°C we need to keep 93 per cent of known and extractable fossil fuel reserves in the ground.

But the Paris Agreement makes no mention of this red line. In fact, it imposes no limits on the use of fossil fuels whatsoever. What is more, the Paris pledges don't even kick in until 2020. In other words, countries are allowed to continue increasing their carbon emissions for five years after the agreement was signed, by which time we will have blown the budget for 1.5°C. On the face of it, five years seem a fair transition period, even given the tight budget. But we have known about anthropogenic climate change since at least the 1960s, and international negotiations to reduce carbon emissions have been under way since 1990. And yet instead of reducing annual carbon emissions, we have *increased* them by 61 per cent over the past two decades. Governments are still subsidising the fossil fuel industry to the tune of $5.3 trillion per year, according to the IMF's most recent estimates, while perversely using the WTO's court to knock down subsidies for alternative technologies such as solar panels.

What might our planet look like if it warms by 3.7°C, or by 4°C, which is our current trajectory? Conservative projections show that it is likely to bring about heatwaves not seen on Earth for some 5 million years. Southern European countries like Italy, Spain and Greece will turn into deserts. By 2100, sea levels will have risen by 1.24 metres, drowning cities including Amsterdam and New York. Forty per cent of species would be at risk of extinction, and huge portions of our rainforests would wither away. Crop yields would collapse by 35 per cent, with key staples like Indian wheat and US corn plummeting by 60 per cent, leading to widespread famine – particularly in the global South. Four degrees will probably mean the total melting of the Greenland ice sheet and possibly the entire West Antarctic Ice Sheet as well, which would then raise sea levels by another six metres and displace hundreds of millions of people around the world.

Climate scientists are sounding the alarm on the spectre of 4°C. According to a 2012 report by the World Bank, 4°C would mean 'extreme heatwaves, declining global food stocks, loss of ecosystems and biodiversity, and life-threatening sea level rise'. According to the Intergovernmental Panel on Climate Change, which avoids any but the most conservative assertions, even our nearer-term prospects are looking bleak. Latin America will see 'gradual replacement of tropical forest by savannah in eastern Amazonia; [and] significant changes in water availability for human consumption, agriculture and energy generation'. In Africa, 'by 2020, between 75 and 250 million people are projected to be exposed to increased water stress; yields from rain-fed agriculture could be reduced by up to 50% in some regions; agricultural production, including access to food, may be severely compromised'. In Asia, 'freshwater availability [is] projected to decrease in Central, South, East, and Southeast Asia by the 2050s; death rates from disease associated with floods and droughts are expected to rise in some regions'.

In sum, 4°C of warming is incompatible with human civilisation as we know it. We might be able to physically withstand the heatwaves and flee the coastal cities, but – given the impending collapse of agriculture – there's no way we would be able to get enough food to eat.

And then there are the feedback loops that we can't even fully predict. The Arctic is set to be ice-free during the summer within a few years, which is already leading to a massive release of methane – enormous plumes of gas, covering millions of square miles, are bubbling to the surface of the sea in quantities twice as great as scientists predicted. Problems like this, which have not yet been fully accounted for, could lead us to as much as 6°C of warming, according to projections from the International Energy Agency. If we can say nothing else about this scenario, we can be certain of this: such a radical transformation of our climate will more than wipe out all the gains in poverty reduction and life expectancy that have been accomplished by development interventions over the past half-century. Scholars of the future who look back on this era will regard the idea of development as a quaint pipe dream of the late Holocene, when the climate was stable enough that it made sense to attempt to imagine a better future for humanity.

*

I sometimes wonder why anyone is talking about development at all any more, at a moment when the whole edifice is at risk of collapsing unless we throw everything we have into the fight against climate change. Certainly anyone who still thinks development is just a matter of increasing GDP growth – and thereby CO_2 emissions – has yet to come to terms with the brutal facts of climate science.

Development agencies have long been trying to solve the problem of global poverty by tinkering around the edges of our economic system. The idea has always been to keep the basic logic of capitalism – exponential growth – in place while trying to make it a little bit less destructive than it otherwise might be. But the climate change emergency forces us to discard this approach and think seriously about the logic of capitalism itself. As Naomi Klein puts it in her most recent book, *This Changes Everything*, 'Our economic system and our planetary system are at war. What the climate needs to avoid collapse is a contraction in humanity's use of resources; what our economic model demands to avoid collapse is unfettered expansion. Only one of these sets of rules can be changed, and it's not the laws of nature.'

But it's not just that capitalism itself appears to be in conflict with the pressing need to stave off a planetary emergency. It's the particular *kind* of capitalism that is at stake, a model that is geared towards slashing government budgets and eroding the power of the state to regulate the economy. How are states to invest in building a zero-carbon infrastructure when they are subjected to austerity and privatisation? How are governments supposed to tax and regulate fossil fuel companies when the very idea of taxation and regulation has been stigmatised as socialist or totalitarian, and even rendered illegal according to some international trade agreements? How are we supposed to subsidise innovation in renewable energies when subsidies have been banned for running against the principles of 'free trade' (with suitable exceptions made for US agribusiness and fossil fuels, of course)? How can states ever hope to respond to the impending humanitarian crisis when their budgets have been cut and public services shut down?

The economic system that we have put in place over the past few decades may have rendered us incapable of meeting the most serious challenge of the 21st century.

PART FOUR

Closing the Divide

Eight

From Charity to Justice

There are a thousand hacking at the branches of evil to one who is striking at the root, and it may be that he who bestows the largest amount of money on the needy is doing the most by his mode of life to produce that misery which he strives in vain to relieve.

Henry David Thoreau

There is a parable that people in public health like to tell as a way of introducing the principles that are central to their field. Imagine you are standing by a river with steep banks and bends that froth with dangerous rapids. Amid the noise of rushing water you hear a faint voice crying out for help, and notice a figure struggling against the waves. A strong swimmer, you summon your courage and plunge into the water, managing to drag the person to safety just in time. While recovering on the shore you notice yet another figure drifting into peril. Refusing to watch them die, you plunge in yet again. But minutes later you catch sight of yet another, and another. Unable to save them all, you rush to find your friends and assemble a team, and together you dedicate yourselves to rescuing people from the river. But as the hours slog by and the disaster shows no sign of abating, it strikes you that perhaps your efforts would be better spent running upstream to find out why so many people are falling into the river in the first place.

For people in public health, the point of this story is simple: prevention is always better than cure. And in order to be effective at prevention, you need to target upstream causes. This might sound straightforward, but it takes work to train yourself to think this way – to learn to pay attention to systems and not just symptoms. We humans are wired such that when we encounter pain and suffering our immediate instinct is to do what we can to make it stop as quickly as possible. For me, the difference between these two approaches becomes clearest when I think of that clinic in Swaziland where my parents worked – the one with the never-ending line of patients winding out the door and into the courtyard. My father likes to tell the story of how one day a wise elder came to visit him and suggested, enigmatically, with a playful glint in his eye: 'Doctor, I can see you are working hard to help these patients. But perhaps you are working at the wrong end of the line?'

The same instinct that leads us to want to put an end to suffering in the most immediate way possible is also what leads us to gravitate towards the most obvious explanation for the misfortunes of others. When we pass a homeless person on the street it is easiest to assume that they are responsible for their own misfortune – they didn't study hard enough in school, they didn't try hard enough at work, they're too lazy and weak-minded to make it. It takes another level of analysis to think about upstream causes: they lost their home because of reckless speculation on the housing market by big banks; their pension disintegrated in the financial crisis; they were victims of unfair dismissal in the absence of decent labour laws; or their employer moved overseas to take advantage of cheaper labour elsewhere. The same is true of poverty on a global scale. It might be easiest to blame poor countries for their own misfortunes, but if we give it enough thought it becomes clear that there is much more to the story.

*

As Oscar Wilde once pointed out, people's emotions are stirred more quickly than their intelligence. 'It is easier to have sympathy with suffering than sympathy with thought,' he suggested. And when it comes to poverty, we would do well to think more about what this crisis demands of us:

> People find themselves surrounded by hideous poverty, by hideous ugliness, by hideous starvation. It is inevitable that they should be strongly moved by all this. Accordingly, with admirable intentions, they very seriously and very sentimentally set themselves to the task of remedying the evils that they see. But their remedies do not cure the disease: they merely prolong it. Indeed, their remedies are part of the disease. They try to solve the problem of poverty, for instance, by keeping the poor alive. But this is not a solution: it is an aggravation of the difficulty. The proper aim is to try and reconstruct society on such a basis that poverty will be impossible. And the altruistic virtues have really prevented the carrying out of this aim. Just as the worst slave-owners were those who were kind to their slaves, and so prevented the horror of the system being realised by those who suffered from it, and understood by those who contemplated it, so the people who do most harm are the people who try to do most good. Charity degrades and demoralises.

There are a number of illuminating insights we can draw from Wilde's words. One is that while charity may indeed improve the lives of the poor in an immediate, temporary sense, it then returns them straight back into the conditions that produced their poverty in the first place. In the end, nothing is actually changed. And once

241

the humanitarian's urge to help is satisfied, they are unlikely to devote any further effort to thinking about the problem or wrestling with its real causes – it defuses their will for change.

But Wilde goes a step further. He argues that charity not only distracts our attention from the ultimate causes of poverty – from the rot at the centre of the system – it also obscures the nature of the problem from those who suffer it. Charity can detract from people's ability to directly challenge the forces that degrade them in the first place and strips them of their political agency. By smoothing over the contradictions of a deeply flawed system, it allows the system to continue a little bit longer. Usually this is unintentional on the part of the humanitarian. But sometimes charity is specifically designed with this end in mind. Some scholars have pointed out that food aid from the West, for example, is carefully calculated to prevent the worst famines, to ensure that people receive at least enough calories to stay alive, because otherwise the injustices of the global economic system would become so apparent that its legitimacy would collapse and political upheaval would almost certainly ensue. To avoid this outcome, the more cynical among the rich are happy to channel some of their surplus into charity.

On this point Wilde makes another critical intervention: 'It is immoral to use private property to alleviate the horrible evils that result from the institution of private property,' he writes. 'It is both immoral and unfair.' Here he draws our attention to yet another problem with the charity paradigm. To the extent that charity is enabled by the accumulation of surplus wealth it can never be a meaningful solution – for the very processes by which wealth is accumulated are those that produce poverty in the first place.

When I graduated from university, many of my friends opted to pursue high-paying careers. Whenever they discussed their choice of work, they would almost invariably offer a moral justification: if I am able to earn millions – as a banker, for example – I will have more money to give away to improve people's lives. On the face of it, this makes perfect sense. Indeed, it is the approach that high-profile philanthropists like George Soros and the Rock-efellers have taken: make mountains of money during the day, and in the evening give a bit away to improve the lives of the poor. But we have to ask the difficult question: where do their riches come from in the first place? Much of Soros' wealth comes from currency speculation, which played a direct role in the 1997 Asian financial crisis that pushed millions of people into poverty. The Rockefeller Foundation won its riches from monopolies in the fossil fuel indus-try. In almost every case we can find that the accumulation that sustains charity comes from processes that cause the very prob-lems they purport to solve.

Starbucks has given charity to help improve the health out-comes of poor people in Ethiopia's coffee-growing communities, but it bears noting that in the past the company has been accused of dramatically underpaying Ethiopian coffee growers. Coca-Cola gives a bit of charity to help impoverished communities in Guate-mala, but the firm has been accused of engaging in violent cam-paigns against trade union organisers in order to prevent wages on its Guatemalan sugar plantations from rising. Fairness is better than charity. In the absence of fairness, charity carries the whiff of a scam. The same argument applies to official Western aid. If the US government wants to reduce global poverty, perhaps instead of doling out aid it should work to end structural adjustment, the tax evasion system and unfair trade laws – some of the major forces that cause poverty in the first place.

*

I have articulated these arguments many times – in the classroom, in public lectures, at conferences and even at events hosted by development agencies themselves. Everywhere I go, even in the very heart of the NGO world, I find that people are eager for the critique – and this is particularly true of the younger genera-tion who have come of age in the wake of the 2008 crash. It seems to resonate with their own suspicions, their own incipient sense

243

that there is something disingenuous about the official narrative. They know from observing their own nations' politics that poverty isn't just a natural phenomenon. They know that it is created by a system that has been carefully designed to benefit some – rich nations, multinational corporations, powerful individuals – at the expense of most of the rest. The official narrative tries to obscure this fact and distracts our attention away from it. It pushes us to focus on apolitical solutions like aid, without addressing underlying causes. It makes the takers in the system seem like givers, and enjoins us to celebrate their generosity. And it tries to convince us that global poverty can be solved without any substantive changes to the status quo.

With 4.3 billion people living in poverty today, and with the divide between rich and poor countries widening, it is time for a different approach. What can we do? How can we change course? On one level, the solutions appear to be relatively obvious. Development will only ever make sense if we begin to change the rules that produce poverty in the first place – if we begin to dismantle the architecture of upward redistribution that defines the world system. To that end, here are five ideas for evolving towards a fairer global economy.

Debt Resistance

Perhaps the most important first step is to abolish the debt burdens of developing countries. This move is crucial in a number of respects. It would roll back the remote-control power that rich countries exercise over poor countries, and restore sovereign control over economic policy at the national level. It would also free developing countries to spend more of their income on healthcare, education and poverty-reduction efforts instead of just handing it over in debt service to big banks. This will be a difficult battle, of course, since creditors stand to lose a great deal. Some that are overexposed to debt in heavily indebted countries might even go bankrupt. But that is a small price to pay for the liberation of potentially hundreds of millions of people. If we abolish the debts, nobody dies – the world will carry on spinning. Debts don't *have* to be repaid, and in fact they shouldn't be repaid when doing so means causing widespread human suffering.

Some NGOs have called for debt 'relief' or even 'forgiveness', but these words send exactly the wrong message. By implying that debtors have committed some kind of sin, and by casting creditors as saviours, they reinforce the power imbalance that lies at the heart of the problem. The debt-as-sin framing has been used to justify 'forgiving' debt while requiring harsh austerity measures that replicate the structural adjustment programmes that contributed to the debt crisis in the first place, effectively saying 'we will forgive your sins, but you will have to pay the price'. In other words, until now, debt forgiveness has largely just perpetuated the problem. If we want to be serious about dealing with debt, we need to challenge not only the debt itself but also the moral framing that supports it.

As of 2008, some $95 million worth of global South debt was scheduled for some degree of relief. This sounds like a lot, but economists at the New Economics Foundation have found that in order to achieve real debt sustainability – and to allow enough budget space for countries to eradicate poverty – it needs to be increased by a factor of six. Another recent report finds that at least $400 billion of debt in 100 different countries needs to be cancelled simply so that states can have enough money to meet the basic needs of their citizens. Both of these studies provide sensible starting points for any debt-cancellation programme. Another approach is to cancel what are known as 'dictator debts' – debts racked up by heads of state with no democratic mandate. Dictator debts presently amount to about $735 billion in thirty-two different countries. Cancelling them would free citizens from having to repay loans that they never agreed to in the first place, and which probably never benefited them.

Alternatively, we could approach debt cancellation from a more general angle. Many developing countries have debt burdens that are primarily piles of interest. For example, if a country took out $5 billion in loans in 1980 at 10 per cent interest and then repaid $500 million each year, by 2000 they would have paid back a total of $10 billion and yet would *still* have more debt to repay, simply because of the power of compound interest. In light of this, we might suggest that poor countries below a certain development threshold that have already paid their debts plus the equivalent of a modest rate of interest – say 2–3 per cent per year at most, enough to cover the creditors' inflation losses – deserve to have the rest of their debt burden written off. This would be the same thing as retroactively imposing interest rate caps on already existing loans, to make them more affordable.

But regardless of how we choose to approach the matter, it is crucial that debt cancellation be free of structural adjustment conditions – otherwise even this seemingly benevolent act becomes just another tool for remote-control power by creditors. Indeed, it would be wise to abolish structural adjustment conditions on development lending in the first place. Such a step is vital to ensuring that developing countries have access to finance going forward while still retaining the sovereignty to use tariffs, subsidies, capital controls, social spending and other measures they might need to manage their economies and reduce poverty.

Of course, it is unlikely that existing lenders – like the World Bank, for instance – will go along with such a plan, as it would mean relinquishing their authority over debtors and would weaken their ability to enforce debt repayment. Instead of battling the World Bank, we could create alternative institutions altogether. The New Development Bank, founded by Brazil, Russia, India, China and South Africa in 2015, might provide just such an alternative. So too might the new Asian Infrastructure Investment Bank, founded by China in 2016. If these banks choose to give finance to other developing countries at zero or low interest, and without structural adjustment conditions, they would help liberate the global South from the grip of Western creditors. That explains why Washington has been less than pleased with their emergence. At the same time, they might not be so benevolent: just as the World Bank has facilitated Western imperialism, so these new banks could end up projecting the economic and geopolitical interests of their founding nations over other regions of the global South. In other words, they might function as a tool of sub-imperialism.

We have to accept, though, that creditors will probably not be willing to cancel debts at anywhere near the necessary level, regardless of how much pressure social movements put on them. If that is true, then the only other option that over-indebted countries have is to simply stop repaying their loans. In the past, debt default has quite often been punished by creditors with invasions and coups, effectively removing this option from the table. Global South countries have been demanding the right to default without threat of military retaliation since at least the 1970s. Enshrining such a right into international law would liberate them to shake off the shackles of their own debt. Yes, this might make it difficult for them to secure new finance from the aggrieved creditors and their allies – but with the New Development Bank and the Asian Infrastructure Investment Bank in play, defaulting countries might have other options open to them.

Global Democracy

The second crucial step towards creating a fairer global economy would be to democratise the major institutions of global governance: the World Bank, the IMF and the WTO. Allowing global South countries – the world's majority – to have fair and equal representation in these institutions would give them a real say in the formulation of policies that affect them.

In the World Bank and the IMF, this would require abolishing the veto power of the United States and reallocating voting power according to a more democratic formula. Right now, votes are apportioned to each country according to their financial shares in the institutions, with rich countries claiming about 60 per cent. To fix this skewed distribution, votes could be apportioned to each country according to the size of their population, or in a way that

247

accounts for their relative development needs. The presidents of the World Bank and the IMF should be decided not by fiat by the US and Europe, as is presently the case, but instead by merit-based candidacy and democratic election, and should be open to candidates of all nationalities. And the immunity of the World Bank and the IMF needs to be revoked so that loan recipients can hold them accountable. This move is essential to eliminating the moral hazard that presently plagues these institutions, which are free to dish out policy prescriptions without heed for the damage they might cause.

The World Trade Organization is already technically democratic, with one vote going to each member country. But in reality richer countries are almost always able to get their way – partly because having bigger markets gives them more bargaining power, and partly because they can afford more and better negotiators. The best way to reform this would be for poorer countries that can't afford a permanent contingent at the WTO headquarters in Geneva, or that can't pay for the staff they need to attend negotiating meetings, to have these costs covered for them by a common fund so that all have a fair chance at getting their voices heard. Another way to democratise the WTO would be to ensure that all proceedings are transparent and accessible to all relevant countries – instead of allowing a few powerful nations to pre-formulate agendas and predetermine decisions in the so-called Green Room meetings from which developing countries are so often excluded. The WTO's courts could also do with a dose of transparency. The secretive tribunals that decide the fate of countries accused of breaking trade rules that harm them could be opened to scrutiny, allowing public media to assess whether the rules and penalties stand up to common-sense notions of fairness.

Ideally, these basic inequities would be rectified before any further demands for market liberalisation are made of developing countries. But even these changes don't quite get at one of the deeper problems that these institutions have. In the World Bank and the IMF, countries are normally represented by their finance ministers or central bank governors, while in the WTO they are represented by trade ministers. These representatives may be selected by the governments of member countries, but that doesn't mean they have the interests of their people at heart. Finance ministers tend to be closely aligned to the interests of the financial community, while trade ministers tend to favour the interests of the business community. Neither have any natural allegiance to the interests of workers, peasants or the environment, and rarely argue for policies in their name. This could be fixed by arranging representation according to some kind of democratic mandate, such as by giving citizens the opportunity to vote on who will represent them at the World Bank, the IMF and the WTO.

Fair Trade

A third vital step would be to make the international trade system fairer. As we have seen, one of the major problems with the WTO is that it demands across-the-board trade liberalisation from all member states – the so-called 'level playing field'. This is theoretically supposed to increase trade flows and improve everyone's lives, but it almost always benefits rich countries at the expense of developing countries. Developing countries lose control over the policy space they need to ensure that they gain from trade. Instead of requiring across-the-board tariff reductions, trade could be conducted with an intentional bias towards poor countries, for the sake of promoting development. One way to do this would be to have all WTO members provide free-market access in all goods to all developing countries either smaller or poorer than themselves (in terms of GDP and GDP per capita). This would allow developing countries to benefit from selling to rich-country markets without having to liberalise their own trade rules in return. This is not unheard of. In fact, we already have a system of special preferences for poor countries – but it is limited, and the WTO has been trying to phase it out since 1994.

Then there are the free-trade agreements. One of the reasons that free-trade agreements end up being so problematic is that they are negotiated in secret. Making the negotiations public, and subject to real democratic scrutiny, would go a long way towards making the final deals fairer. We shouldn't have to rely on Wiki-Leaks to provide this information in a partial and ad hoc way. Having full access to the draft proposals would allow vulnerable groups and advocacy organisations in rich and poor countries alike to push back against clauses that are harmful to people and the environment. Indeed, ideally all existing agreements should be suspended and renegotiated under more transparent and democratic conditions.

There has been a growing uproar about the investor-state dispute settlement mechanisms that are included in most FTAs, which allow foreign corporations to sue sovereign states for regulations that compromise their profits. As these mechanisms have such little legitimacy, it would make sense to place a moratorium on all future cases and require plaintiffs to pursue their concerns through national court systems, which are transparent, public and accountable. This is essential to restoring the ability of developing countries – and all sovereign states – to create regulations in the interest of workers, the environment or public health *even if* such regulations happen to harm the potential profits of foreign investors.

The TRIPS Agreement, while having little to do with trade in the strict sense, is also in desperate need of reform. The period of patent protection under TRIPS is presently twenty years, longer than it has ever been. This could be halved without negatively impacting incentives for research and development. Relaxing patent rules would allow poor countries to access the technologies they need for development – not only industrial technologies but also things like textbooks and software. And there is a strong case to be made that the most essential technologies – like public health medicines – should be exempt from the patent system altogether. Ensuring that developing countries have the legal right to produce or import generic versions of life-saving medicines would go a long way towards saving lives, and would prevent the kind of needless catastrophe that unfolded with the AIDS crisis.

In addition to shortening patent durations and securing exemptions for essential goods, stricter rules on 'originality' would prevent corporations from patenting seeds, plants, medicines and genetic materials that either already exist naturally in the world or have been developed over thousands of years by humans through collective effort and traditional knowledge. This is particularly important for small farmers across the global South, many of whom are already being barred from saving and using their own indigenous seed varieties and forced to purchase them instead from agribusiness companies. It is vital that natural substances and public knowledge remain in the public domain, so that people have equal access to the bounty of life and the yields of humanity's collective intelligence.

Finally, the agricultural subsidy regime – one of the most hotly contested features of the international trade system – needs urgent attention if global South countries are going to have a fair shot at development. The first step to reforming it is to cut back the subsidies that the governments of rich countries presently dish out to their farmers, allowing them to overrun competitors in the global South who might otherwise have the upper hand, and flooding poor countries with cheap grain that undercuts the market share of small farmers. Even abolishing only half of the OECD's agricultural subsidies – for example, the portion that is handed out to the biggest exporters – would help level the playing field and create much-needed breathing room for farmers in the global South. But in addition to curtailing subsidies in rich countries, we need to ensure that the governments of poor countries have the freedom to give subsidies to their own farmers. This is necessary in order for infant agricultural businesses to grow strong enough to compete on the world stage, as well as to ensure that small farmers have the support they need to maintain their own livelihoods and help feed their fellow citizens. Indeed, subsidies for small farmers in the South is essential to curbing global hunger.

Just Wages

If we are going to have a global labour market, where companies can roam the planet in search of ever-cheaper workers, it stands to reason that we need a global system of labour standards as well. This is where a fourth intervention might lie: putting a stop to the global race to the bottom for cheap labour by guaranteeing a base-line level of human fairness. The single most important component of such an intervention would be a global minimum wage. On the face of it, this might sound problematic. For one, it wouldn't make any sense for workers in Tanzania to earn the same as workers in Britain, for example, since the cost of living differs markedly between these two countries. Plus, what if raising wages in cheap-labour countries ruins their competitive advantage and causes businesses to flee, increasing unemployment and poverty?

The current recommendation for a global minimum wage would deal with these difficulties by setting the bar at 50 per cent of each country's median wage, so it would be tailored to local economic conditions, costs of living and purchasing power. As wages increase across the spectrum, the minimum wage would automatically move up. For countries where wages are so low that 50 per cent of the median would still leave workers in poverty, there would be a second safeguard: wages in each country would have to be above the national poverty line.

Under this proposal, countries that presently enjoy a comparative advantage through cheap labour would retain that advantage, so there would be minimum disruption to their economies. This system would go a long way towards eliminating poverty – at least the poverty of the working population. It would also help reduce inequality, not only within countries but also between them. Raising wages also has positive economic benefits: putting more money into the hands of ordinary workers stimulates demand and thus facilitates local economic growth, and it does so in a way that doesn't depend on debt (unlike microfinance).

Of course, some might object that raising wages in poor countries might drive up the prices of their exports too much, leading to a drop in consumer demand and ultimately a rise in unemployment. But this fear is not well founded. There is no evidence that raising minimum wages has any negative effect on employment. Indeed, a recent study found that *doubling* the wages of sweatshop workers in Mexico would raise the price of clothes sold in the US by only 1.8 per cent – too little for most consumers in rich countries to notice. In fact, you could raise sweatshop wages by a factor of ten and consumers still wouldn't be fazed: a study by the National Bureau of Economic Research shows that people are willing to pay up to 15 per cent more on a $100 item — and 28 per cent more on a $10 item — if it is made under 'good working conditions'. There is a lot of room for wage growth before it begins to have any troublesome economic effects.

It might sound like a bureaucratic nightmare to manage, but the UN's International Labor Organization has already claimed that it has the will and the capacity to govern a global minimum wage system. A global minimum wage would go a lot further than the 'fair trade' fad that has become popular among Western consumers. Every time I walk into a store and see items labelled fair trade, I'm always struck by what their presence implies: that the rest of the 'normal' products are *un*fair. We shouldn't have to choose between fair and unfair products. When we buy the things we need to sustain and enjoy our lives, we should be able to be confident that we are not colluding in the exploitation of other human beings.

Reclaiming the Commons

The fifth step would be to deal with the three mechanisms of plunder that I discussed in the previous chapter: tax evasion, land grabbing and climate change – all of which have to do with reclaiming public resources and protecting the commons.

253

Tax evasion drains hundreds of billions of dollars out of developing countries each year. Fixing the international tax system is vital to putting an end to this theft – and doing so would yield formidable funds for development and poverty eradication. The issue does appear in the UN's Sustainable Development Goals, which state: 'Strengthen domestic resource mobilization, including through international support to developing countries, to improve domestic capacity for tax and other revenue collection' (17.1). While improving tax collection in developing countries is an important step, this approach makes it seem as though poor countries are to blame for their own misfortunes. The real culprits – the individuals and multinational corporations that offshore their income, the bankers who assist them and the rich-country governments and international institutions that make it all possible – are let off the hook.

First of all, the most effective way to improve domestic tax collection would be to start at the global level: change the WTO's customs invoicing standards, which presently make it very easy for companies to steal money through trade misinvoicing and transfer mispricing. This could be done by allowing customs officials to hold up transactions whose prices diverge suspiciously from standardised norms. Another method would be to close down the secrecy jurisdictions that serve as tax havens in the first place. Requiring global financial transparency would put an end to shell companies and anonymous accounts, and revealing the 'beneficial owners' of all companies, trusts and foundations would allow their income and wealth to be taxed by their home countries.

Another popular proposal is to require multinational companies to report their profits in the countries where their economic activity actually takes place, rather than the current practice of providing a single consolidated balance sheet for all operations and filing it in a separate low-tax jurisdiction. This is known as 'country-by-country reporting'. To bolster this system further, we could prevent tax evasion through transfer mispricing by taxing multinationals as single firms rather than as a collection of independent subsidiaries. Another interesting option might be to impose a global minimum tax on corporations, which would eliminate their incentive to evade national taxes altogether. It would also put a floor on competition between countries in their race to attract investment by offering ever-lower taxes. And to help seal it all up, it would make sense to introduce harsh penalties for bankers and accountants who facilitate tax evasion and other illicit flows.

*

Then there are land grabs. To put an end to land grabs, it would make sense to place a moratorium on all deals that involve major transfers of land from small farmers, collective use or ecosystem services to commercial use, until such deals can be conducted transparently and with the full involvement of affected communities. Because many land grabs are made with an eye towards profiting from rising food prices, to really get at the root of this problem would require preventing financial firms and investors from speculating recklessly on food. Not only would this remove the incentives that spur many of the most harmful land grabs, it would also help keep food affordable and prevent needless hunger.

There is also the matter of the New Alliance for Food Security and Nutrition, which has spurred land grabs in the name of reducing hunger, operating under the assumption that corporations can produce food more efficiently. But by dispossessing small farmers it paradoxically risks *increasing* hunger. The weight of evidence suggests that the best strategy for tackling hunger is in fact the opposite approach: land reform in favour of the small farmers whose produce already feeds the vast majority of the world's population. Indeed, that's how China eradicated so much hunger during the 1990s. In 2014, the UN special rapporteur on the right to food affirmed this point, calling for strong protections against agribusiness land grabs and laws that ensure small farmers have rights to use, save and exchange seeds.

Because the UN REDD programme and other carbon-trading

schemes have become another driver of land grabs in the developing world – triggering what analysts are calling 'carbon colonialism' – it would make sense to re-evaluate all such transactions to ensure that they don't force people off their land in the name of climate change mitigation. Because indigenous people who inhabit forests are particularly vulnerable to dispossession under carbon trading schemes, special care needs to be taken to ensure that their rights to land and forest resources are respected – and this should not have to require granting them formal title deeds, which often paradoxically renders people even *more* vulnerable to dispossession.

*

On climate change, the solutions are more obvious. The 2016 Paris Agreement under the United Nations Framework Convention on Climate Change commits to keeping us under 1.5°C of warming over pre-industrial levels. Unfortunately, though, the Paris Agreement doesn't go far enough to put us on track to satisfy this obligation. The agreement relies on pledges for emissions reductions from signatory countries, but even if all of these pledges are fulfilled we will still breach 3 or even 4°C of warming, with catastrophic consequences. And this is before we factor in the possibility that the United States under a Trump administration will withdraw from its pledges altogether. We are presently on track to use the entire carbon budget for 1.5°C by as early as 2020, and the country pledges will not even be reviewed until 2023.

Keeping below 1.5°C may no longer be an option, but we can still keep below 2°C if we adopt a much more aggressive approach. To have a strong chance of accomplishing this, rich countries will have to hit zero carbon emissions by 2035, and poor countries will have to follow suit by 2050. By applying stringent standards on energy efficiency and tightening them every year, rich countries might be able to reduce their energy demands by as much as 40–70 per cent in ten years. And if the top 10 per cent of individuals with the biggest carbon footprints reduce their emissions down to the level of even just the average European, rich countries could cut their emissions by 33 per cent – and this could theoretically be achieved in a single year. Cuts on this order will be essential to preventing runaway climate change.

Bizarrely, the Paris Agreement makes no reference to fossil fuels or fossil fuel companies. This is a fatal oversight, as one of the most powerful steps towards climate change mitigation would be to end subsidies for fossil fuel companies, which presently amount to $5.3 trillion per year. Ending these subsidies would help make fossil fuels less competitive compared with renewable alternatives. And we could advance this further still by reinvesting this $5.3 trillion in renewable energies like solar, wind and tidal power – avoiding biofuels, since the land required for biofuel production means this strategy ends up driving land grabs, and as land is converted from food production to energy production it creates problems for food security. Breaking the back of the fossil fuel industry, which exerts undue influence over policymaking around the world, is essential to real progress against climate change. In addition to cutting subsidies, another approach is to get universities, foundations, cities and other entities to divest their endowments from fossil fuel holdings – a campaign that is already gaining significant traction around the world.

At the same time, it is vital to ensure that developing countries receive due compensation for the damage caused by climate change, as well as financial and technical support to help them transition to renewable energy systems. A number of studies have already delineated fair ways to divide the responsibility for these financial transfers, accounting for each country's historical emissions and present resources. The Climate Fairshares project, by the Stockholm Environment Institute and Friends of the Earth, offers what are probably the best proposals to date.

*

By targeting the deep structural causes of global poverty and inequality, and by making the international economic system fairer, more rational and more democratic, these interventions would have a monumental impact. Best of all, this approach *wouldn't require a single dollar of foreign aid.* Instead of relying on charitable window dressing, it goes to the root of our global problems by redistributing both power and resources. But implementing these interventions will require the political courage to stand up to the interests of the very powerful actors who extract so much material benefit from the present system, for they will not concede voluntarily. It will be a difficult battle, but not impossible. Indeed, it is already being fought – and not without success.

The Jubilee Campaign and Strike Debt are proving to be a formidable force calling for debt cancellation in the global South. So too are the South Centre and the Third World Network, which are building solidarity among global South governments and civil society organisations respectively, to tackle not only debt but also structural adjustment, unfair trade rules, intellectual property issues and the imbalance of power in global governance institutions. The Bretton Woods Project is pushing hard for increased transparency and democracy in the World Bank and the IMF. And the Bolivarian Alliance for the Peoples of Our America (ALBA) is building a real-life alternative to the neoliberal Washington Consensus by organising regional economic integration in Latin America and creating an alternative currency for trade, with a focus on cooperation rather than competition and with an eye towards improving social welfare rather than just corporate profits. The battle for a global minimum wage is still in its infancy, but there are impressive movements building in this direction – for example, the Asian Floor Wage campaign is fighting to establish a transnational minimum wage for garment workers across Asia, one of the most vulnerable workforces in the world.

The Tax Justice Network is probably the most effective force in the battle against tax evasion and illicit financial flows, and has already succeeded in getting some initial reforms enacted by national governments. On the land front, the global network of small farmers known as La Via Campesina is organising against land grabs, agribusiness monopolies and seed patents, along with regional organisations such as Ekta Parishad in India and NGOs like GRAIN. The Indigenous Environmental Network is putting up a strong fight against REDD and other carbon-trading schemes that dispossess indigenous people. And the real momentum against climate change is building in unexpected ways, with Native Americans using their territorial rights to block fossil fuel projects (like Standing Rock and Idle No More), citizens taking to the streets to demand stronger action from their governments, and students pressuring their universities to divest from fossil fuels. As this book goes to press, 690 institutions around the world – including universities, faith-based organisations, foundations, pension funds and governments – have divested their wealth from fossil fuels, pulling some $5.44 trillion out of the industry and redirecting much of this into renewables.

None of the people involved in this struggle are asking for charity, nor are they calling for bigger aid disbursements. They are taking matters into their own hands, building solidarities, challenging power interests, tackling root causes and, in many cases, even putting their lives on the line in the process. If we are to have a fair shot at a better world, it will be down to their hard work and courage.

Nine

The Necessary Madness of Imagination

> You cannot carry out fundamental change without a certain amount of madness. In this case, it comes from nonconformity, the courage to turn your back on the old formulas, the courage to invent the future.
>
> Thomas Sankara

Let's imagine, for a moment, that we succeed. Poor countries are liberated from the shackles of structural adjustment; they win an equal voice in the institutions of global governance; and the rules of international trade are rebalanced to give them a fair shot. All of a sudden they find themselves free to determine their own economic policies in their own national interests, without threat of coercion or invasion, and they resort to the developmentalist agenda that worked so well for them in the 1960s and 1970s. They nationalise their oil reserves and their mines, and they reclaim control over their telecommunication and water infrastructure. They protect their domestic industries with strong tariffs, and nurture companies until they can compete effectively on the world stage. They break up the big foreign agribusinesses, ensure that small farmers have stable access to land, and offer subsidies to promote national food security. As domestic industries grow, more jobs are created, labour unions win decent salaries for workers, and a middle class begins to rise. Income growth rates inch their way up, poverty falls and hunger becomes a thing of the past. With the tax havens closed, government revenues increase and – without a crushing debt burden to pay off – there is room for social spending on universal healthcare and education. Universities increase their enrolment and, with better public health systems and access to generic medicine, tropical diseases are kept in check at last.

It is a compelling vision. And in the context of a fairer global economic system, all of this is theoretically possible. But there is one problem that we haven't yet accounted for. The standard developmentalist model hopes that poor countries will be able to grow their industrial economies – and their incomes – to the point of catching up with rich countries. Such growth requires an increase in resource consumption, of course, along with an increase in waste, pollution and emissions. This is a normal and perhaps to some extent inevitable process. But unfortunately our planet doesn't have enough ecological capacity for it to happen – in terms of both resources and the ability to absorb our greenhouse gas emissions. Scientists tell us that even at existing levels of aggregate global consumption we are already overshooting our planet's ecological capacity by about 60 per cent each year.

This overshoot is due almost entirely to overconsumption in rich countries. According to data compiled by researchers at the Global Footprint Network in Oakland, our planet only has enough ecological capacity for each of us to consume 1.8 'global hectares' annually – a standardised unit that accounts for resource use, waste, pollution and emissions. Anything over this means a degree of resource consumption that the Earth cannot replenish, or waste that it cannot absorb; in other words, it locks us into a pathway of progressive degradation. The figure of 1.8 global hectares is roughly what the average person in Ghana or Guatemala consumes. By contrast, Europeans consume 4.7 global hectares per person, while in the US and Canada the average person consumes 8 – many times their fair share. To get a sense of how extreme this overconsumption is: if we were all to live like the average citizen of the average high-income country, we would require the ecological capacity equivalent to 3.4 Earths.

For most of us it is difficult to comprehend what this overshoot means, insulated as we are from its effects. But the scientific data is piling up around us. Take deforestation, for example. Only sixty years ago our planet was carpeted with 1.6 billion hectares of mature tropical forests. Since then more than half have been destroyed by human industry. Then there are the soils. Forty per cent of our planet's agricultural soil is seriously degraded, mostly as a result of intensive industrial farming techniques and chemical fertilisers that strip the soil of its fertility, which means that agricultural yields will begin to collapse in the not-too-distant future. Or look at fish: around 85 per cent of global fish stocks are over-exploited or depleted. Haddock have fallen to 1 per cent of their former volume. Halibut to one-fifth of 1 per cent. Most of this is due to overfishing, but some of it is also due to the rapid acidification of the oceans, triggered by high concentrations of CO_2 in the atmosphere. And it's not just fish. Scientists tell us that up to 140,000 species of plants and animals are disappearing each year due to our over-exploitation of the Earth's ecosystems. This rate of extinction is 100 to 1,000 times faster than before the Industrial Revolution – so fast that scientists have classed this as the sixth mass extinction event in the planet's history, with the last one having occurred some 66 million years ago.

And all of this is just at our existing levels of aggregate economic activity – with the existing levels of consumption in rich and poor countries. If poor countries increase their consumption, which they will have to do to some extent in order to eradicate poverty, they will only tip us further towards disaster. Unless, that is, rich countries begin to consume less.

The Conundrum of Growth

Getting rich countries to consume less might sound like a simple thing to do. It would certainly be a fair and sensible move. But given the present structure of the economy it is almost literally unthinkable. Indeed, almost the entire economics profession and nearly all of our politicians are focused on exactly the opposite agenda: to increase GDP growth. And increasing GDP growth means ramping up production and consumption each year. Of all the economic ideas out there today, this is perhaps the most hegemonic. It is so commonly accepted that almost nobody thinks to question it.

We tend to take the GDP measure for granted as though it has always existed. Most people don't realise that it was invented only recently. It has a history. During the 1930s, the economists Simon Kuznets and John Maynard Keynes set out to design an economic aggregate that would help policymakers figure out how to escape the Great Depression. The goal was to calculate the total monetary value of all the goods and services produced in the economy so they could see more clearly what was going wrong and what needed to be done to fix it. Kuznets argued for a measure that would help society maximise well-being and track the progress of human welfare; he wanted GDP to exclude negative things like advertising, commuting and policing, so that if those things went up governments would not be able to say that people's lives were getting better when in fact they were not. But when the Second World War struck, Keynes broke from this vision and insisted that we should count all money-based activities – even negative ones – so we would be able to identify every ounce of productivity that was available for the war effort. In the end Keynes won, and his version of GDP came into use.

GDP was intended to be a war-time measure, which is why it is so single-minded – almost even violent. It tallies up all money-based activity, but it doesn't care whether that activity is useful or destructive. If you cut down a forest and sell the timber, GDP goes up. If you strip a mountain range to mine for coal, GDP goes up. If you extend the working day and push back the retirement age, GDP goes up. But GDP includes no cost accounting. It does not measure the cost of losing the forest as a sinkhole for carbon dioxide, or the loss of the mountain range as a home for endangered species, or the toll that too much work takes on people's bodies and minds and relationships. And not only does it leave out what is bad, it also leaves out much of what is good – for it does not count useful activities that are not monetised. If you grow your own food, clean your own house or take care of your ageing parents, GDP says nothing, for these activities don't involve transacting money. It only counts if you buy these services.

Of course, there's nothing inherently wrong with measuring some things and not others. GDP itself doesn't have any impact in the real world. GDP *growth*, however, does. As soon as we start focusing on GDP growth, we're not only promoting the things that GDP measures, we're promoting the indefinite increase of those things. And that's exactly what we started to do in the 1960s. GDP came into widespread use during the Cold War for the sake of adjudicating the grand pissing match between the West and the USSR. Suddenly, politicians on both sides became feverish about promoting GDP growth. Kuznets was careful to warn that we should never use GDP as a normal measure of economic success, for it would incentivise too much destruction. And yet that is exactly what we began to do – and then it was swiftly pushed around the rest of the world by the World Bank and the IMF. Today, nearly every government in the world, rich and poor alike, is focused obsessively on the single objective of increasing GDP growth.

According to the standard narrative, we need GDP growth rates of at least 2 or 3 per cent per year in order to have a healthy, functioning global economy. Anything less, and economists tell us we're in crisis; if growth drops towards zero, the whole system – we're told – will fall apart. So what does this degree of growth look like? Well, in 2015 global GDP stood at $73 trillion. Growing that by 3 per cent means adding more than $2 trillion; that's how much we have to add to global economic production next year, just to stay afloat. To put that in perspective, $2 trillion is roughly the GDP of the United Kingdom. Imagine all the cars, all the televisions, all the houses, all the factories, all the barrels of oil and everything else that is produced in Britain every year. Keep that mountain of stuff in your mind. That's how much we have to *add* next year *on top of* what the world is already producing. And because growth is exponential – not linear – we have to add even more than that the next year, and more still the year after.

The multiplier of compound growth is extremely powerful. A 4.5 per cent rate of growth – which is roughly the aggregate rate that the governments of the world want to achieve – doubles a 'thing' every sixteen years. Within thirty-two years the thing is quadrupled. If Ancient Egypt had started with one cubic metre of possessions and grew them by 4.5 per cent per year, by the end of its 3,000-year civilisation it would have needed 2.5 billion solar systems to store all its stuff. It doesn't take a scientist to realise that endless exponential growth is absurd, in the true sense of the word. To imagine that we can continue on this trajectory indefinitely is to disavow the most obvious truths about our planet's material limits. As David Attenborough once so eloquently put it, 'Anyone who thinks that you can have infinite growth on a finite planet is either a madman or an economist.'

If we are overshooting our planet's ecological capacity at our existing levels of economic activity, what happens when we factor in exponential growth? Even the near future looks quite bleak. Scientists tell us that by 2050 our mature tropical forests will have disappeared. Species biodiversity will have declined by another 10 per cent. Stocks of all presently fished seafood will have collapsed by an average of more than 90 per cent from 1950 levels. Most major metal reserves will be exhausted, including gold, copper, silver and zinc, along with many of the key metals used in renewable energy technologies, like lead, indium and antimony. If Silicon Valley entrepreneurs like Elon Musk are to be believed, we might be able to replace some of these metals by mining the moon and asteroids. But extraterrestrial extraction won't help us much with the forests and the fish. Nor will it do much for our soil crisis: at present rates of depletion, the topsoils of the world's farmlands will be more or less useless by 2050, and by 2075 they will be gone.

Despite these obvious problems, for some reason we have come to believe that GDP growth is equivalent to human progress. We assume that when GDP goes up, it makes our lives better: it raises our incomes, it creates more jobs, it means better schools and hospitals and so on. This may have been true in the past, when the world was relatively empty of people and the human footprint was small relative to the bounty of the Earth. Unfortunately, it no longer holds. In the United States GDP has risen steadily over the past half-century, yet median incomes have stagnated, the poverty rate has increased and inequality has grown. The same is true on a global scale: while global real GDP has nearly tripled since 1980, the number of people living in poverty, below $5 per day, has increased by more than 1.1 billion. Why is this? Because past a certain point, GDP growth begins to produce more negative outcomes than positive ones – more 'illth' than wealth. The reason is because there are no longer any frontiers where accumulation doesn't directly harm someone else, by, say, enclosing the land, degrading the soils, polluting the water, exploiting human beings or changing the climate. We have reached the point where GDP growth is beginning to create more poverty than it eliminates.

When the entire global political establishment puts its force behind the goal of GDP growth, human and natural systems come under enormous pressure. In India it might come in the form of land grabs. In the UK, it's privatisation of public services. In Brazil it looks like deforestation in the Amazon basin. In the US and Canada it brings fracking and tar sands. Around the world it means longer working hours, more expensive housing, depleted soils, polluted cities, wasted oceans and – above all – climate change. All for the sake of GDP growth. People who push against these destructive trends will tell you how futile it feels. It is futile because our governments don't care. They don't care because according to their most important measure of progress, the destruction counts as good, and must continue at all costs. This is not because humans are inherently destructive. It is because we have created a rule that encourages us to behave in destructive ways. As Joseph Stiglitz has put it, 'What we measure informs what we do. And if we're measuring the wrong thing, we're going to do the wrong thing.'

It is worth pointing out that, as long as GDP growth remains the main objective of the global economy, the solutions we covered in the previous chapter may prove to be impossible to achieve. The pressure to increase GDP translates into pressure for more debt, more structural adjustment, more 'free trade' and so on, as the system groans and writhes in a desperate search for frontiers of accumulation, more things to be monetised. It is like an iron law. It is necessary for the very continuation of our economy's existence – at least as the economy is presently organised.

False Promises

When ecologists and climate scientists present projections of what our world will look like if we carry on with GDP growth, they are quite often shouted down by economists who insist that technological innovations and efficiency improvements will help us 'decouple' economic growth from material throughput. Don't worry, they say, we will be able to keep GDP growing indefinitely without ruining the planet.

From one perspective, this appears to be correct. The 'domestic material consumption' of Britain, Japan and many other rich countries has been decreasing since at least 1990, and in the United States it has more or less flattened out. Domestic material consumption is the standard measure of all the physical stuff that countries extract and produce and consume, including goods imported from abroad. The fact that it is decreasing doesn't mean that these countries are consuming fewer products; they are not.

Rather, it means that the material 'footprint' of their consumption is decreasing, and is having less of a negative impact on the planet – all while GDP continues to go up. In other words, growth is decoupling from material throughput. It seems like excellent news, and this is the kind of data that economists draw on when they paint their very beguiling vision of a future lightweight economy.

But the reason domestic material consumption in rich countries has been shrinking is because the standard measurement ignores one crucial piece of the puzzle: while it includes the imported goods that a country consumes, it does not include the material footprint involved in producing and shipping those goods. Having been outsourced to other countries – mostly in the global South – this side of material consumption has been conveniently shifted off the balance sheet. If we bring it back into the picture, we see that the material consumption of rich countries has in fact been increasing dramatically in recent decades, even outpacing GDP growth. Another way to think about this is to look at the material throughput of the global economy as a whole, which gives us a picture of total extraction and consumption regardless of where in the world it happens. If we use this approach, we see that global material extraction and consumption grew by 94 per cent between 1980 and 2010, accelerating in the last decade to reach as high as 70 billion tons per year. And it is still going up: by 2030, we're projected to breach 100 billion tons of stuff per year.

What will this look like in the real world? Well, the number of cars on the road is set to double by 2030, for example. The number of commercial aeroplanes in the skies will double by 2035. By 2040 we'll have doubled the amount of stuff we ship around the world by sea. Our generation of solid waste – the stuff that gets shovelled into landfills – is on pace to triple by 2100 to 11 million tons per day. That's a lot, when you consider the fact that waste from our cities alone is already enough to fill a line of trucks 5,000 kilometres long every day. Think about it: a line of garbage trucks strung bumper to bumper across the whole continental United States – from Los Angeles to New York City – filled with trash, every day.

Keep in mind that so far we have only considered the impact of growth on our planet's physical resources. We haven't even begun to talk about what it is going to do in terms of climate change. We know that we've already breached the safe limit of CO_2 concentration in the atmosphere, which scientists say is about 350 ppm. Just recently we hit the 400 ppm mark, which will guarantee us at least 1.5°C of global warming over pre-industrial levels. On our present growth trajectory, we're cruising for around 4°C of warming, even if we factor in countries' pledges to cut emissions under the Paris Agreement. As we saw in the previous chapter, this means rising seas, swamped cities, increased floods and droughts, crop collapse, epidemic disease, famine and mass displacement, even according to the most sober scientific analysis. It looks very unpleasant indeed. And of course the great irony is that this degree of global warming is going to cause economic growth to collapse, costing at least 5 per cent of global GDP per year indefinitely, and possibly as much as 20 per cent.

Here again some have assured us that we needn't worry. We can continue with business-as-usual growth, maintain the living standards of the rich world and still be safe from climate change – so long as we shift quickly to renewable energies and begin to use negative-emissions technology to pull carbon back out of the atmosphere.

The dominant proposal out there is called BECCS: bio-energy carbon capture and storage. The basic idea is that we develop enormous tree plantations that will absorb carbon out of the atmosphere. Then we cut down the trees, convert them into wood pellets, ship them around the world and burn them in power stations to create energy, while capturing the carbon that the power stations produce and storing it deep in the ground. It sounds fine on paper, but there's one problem: we don't have the technology yet, and even the most optimistic engineers admit that it won't be ready in time to save us from climate change. Plus, even if we somehow managed to get BECCS online tomorrow, we don't have enough land on the planet to make it work. We would need to create a plantation three times the size of India to harvest year after year, decade after decade, and without taking away from the agricultural land that we need to feed the world's population.

BECCS and other such plans aside, there's something else we need to keep in mind here: when it comes to climate change, energy use is only part of the problem. Fossil fuels account for about 70 per cent of our present greenhouse gas emissions. So even if we're able to get off fossil fuels tomorrow and switch to perfectly clean and renewable energy, we still have to deal with that other 30 per cent.

Where do those non-fossil-fuel emissions come from? Deforestation is a major cause. Not only does deforestation actively release carbon into the atmosphere, it also deprives us of the sinks we need to absorb our emissions. To make matters worse, most deforested land is being converted to industrial agriculture, with intensive chemical fertilisers that degrade the soils. As the soils deplete, they lose their capacity to store carbon, releasing huge plumes of CO_2 into the atmosphere. Then there is industrial livestock farming, which produces 90 million tons of methane per year and most of the world's anthropogenic nitrous oxide. Both of these gases are vastly more potent than CO_2 when it comes to global warming. Livestock farming alone contributes more to global warming than all the cars, trains, planes and ships in the world. There are also a number of industrial processes that contribute significantly to climate change, such as the production of cement, which requires chemical reactions that produce greenhouse gases. So too with steel, iron and plastics. And then there are our landfills, which pump out huge amounts of methane – some 16 per cent of the world's total.

So the problem isn't just the type of energy we're using, it's what we're doing with it. What would we do with 100 per cent clean energy? Exactly what we're doing with fossil fuels: raze more forests, build more meat farms, expand industrial agriculture, produce more cement and heap up more landfills with waste from the additional stuff we would produce and consume, all of which will pump deadly amounts of greenhouse gas into the air. We will do these things because our economic system demands endless exponential growth. Switching to clean energy will do nothing to slow this down.

The Degrowth Imperative

If we peel back the false promises of dematerialisation and carbon capture, it becomes clear that the problem is much deeper than most are willing to admit. Our present economic model of exponential GDP growth is no longer realistic, and we have to face up to this fact. This presents us with a very difficult conundrum when it comes to development and poverty reduction. How can we eradicate poverty if we're already bumping up against our ecological limits?

Thankfully, for the first time in history, we have the data we need to think about this. Let's start with the international agreement to limit global warming. We know that it is very unlikely that we will be able to keep within 1.5°C warming over pre-industrial levels. But we still have a chance of keeping within the 2°C threshold, which the Paris Agreement on climate change sets as an absolute cap. If we want to keep beneath this cap, we can emit no more than another 805 gigatons of CO_2. Now, let's accept that poor countries will need to use a portion of this carbon budget in order to grow their incomes enough to eradicate poverty; after all, we know that for poor countries human development requires an increase in emissions, at least up to a relatively lowish point. This principle is already widely accepted in international agreements, which recognise that all countries have a 'common but differentiated responsibility' to reduce emissions: because poor countries did not contribute much to historical emissions, they have a right to use more of the carbon budget than rich countries do – at least enough to fulfil basic development goals. This means that rich countries have to figure out how to make do with the remaining portion of the budget.

Kevin Anderson and Alice Bows, two of Britain's leading

climate scientists, have been devising potential scenarios for how to make this work. If we want to have a 50 per cent chance of staying under 2°C, there's basically only one feasible way to do it – assuming, of course, that BECCS is not a real option. In this scenario, poor countries can continue to grow their economies at the present rate until 2025, using up a disproportionate share of the global carbon budget. That's not a very long time, so this strategy will only work to eradicate poverty if the gains from growth are distributed with a heavy bias towards the poor. Meanwhile, the only way for rich countries to keep within what's left of the carbon budget is to cut emissions aggressively, by about 10 per cent per year. Efficiency improvements and clean energy technologies will contribute to reducing emissions by at most 4 per cent per year, which gets them part of the way there. But to bridge the rest of the gap, rich countries are going to have to downscale production and consumption by around 6 per cent each year. And poor countries are going to have to follow suit after 2025, downscaling economic activity by about 3 per cent per year.

This might sound scary, but it's really not. We already have plenty of data showing that it's possible to reduce production and consumption at the same time as *increasing* human development indicators like happiness, education, health and longevity. For example, Europe has higher human development indicators than the United States in virtually every category, with 40 per cent less GDP per capita and 60 per cent fewer emissions per capita. The excess of the United States wins them nothing when it comes to what really matters.

How much do we really need to live long and happy lives? We can approach this as an empirical question. In the US, life expectancy is seventy-nine years and GDP per capita is $53,000. But many countries have achieved similar life expectancy with a mere fraction of this income. Costa Rica has a higher life expectancy than the US with GDP per capita of only $10,000. Of course, we might expect that some of the excess income and consumption we see in the rich world yields improvements in quality of life that are not captured by life expectancy. But even if we look at measures of overall happiness and well-being, a number of low- and middle-income countries rank highly. According to the UN's World Happiness Report, Costa Rica matches the United States. Brazil beats Britain, and with only a quarter of the income. This fits with findings from the growing field of 'happiness economics', which tells us that happiness only increases with income up to a certain point – a point that rich countries have long since surpassed. In the United States, for example, happiness rates peaked in the 1950s, with a GDP per capita of only about $15,000 (in 2010 dollars), and have plateaued since then. After that, what makes us happier isn't more income, but greater equality, good relationships and strong social guarantees.

In light of this, perhaps we should regard countries like Costa Rica not as underdeveloped, but rather as appropriately developed. We should look at societies where people live long and happy lives at low levels of income and consumption not as backwaters that need to be developed according to Western models, but as exemplars of efficient living – and begin to call on rich countries to cut their excess consumption.

This would likely prove to be a strong rallying cry in the global South, but it might be tricky to convince Westerners. Tricky, but not impossible. According to recent consumer research, 70 per cent of people in middle- and high-income countries believe overconsumption is putting our planet and society at risk. A similar majority also believe we should strive to buy and own less, and that doing so would not compromise our happiness. In other words, this consciousness is already building. People are ready for a different world.

Inventing the Future

If scientists are correct in saying that our model of exponential GDP growth lies at the very core of our crisis, then that's where we need to start when it comes to imagining an alternative future.

One crucial first step would be to get rid of GDP as a measure of economic progress and well-being and replace it with something different. There are many alternative measures of success on offer. The Genuine Progress Indicator (GPI), for example, starts with GDP but then adds positive factors such as household and volunteer work, subtracts negatives such as pollution, resource depletion and crime, and adjusts for inequality. A number of US states, like Maryland and Vermont, have already begun to use GPI as a measure of progress, albeit secondary to GDP. Costa Rica is about to become the first country to do so, and Scotland and Sweden may soon follow.

Measuring GPI gives us a completely different picture of society than GDP. If we plot global GPI and GDP together, just for comparison, we see that GPI increased together with GDP up through the mid-1970s and then levelled off – and even began to decrease – while GDP continued to rise.

This illustrates how growing GDP no longer translates into a better society. The consequences of shifting to something like GPI are profound. If our governments were driven to maximise

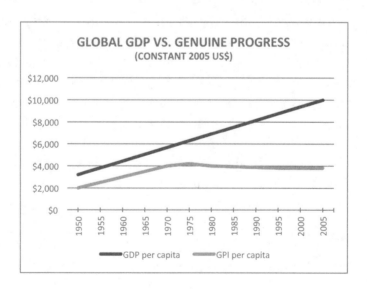

GPI, they would be incentivised to create policies that would facilitate good economic outcomes while diminishing bad ones. It doesn't have to be GPI, though. It could be anything: the Happy Planet Index designed by the New Economics Foundation, which balances life expectancy, happiness and ecological footprint; or the OECD's Better Life Index, which focuses on eleven dimensions of social and environmental well-being; or any number of indicators that haven't yet been imagined. As soon as we shake ourselves free from the tyranny of GDP, we can have an open discussion about what we really value, and how we want to measure progress. In some ways, this is the ultimate democratic act. And what is certain is that the result will look very different from GDP. In fact, it probably won't involve perpetual growth at all, because growing *anything* in perpetuity – even good things – is philosophically absurd.

GDP growth is not the only imperative that pushes constant economic expansion, however. It might be the primary *public* imperative, but there is also a private one: the imperative for corporations to maximise shareholder returns. Like GDP, this imperative has not been around for ever. We can trace it back to 1919, with the landmark US Supreme Court case *Dodge v. Ford Motor Company*. At the time, the Ford Motor Company had a sizeable capital surplus, and Henry Ford had decided to devote some of it to raising his workers' wages, which were already considered to be quite high. The Dodge brothers, two of the company's biggest shareholders, sued Ford for this move, claiming that Ford's capital actually belonged to his shareholders, and that unnecessarily raising wages was effectively stealing from them. The court ruled in their favour, and a precedent was set. Business decisions would have to be made in the interests of shareholder returns first. If CEOs want to spend money to increase wages or protect the environment in a manner that results in decreased shareholder returns, they can't, for it is effectively illegal to do so. Today, corporations are largely ruled by this imperative, which makes them much more rapacious than they otherwise might be. Abolishing it will be an important step towards giving them the space to consider other priorities.

*

Ditching the GDP measure and shareholder-value laws is a crucial first step, but it is not enough in and of itself. It might help us refocus our attention, but it doesn't address the main underlying driver of growth, which is a little bit deeper and more difficult to see, and that is debt. Right now, one of the reasons our economies *have* to grow is because of debt. Debt comes with interest, and interest means that debt grows exponentially. For a country to pay down its debt over the long term, it has to grow its economy enough to match the growth of its debt. The same is true of a business. If you want to start a business, you'll probably have to take out a loan. Then, because you have that debt, you can't just be satisfied with earning enough to pay your employees and feed your family – you also have to turn enough profit to pay off your loan with compound interest. Regardless of whether you're a country or a business – or even an individual – you'll find that, without growth, debt piles up and eventually causes a financial crisis. If you don't grow, you collapse.

One way to relieve this pressure is simply to cancel some of the debt. Cancelling the debt of sovereign nations, which we looked at in the previous chapter, would liberate them from the pressure to plunder their own resources and exploit their citizens in the hunt for income to repay debt. Cancelling the debt of individuals would allow them to work less. Here again, debt cancellation would mean that creditors would lose out – like the Wall Street banks that own so much of the debt. Still, we might decide that this is a reasonable sacrifice to make.

But even debt cancellation would only provide a short-term fix; it wouldn't really address the root problem, which is the fact that the global economic system runs on money that is itself debt. When you walk into a bank to take out a loan, you assume that the bank is lending you money it has in its reserve – real money that it stores in a basement vault, for example, collected from other people's deposits. But that's not how it works. Banks are only required to hold reserves worth about 10 per cent of the money they lend out. This is known as 'fractional reserve banking'. In other words, banks lend out about ten times more money than they actually have. So where does that extra money come from, if it doesn't actually exist? The banks create it out of thin air. They *loan it into existence*. About 90 per cent of the money that is presently circulating in our economy is created in this manner. In other words, almost every single dollar that passes through your hands represents somebody's debt. And every dollar of debt has to be paid back *with interest* – with more work, more production or more extraction.

The fact that our economy runs on debt-based currency is one big reason that it needs constant growth. Restricting the fractional reserve banking system would go a long way to diminishing the amount of debt sloshing around in our economies, and therefore to diminishing the pressure for growth. One easy way to do this would be to require banks to keep a bigger fraction of reserves behind the loans they make. But there's an even more interesting approach we might try: we could abolish debt-based currency altogether. Instead of letting commercial banks create our money, we could have the state create it – free of debt – and then spend it into the economy instead of lending it into the economy. The responsibility for money creation could be placed with an independent agency that is democratic, accountable and transparent. Banks would still be able to lend money, of course, but they would have to back it with 100 per cent reserves, dollar for dollar.

This is not a fringe proposal. It made headlines in 2012 when it was proposed by a couple of progressive IMF economists, who pointed out that such a system would dramatically reduce both public and private debt and therefore make the global economy more stable. In the United Kingdom, a campaigning group called Positive Money has generated quite a bit of popular excitement around the idea.

*

Changes like these would do a lot to liberate us from the tyranny of growth. But remember: the goal is not just to stop the unnecessary expansion of our economies, it is also to figure out how to actively *downsize* aggregate consumption – especially in rich countries – to get it back within sustainable levels. And this requires some rather creative thinking.

A first step in tackling this issue would be to take a serious look at the advertising industry, which is a major driver of unnecessary consumption. This hasn't always been a problem. As late as the early 20th century, consumption was a more or less perfunctory act: you basically bought what you needed. Advertisements did little more than inform you of the useful qualities of an object. But retail companies realised they couldn't expand indefinitely if everyone was buying only what was necessary. Limited needs mean limited profits. Companies needed a 'fix' for this obstacle – a way to surmount the limit of market saturation – and they found it in the new theories of advertising being developed at the time by Edward Bernays. Bernays, the nephew of psychoanalyst Sigmund Freud, taught retailers that they could get people to buy things they didn't need by manipulating their emotions. For example, you could seed anxiety in people's minds, and then present your product as a solution to that anxiety. Or you could sell things on the promise that they would provide social acceptance or class distinction. This kind of advertising quickly became indispensable to American retailers desperate to keep demand perpetually high.

Today, advertising is an enormous part of our economy. According to a recent report, the United States spent a total of $321 billion (2015 dollars) in advertising in 2007 alone, and this figure has been rising at about 5 per cent each year since then – much faster than the rate of economic growth. This frenzy of advertising has driven consumption to dizzying heights, to the point where the average American now consumes twice as much as they did in the 1950s.

In light of this, one easy solution to overconsumption would be to ban advertising – at least in public spaces, where people don't have a choice about what they see. This may sound impossible, but São Paolo, a city of 20 million people, has already done it. The result? Happier people: people who feel more secure about themselves and more content with their lives, in addition to consuming less. Paris recently made moves in this direction, too, curbing outdoor ads and even banning them outright in the vicinity of schools. Another, more aggressive option is to replace advertising with public messaging that encourages reduced consumption. China is pioneering this approach in its new campaign to cut the country's meat consumption in half by 2030 – a widely celebrated strategy for reducing greenhouse gas emissions. Or you could outright ban particularly unnecessary and destructive products, like bottled water, as some cities in Australia and the United States have done. Other simple ways to curb consumption might include regulating credit cards, raising taxes on luxury products and outlawing the use of 'planned obsolescence' by manufacturers who seek to increase turnover by building shoddy, throwaway products.

But what about jobs? If we scale back production and consumption, won't that trigger a crisis of unemployment? It's a good question, and one we must take seriously. After all, our politicians are always calling for more economic growth because they want to get the employment figures up – that's what gets them votes. But there are creative ways to scale back our economic activity *and* make sure everyone has meaningful work at the same time. The key proposal out there is to reduce the length of the working week, from forty-seven hours (the average in the United States) down to thirty or even twenty hours. We can do this by eliminating unnecessary or harmful industries (the kinds of industries that would atrophy anyway if we measured our economic progress by something like GPI instead of GDP) and distributing the remaining work by promoting job-sharing. Research by the New Economics Foundation in London suggests that a shorter working week not only reduces the physical and psychological ills associated with overwork, but also helps reduce consumption and greenhouse gas emissions. Working less means having more time to do things like caring for young or elderly relatives, growing your own food and doing your own cooking, cleaning, gardening and other activities that we often end up outsourcing to companies. It allows you to get to know your neighbours, which creates possibilities for sharing skills and possessions.

Another idea – and one that has really captured the public imagination over the past few years – is to introduce a basic minimum income. People have been proposing a basic income for a wide variety of reasons – most commonly as a strategy for poverty reduction. Over the past decade or so we've amassed an extraordinary amount of data showing that direct cash transfers to poor people in the global South is the single most effective way to reduce poverty. Unlike microfinance, which has had zero aggregate impact on poverty rates and tends to increase personal debt burdens, direct cash transfers are a form of positive money that stimulates local economies and creates sustainable livelihoods. Such schemes have been tried in South Africa, India, Indonesia, Mexico and many other countries, all with outstanding results. This approach is going to be increasingly necessary in the global South as automation eats rapidly into two of the region's biggest employment sectors: textiles and small consumer electronics. As these industries go to the robots, there could be a significant collapse in (already meagre) living standards unless alternative livelihoods are created.

In the United States and Europe, a basic income makes sense for a whole different set of reasons. Yes, it would reduce poverty. It would also improve working conditions and wages, as employers would have to offer a better deal in order to attract workers. But perhaps more importantly, it would smooth out what have become gross levels of inequality. This is important not just for moral reasons, but also because greater equality reduces the pressure for economic growth. This might seem a bit counterintuitive at first, but keep in mind that one of the reasons growth is so appealing to politicians is that it allows them to sidestep the thorny problem of distribution. As long as the pie is growing there's less pressure to redistribute existing resources. Even the promise of growth acts as a kind of damper on redistributive politics. Henry Wallich, a former member of the US Federal Reserve Board, once put it like this: 'Growth is a substitute for equality of income. So long as there is growth, there is hope, and that makes large income differentials tolerable.' There is a secret that lies within this formula. If growth is a substitute for equality, then equality is a substitute for growth. A basic income would help immensely towards this end. And that's on top of the fact that a basic income would in and of itself help slow our overheated production down a bit by releasing people from the pressure of having to work for forty or even sixty hours a week simply in order to stay alive.

A basic income could be funded in a variety of ways, including progressive taxes on commercial land use, like the land value tax made famous by the American economist Henry George, or taxes on capital gains, foreign currency transactions and financial transactions, such as the Robin Hood tax suggested by Nobel Prize-winning economist James Tobin. Another approach might be to tax the $32 trillion of private wealth that is presently hidden away in offshore tax havens, and use the proceeds for direct cash transfers.

In the US state of Alaska, natural resources are considered a commons, so every resident receives an annual dividend from the state's oil revenues as a basic income. The Alaska model is popular and effective, and scholars have pointed out that the same approach could be applied to other natural resources, such as forests and fisheries. It could even be applied to the air, with a carbon tax whose yields would be distributed as a basic income to all.

Regenerating Hope

Unfortunately, it is not likely that degrowth will happen as quickly as we need it to. Social change can be slow. The idea is gradually taking hold, but it could take a generation to move our collective consciousness on this issue, and we don't have that kind of time. That said, we might have a way out. And it has to do with soil.

Soil is the second biggest reservoir of carbon on the planet, next to the oceans. It holds four times more carbon than all the plants and trees in the world. But human activities like deforestation and industrial farming – with its intensive ploughing, monoculture and heavy use of chemical fertilisers and pesticides – are degrading our soils at breakneck speed, killing the organic materials that they contain. Forty per cent of agricultural soil is now classed as 'degraded' or 'seriously degraded'. In fact, industrial farming has so damaged our soils that a third of the world's farmland has been destroyed in the past four decades. And as our soils degrade, they are losing their ability to hold carbon, releasing enormous plumes of CO_2 into the atmosphere.

Fortunately, there is a solution emerging. Scientists and farmers around the world are pointing out that we can regenerate degraded soils by switching from intensive industrial farming to more ecological methods – not just organic fertiliser, but also no-tillage, composting and crop rotation. And here's the brilliant part: as the soils recover, they not only regain their capacity to hold CO_2, they begin to actively pull additional CO_2 out of the atmosphere. The science on this is quite exciting. A recent study published by the US National Academy of Sciences claims that regenerative farming can sequester 3 per cent of our global carbon emissions. An article in *Science* suggests it could be up to 15 per cent. And new research from the Rodale Institute in Pennsylvania, although not yet peer-reviewed, says sequestration rates could be as high as 40 per cent, and if we apply regenerative techniques to the world's pastureland as well, we could capture more than 100 per cent of global emissions.

In other words, regenerative farming may be our best shot at actually cooling the planet. And it comes with a very useful side-effect: regenerative methods actually produce higher yields than industrial methods over the long term, by enhancing soil fertility and improving resilience against drought and flooding. So as climate change makes farming more difficult, this may be our best bet for food security, too. Of course, regenerative farming doesn't offer a permanent solution to the climate crisis, for soils can only hold a finite amount of carbon. We still need to get off fossil fuels as quickly as possible, and – most importantly – we have to kick our obsession with endless exponential growth and downsize our material economy to bring it back in tune with ecological cycles. But it might buy us some time to get our act together.

I pick this example because it is fundamentally different to most of the other negative-emissions and geoengineering schemes out there, which end up embodying the very same logic that got us into this mess in the first place, treating Earth as something to be subdued and dominated. The solution to climate change won't be found in the latest schemes to bend our living planet to the will of man. Perhaps instead it lies in something much more down to earth – an ethic of care and healing, starting with the soils on which our existence depends. Regenerative farming holds out a first-step solution to our crisis that doesn't require shiny new technology. Rather, it requires remembering some of the ancient wisdom that got our species through the last 200,000 years, and which may be our only hope of getting through the next 200,000: the knowledge that our existence is tied up with the existence of all other living things, from the fish and the trees to the bees and seeds, right down to the microorganisms that make up the soil on which we depend. And on this point we have much to learn from people on the periphery of the world system – the ones our governments have so long referred to as 'underdeveloped'.

*

If rich countries organise a planned shrinkage of their material economies, with the goal of maintaining and even improving their quality of life, this will free up the ecological space that poor countries need to achieve basic standards of human well-being. But even so, the global South will still have a decision to face. Will they follow the standard development model laid down by the West, with its focus on extraction, consumption and growth? Or will they seize the opportunity to set out on a different path entirely?

In the early 1960s, just as the colonial project was collapsing, Frantz Fanon, the revolutionary intellectual from Martinique, penned words that today carry a new and even more powerful resonance than they did when they were written so many years ago:

> Come, then, comrades, the European game has finally ended; we must find something different. We today can do everything, so long as we do not imitate Europe, so long as we are not obsessed by the desire to catch up with Europe. Europe now lives at such a mad, reckless pace that she has shaken off all guidance and all reason, and she is running headlong into the abyss; we would do well to avoid it with all possible speed. The Third World today faces Europe like a colossal mass whose aim should be to try to resolve the problems to which Europe has not been able to find the answers. But let us be clear: what matters is to stop talking about output, and intensification, and the rhythm of work. No, we do not want to catch up with anyone. What we want to do is to go forward all the time, night and day, in the company of Man, in the company of all men. So, comrades, let us not pay tribute to Europe by creating states, institutions and societies which draw their inspiration from her. Humanity is waiting for something other from us than such an imitation.

We are already seeing this 'something other' emerge in pockets across the global South, sprouting up like shoots through concrete. Bhutan has famously rejected GDP growth and replaced it with Gross National Happiness as its measure of social progress. But this is only the very tip of the iceberg – the bit that makes its way into our media, almost as a quaint curiosity. Across Latin America, indigenous activists have brought the concept of 'sumak kawsay' to prominence – an indigenous Quechua term that translates as 'living in harmony and balance'. Instead of the Western model of development, which relies on a deep conceptual distinction between subject and object, self and other, humanity and the natural world, *sumak kawsay* calls us to recognise that we are interconnected, that we are part of a whole, that our well-being is inextricable from that of our ecosystems. This philosophy rejects the linear thinking that lies at the heart of the industrial development model, and calls us to think more relationally. The concept has gained such traction that Ecuador included it in its 2008 constitution – followed by Bolivia in 2009 – recognising the inalienable rights of ecosystems to survive and flourish. Neither experiment has been perfect, of course – cynical politicians in both Ecuador and Bolivia have used *sumak kawsay* to cloak their own extractivist agendas – but the idea itself continues to flourish.

And it's not only in Latin America. In India, impoverished communities in rural areas are asserting the principle of 'ecological *swaraj*'. Rather than submitting to plans handed down by central governments in distant capitals, people are using direct democracy to make decisions about their resources and environments, seeking regeneration and harmony with their surrounding ecology. In the Middle East, communities in the mountains of northern Iraq and in Rojava in Syria are experimenting with similar ideas. As central governments withdraw from these regions in order to battle ISIS and other factions vying for regional power, people are taking the opportunity to organise a kind of socio-ecological revolution marked by direct democracy, gender equality and regenerative farming, marking a decisive break with the Western development model.

Who knows what all of this might lead to. Once people begin to reject the single story of development, the future is fertile and rich with possibility. We need only have the courage to invent it.

Endnotes

One: The Development Delusion

p. 8 'The media went crazy ...' The history of Benjamin Hardy's involvement in the formulation of Point Four is recounted by Robert Schlesinger in *White House Ghosts: Presidents and their Speechwriters* (New York: Simon & Schuster, 2008).

p. 11 'And it has become ...' Net official development assistance was $135 billion in 2013, according to OECD data, which is roughly equivalent to the total net income of US banks in the same year.

p. 14 'These statistics are certainly worth ...' These reductions in child and maternal mortality are important gains, but we need to ask what happened in the decades prior to 1990 that pushed mortality rates to such high levels in the first place, and we need to ask whether it was really Western aid that has since caused them to decline.

p. 15 'More realistic estimates put...' FAO, *The State of Food Insecurity in the World 2012* (Rome: The Food and Agriculture Organization of the UN, 2012).

p. 15 'It is hard to imagine...' E. Holt-Gimenez et al., 'We already grow enough for 10 billion people ... and still can't end hunger', *Journal of Sustainable Agriculture* 36(6), 2012, pp. 595–8.

p. 15 'If we look at absolute . . .' According to the $1.25 (2008 PPP) poverty line. Source: PovcalNet.

p. 15 'Many scholars are now saying . . .' I discuss this scholarship in more depth in Chapter 2. See P. Edward, 'The ethical poverty line: a moral quantification of absolute poverty', *Third World Quarterly* 37(2), 2006, pp. 377–93; R. Lahoti, and S. Reddy, '$1.90 per day: what does it say?' Institute for New Economic Thinking, 6 October 2015, https://www.ineteconomics.org/perspectives/blog/1-90-per-day-what-does-it-say; David Woodward, *How Poor Is 'Poor'? Toward a Rights-Based Poverty Line* (London: New Economics Foundation, 2010).

p. 16 'These numbers represent almost . . .' All of the figures cited here are according to the World Bank's PovcalNet.

p. 16 'On the contrary, over the . . .' As measured in GDP per capita, 1990 Int. GK$, according to the Maddison Project database, 2013.

p. 16 'The gap between the . . .' As measured in GDP per capita, 2005 US$, according to World Development Indicators.

p. 17 'Others guessed that . . .' The argument that underdevelopment has to do with climate and geography has been made by Jared Diamond, *Guns, Germs, and Steel: The Fates of Human Societies* (New York: W. W. Norton, 1997).

p. 18 'Maybe it has to do with . . .' The argument that the fortunes of rich countries and poor countries is down to the quality of their institutions has been made most famously by Daren Acemoglu and James Robinson, *Why Nations Fail: The Origins of Power, Prosperity, and Poverty* (New York: Crown Business, 2012). Their argument has been criticized for not paying attention to geopolitics.

p. 19 'Europe's development couldn't have happened . . .' Kenneth Pomeranz, *The Great Divergence: China, Europe, and the Making of the Modern World Economy* (Princeton, NJ: Princeton University Press, 2009).

p. 19 'Average living standards in India . . .' Ha-Joon Chang, *Bad Samaritans* (New York: Bloomsbury Press, 2008), p. 25.

p. 22 'Global South countries lost . . .' Robert Pollin, *Contours of Descent* (New York: Verso, 2005), p. 133.

p. 22 'Today, power imbalances like these . . .' This figure comes from the United Nations' Trade and Development Report, 1999 (pp. ix and 143). The report estimates that if the Uruguay Round was fairer to poor countries (i.e., if rich countries reduced their tariffs against exports from poor countries), the latter could earn an extra $700 billion in export revenues, solely in low technology and resource-based industries, with big benefits for employment. Earnings from agricultural exports would make this figure considerably higher.

p. 23 'But perhaps it would be . . .' As in the title of Walter Rodney's famous 1972 book, *How Europe Underdeveloped Africa*.

p. 23 'And for evidence they invariably . . .' Official development assistance from DAC countries to developing countries totalled $128 billion in 2012, according to OECD data.

p. 25 'But more than twice that . . .' Global Financial Integrity, *Financial Flows and Tax Havens: Combining to Limit the Lives of Billions of People* (Washington, DC: Global Financial Integrity, 2016). The GFI study cites $2.97 trillion in net outflows between 1980 and 2012 through recorded transfers (mostly driven by countries with large current account surpluses, like China), $6.6 trillion through capital flight through leakages in the balance of payments, and $6.8 trillion through trade misinvoicing in goods. They estimate that another $6.8 trillion was lost through 'same-invoice faking' or 'abusive transfer pricing' in goods. Including trade in services, trade misinvoicing and abusive transfer pricing rise to $8.5 trillion each. This makes for a total of about $26.5 trillion in net outflows since 1980. For more on GFI's methodology, see Chapter 7 and accompanying notes. Note that GFI's calculations of net resource transfers do not include inward capital flight. GFI holds that because capital flight into developing countries does not contribute to development, it cannot be compared with outward capital flight, which actively undermines development. In addition, GFI argues that it does not make sense to net out capital flight in both directions because it does not make sense to speak of 'net crime'.

p. 25 'Today, poor countries pay over . . .' Developing countries paid $211 billion (INT, current US$) in interest payments on total external debt in 2015. Source: World Bank, International Debt Statistics.

p. 25 'Foreign investors take nearly . . .' International investors repatriated $486 billion in profits in 2012. Jesse Griffiths, 'The State of Finance for Developing Countries, 2014', Eurodad, 2014.

p. 25 'And there are many smaller . . .' Meena Raman, 'WIPO Seminar Debates Intellectual Property and Development', Our World is Not For Sale network, 10 May 2005.

p. 26 'But by far the biggest . . .' $23.6 trillion includes capital flight through leakages in the balance of payments, plus through trade misinvoicing and same-invoice faking in goods and services. Global Financial Integrity, *Financial Flows and Tax Havens: Combining to Limit the Lives of Billions of People* (Washington, DC: Global Financial Integrity, 2015).

p. 26 'A similarly large amount . . .' These figures on trade misinvoicing and abusive transfer pricing include estimates for both goods and services. Global Financial Integrity, *Financial Flows and Tax Havens: Combining to Limit the Lives of Billions of People* (Washington, DC: Global Financial Integrity 2015).

p. 27 'Comparing aid to various outflows . . .' The sources for the figures used in this graph are all as cited in the text. Note that they apply to different years, however. The figure for aid is for 2012. The figure for debt service is for 2013. The figures for trade misinvoicing, abusive transfer pricing and capital flight are for 2012. The figure for tax holidays is for 2013. The figure for TRIPS was published in 2015. The figure for climate change was published in 2010. The figure for structural adjustment is the annual average across twenty years during the 1980s and 1990s, in current dollars. The figure for the WTO Uruguay Round is for 2005. The figure for undervalued labour is for 1996, rendered in 2013 dollars.

p. 28 'In the mid-1990s . . .' Gernot Köhler, 'Unequal Exchange 1965–1995: World Trend and World Tables', 1998, wsarch.ucr.edu/archive/papers/kohler/kohler3.htm. See also Gernot Köhler and Arno Tausch, *Global Keynesianism: Unequal Exchange and Global Exploitation* (New York: Nova Science Publishers, 2002). Köhler calculates unequal exchange in 1995 as $1.752 trillion in current dollars. Köhler's method is to calculate the difference between nominal exchange rates and real exchange rates (i.e. corrected for purchasing power) for goods traded. For example, imagine a nominal exchange rate between the US dollar and the Indian rupee of 1:50. Now imagine that India sends R1,000 worth of goods to the US, and receives $20 worth of goods in return. That would be a perfectly equal exchange. Or at least so it would appear. The problem is that the nominal exchange rate isn't exactly accurate. In India, R50 can buy much more than the equivalent of $1 worth of goods. For instance, perhaps it can buy closer to $2 worth. So the *real* exchange rate, in terms of purchasing power, is 1:25. This means that when India sent R1,000 worth of goods to the US, it was really the equivalent of sending $40 worth, in terms of the value that R1,000 could buy in India. And yet India received only $20 in return, which in real terms is worth only R500. In other words, because of the distortion between real and nominal exchange rates, India sent $20 (R500) more than it received. One way to think of this is that India's export goods are worth more than the price they receive on the world market. Another way is that India's labour is underpaid relative to the value it produces. The problem with this method, of course, is that it relies on PPP calculations, which can be inaccurate. Other scholars have made more recent estimates of unequal exchange. Zak Cope estimates that unequal exchange in 2009 was between $2.8 trillion and $4.9 trillion, depending on the method used. See Zak Cope, *Divided World Divided Class: Global Political Economy and the Stratification of Labour Under Capitalism* (Montreal: Kersplebedeb, 2012).

p. 28 'For example, ActionAid reports that . . .' Luke Balleny, 'Corporate tax breaks cost poor nations $138 billion a year – report', Reuters, 4 July 2013.

p. 28 'Remittances sent home by immigrant workers . . .' Remittances totalled $432 billion in 2015, and fees averaged 7.68 per cent.

p. 29 'Global South economies lose . . .' H. Kharas, *Measuring the Cost of Aid Volatility*, Wolfensohn Center for Development working paper no. 3 (Washington, DC: Brookings Institution, 2008). Kharas calculates that aid volatility causes losses equal to 20 per cent of the total value of aid.

p. 29 'Then there are forms of extraction . . .' According to the Land Matrix database (www.landmatrix.org), with data accurate as of January 2017.

p. 29 'And then, of course, there are . . .' According to the Climate Vulnerability Monitor's 2012 report.

p. 29 'Indeed, some of this damage . . .' There have been attempts by some NGOs to campaign on these more structural issues: the Make Trade Fair campaign run by Oxfam, for instance, or the Jubilee Debt campaign. Even Make Poverty History had trade and debt in the mix, and Christian Aid and ActionAid have campaigned on tax evasion for several years, gradually dragging

291

more conservative NGOs to at least acknowledge the problem. But such efforts are almost completely drowned out by the dominant framing of charity and aid that the very same NGOs promote.

Two: The End of Poverty . . . Has Been Postponed

p. 36 'The same is true . . .' Gains against maternal mortality fell far short of the target; and because it is so difficult to measure, experts have raised questions about the validity of even the modest improvements that the UN has claimed. See Amir Attaran, 'An immeasurable crisis: a criticism of the Millennium Development Goals and why they cannot be measured', *PLoS Medicine* 2(10), 2005. Of maternal mortality, the author notes: 'The limitations of current estimation techniques are so profound that UNICEF and WHO scientists warn that "it would be inappropriate to compare the 2000 estimates with those for 1990 . . . and draw conclusions about trends."' Child mortality is, on the other hand, much easier to measure.

p. 37 'The new commitment was to . . .' Article 19 of the Millennium Declaration. Emphasis mine.

p. 38 'This backdating took particular advantage . . .' 165 million people at the $1.08 (1993 PPP) poverty line, and 400 million at the $1.25 (2005 PPP) poverty line.

p. 38 'and deceptively chalked them up as . . .' Thomas Pogge has been instrumental in highlighting the sleight of hand practised by the Millennium Campaign. For example: 'Millions Killed by Clever Dilution of Our Promise', CROP Poverty Brief, August 2010; 'How World Poverty is Measured and Tracked', in Elcke Mack, Michael Schramm, Stephan Klasen and Thomas Pogge (eds), *Absolute Poverty and Global Justice* (Aldershot: Ashgate, 2009), pp. 51–68; 'The first United Nations Millennium Development Goal: a cause for celebration?', *Journal of Human Development* 5(3), 2004, pp. 377–97.

p. 38 'This also meant that they . . .' I am indebted to Thomas Pogge for bringing all of this to my attention.

p. 39 'But that's not the only . . .' Sanjay Reddy and Thomas Pogge have been instrumental in articulating this argument in *How Not to Count the Poor* (mimeo, Columbia University Academic Commons, 2005).

292

p. 39 'It seemed reasonable, he thought . . .' M. Ravallion et al., 'Quantifying absolute poverty in the developing world', *Review of Income and Wealth* 37(4), 1991, pp. 345–61.

p. 40 ' "The absolute number of those . . ." ' World Bank, *World Development Report 1999/2000* (New York: Oxford University Press, 1999), p. 25. Emphasis mine.

p. 40 'Not only that, it also . . .' See William Easterly, 'The lost decades: developing countries' stagnation in spite of policy reform 1980–1998', *Journal of Economic Growth* 6, 2001, pp. 135–57.

p. 40 ' "Over the past few years . . ." ' Wolfensohn in speech to G20 finance ministers and central governors, Ottawa, 17 November 2001.

p. 41 'Then, three years later . . .' Shohua Chen and Martin Ravallion, *How Have the World's Poorest Fared since the Early 1980s?*, World Bank Policy Research Working Paper 3341, June 2004.

p. 42 'The World Bank's economists claimed . . .' Reddy and Pogge, *How Not to Count the Poor*. See Ravallion's response: 'How Not to Count the Poor? A Reply to Reddy and Pogge', in Sudhir Anand et al. (eds), *Debates on the Measurement of Poverty* (Oxford: Oxford University Press, 2008).

p. 43 'This is a crucial point . . .' Robert Wade, *Economic Theory and the Role of Government in East Asian Industrialization* (Princeton, NJ: Princeton University Press, 1990).

p. 43 'The UN was forced to . . .' FAO, *The State of Food Insecurity in the World 2008* (Rome: The Food and Agriculture Organization of the UN, 2008), p. 8.

p. 44 'The 2013 report of . . .' United Nations, *Millennium Development Goals Report 2013*, p. 10.

p. 44 'In addition, the FAO revised . . .' FAO, 'Food Security Methodology', FAO (2012). This second phase of changes was reflected in the 2012 report.

p. 44 'They also adjusted the hunger . . .' The FAO also used revised data on average population heights, which are used in turn to calculate the minimum dietary energy requirements (MDER) for each country (i.e. the calorie threshold at which hunger is measured). The new calorie thresholds were adjusted significantly downwards across the board, but with greater reductions (over the previous thresholds) at the end of the period than at the beginning, with the result that – all other things being equal – the number of hungry people would appear to slope downwards more rapidly than under the previous measurements. Compare the new MDER (http://www.docs-library.com/xls/1/7/2217-2548.html) with the old MDER (http://www.fao.org/fileadmin/templates/ess/documents/food_security_statistics/MinimumDietaryEnergyRequirement_en.xls).

p. 44 'The UN counts people as . . .' FAO, *The State of Food Insecurity in the World 2012* (Rome: The Food and Agriculture Organization of the UN, 2012), p. 12.

p. 45 'The average rickshaw driver . . .' 'A Recovery with a Human Face', UNICEF e-discussion, accessed 12 October 2015, http://www.recoveryhumanface.org/. See Thomas Pogge's posts in June 2015.

p. 45 'The FAO itself recognises . . .' FAO, *State of Food Insecurity 2012*, p. 12.

p. 45 'This is two to three . . .' See also F. Moore Lappé, J. Clapp, M. Anderson, R. Broad, E. Messer, T. Pogge and T. Wise, 'How we count hunger matters', *Ethics and International Affairs* 27(3), 2013, pp. 251–9.

p. 46 'So people who have . . .' FAO, *State of Food Insecurity 2012*, p. 23.

p. 46 '"The reference period should be . . ."' FAO, *State of Food Insecurity 2012*, p. 50.

p. 46 'In other words, the FAO's . . .' I am indebted to Thomas Pogge (personal correspondence) for drawing my attention to this issue.

p. 46 'And this tragedy persists . . .' 'World Hunger and Poverty Facts and Statistics 2015', World Hunger Education Service, Washington DC, http://www.worldhunger.org/2015-world-hunger-and-poverty-facts-and-statistics/.

p. 46 'In the US and Europe . . .' Rebecca Smithers, 'Almost half of the world's food thrown away, report finds', *Guardian*, 10 January 2013.

p. 46 'The UN finds that cutting . . .' Kate Lyon, 'Cutting food waste by a quarter would mean enough for everyone, says UN', *Guardian*, 12 August 2015.

p. 47 '"The morally relevant comparison . . ."' T. Pogge, 'The end of poverty?', *Mark News*, 29 May 2014.

p. 47 'But the World Bank . . .' World Bank, *World Development Report 1999/2000*, p. 237.

p. 48 'But empirical research in India . . .' 'Poverty in India 2.5 times the official figure: study', NDTV India, 20 February 2014.

p. 48 'So not only does the . . .' Vijay Prashad, 'Making poverty history', *Jacobin*, 10 November 2014, https://www.jacobinmag.com/2014/11/making-poverty-history/.

p. 48 'In Niger, babies born . . .' Adam Wagstaff, 'Child health on a dollar a day: some tentative cross-country comparisons', *Social Science and Medicine* 57(9), 2003, pp. 1529–38.

p. 48 'Even this minor shift would . . .' 'Asians poorer than official data suggest, says ADB', *Financial Times*, 20 August 2014.

p. 48 'But the US government itself . . .' USDA, *Thrifty Food Plan 2005* (Washington DC: United States Department of Agriculture, 2005).

p. 49 'According to British economist . . .' David Woodward, 'How poor is too poor?', *New Internationalist*, 1 July 2010.

p. 49 'Recent studies place this . . .' P. Edward, 'The Ethical Poverty Line: a moral quantification of absolute poverty', *Third World Quarterly* 27(2), 2006, pp. 377–93.

p. 50 'Economists Rahul Lahoti and . . .' R. Lahoti and S. Reddy, '$1.90 per day: what does it say?', Institute for New Economic Thinking, 2015. Lahoti and Reddy put the food poverty line at $5.04 at 2011 PPP; I have adjusted here to 2005 PPP, to enable the comparison.

p. 50 'The New Economics Foundation . . .' David Woodward, *How Poor Is 'Poor'? Toward a Rights-Based Poverty Line* (London: New Economics Foundation, 2010).

p. 50 'As it turns out, $5 . . .' Andrew Sumner, 'Did global poverty just fall a lot, quite a bit, or not at all?', *Global Policy Journal*, accessed 16 June 2014, http://www.globalpolicyjournal.com/blog/16/06/2014/donors%E2%80%99-dilemma-did-global-poverty-just-fall-lot-quite-bit-or-not-all.

p. 50 '"In more developed regions . . ."' 'There are multiple international poverty lines. Which one should I use?', World Bank.

p. 50 'Harvard economist Lant Pritchett . . .' L. Pritchett, 'Monitoring progress on poverty: the case for a high global poverty line', 2013, www.developmentprogress.org.

p. 50 'Even with China factored in . . .' At the IPL of $2.50 (2005 PPP), the World Bank calculations show that the poverty headcount increased by 852 million between 1981 and 2005, excluding China.

p. 50 'At the $10-a-day line . . .' World Bank Development Indicators 2008.

p. 51 'In 2016 the World Bank's . . .' B. Milanović, *Global Inequality: A New Approach for the Age of Globalization* (Cambridge, Mass.: Belknap Press, 2016).

p. 52 'In fact, the economists . . .' S. Anand and P. Segal, 'The global distribution of income', in Anthony B. Atkinson and Francois Bourguignon (eds), *Handbook of Income Distribution* (Amsterdam: Elsevier, 2014).

p. 52 'This is important because . . .' Robert Wade, *Economic Theory and the Role of Government in East Asian Industrialization* (Princeton, NJ: Princeton University Press, 1990).

p. 53 'Sudhir Anand and Paul Segal . . .' 'The global distribution of income'.

p. 55 'In 2015, the economist . . .' David Woodward, '*Incrementum ad absurdum*: global growth, inequality and poverty eradication in a carbon-constrained world', *World Economic Review* 4, 2015, World Economic Association.

p. 56 ' "There is simply no way . . ." ' David Woodward, 'How progressive is the push to eradicate extreme poverty?', *Guardian*, 7 June 2013.

Three: Where Did Poverty Come From? A Creation Story

p. 64 'But archaeological records show . . .' Richard Steckel and Jerome Rose (eds), *The Backbone of History: Health and Nutrition in the Western Hemisphere* (Cambridge: Cambridge University Press, 2002). Life expectancy figures for foragers are often skewed downwards by higher infant mortality rates compared to their settled counterparts. If we correct for this, some researchers find that forager lifespans reached well into the seventies. See: M. Gurven and H. Kaplan, 'Longevity among hunter-gatherers: a cross-cultural examination', *Population and Development Review* 33, 2007, pp. 321–65. Also, Marshall Sahlins draws on a variety of historical and ethnographic sources to argue that forager societies enjoyed significantly longer life expectancies than state societies. See 'The original affluent society' in his *Stone Age Economics* (Chicago: Aldine-Atherton, 1972).

p. 64 'They were healthier, stronger, taller . . .' Steckel and Rose (eds), *The Backbone of History*. See also: Karl Widerquist and Grant McCall, *Prehistoric Myths in Modern Political Philosophy* (Edinburgh: Edinburgh University Press, 2017); Jared Diamond, *Guns, Germs and Steel: The Fates of Human Societies* (New York: W. W. Norton, 1997); Yuval Noah Harari, *Sapiens: A Brief History of Humankind* (London: Random House, 2014).

p. 64 'In the Americas of the . . .' According to George Murdoch's Ethnographic Atlas (representing data from 1500 to 1960, with the majority from the 19th century), only about 20 per cent of societies in America north of the Isthmus lived in compact, permanent settlements and depended on agriculture for the majority of their subsistence. Only 1 per cent of societies are classed as 'complex' states.

p. 65 'Asia exceeded Europe in many . . .' These figures come from data collated by Kenneth Pomeranz from a variety of leading extant sources. See his *The Great Divergence* (Princeton, NJ: Princeton University Press, 2000), p. 36ff. The initial figure for England accounts for infant mortality. Data on life expectancy in India at the time is not good enough to be conclusive. The figure for the English working class comes from Edwin Chadwick's report on *The Sanitary Condition of the Labouring Population*, cited in Friedrich Engels, *The Condition of the Working Class in England in 1844* (1845).

p. 65 'In fact, by the time . . .' Immanuel Wallerstein, *The Modern World System* (New York: Academic Press, 1974).

p. 66 'In his journals, Columbus reported . . .' Quoted in Howard Zinn, *A People's History of the United States* (New York: HarperCollins, 2003), 3.

p. 66 'They lived in communal buildings . . .' Quoted in Zinn, *A People's History*, p. 1.

p. 66 'Columbus was eager to exploit . . .' Quoted in Zinn, *A People's History*, p. 1.

p. 68 '"They lifted up the gold . . ."' Quoted in Eduardo Galeano, 'Open Veins of Latin America', *Monthly Review Press*, 1973, pp. 18–19.

p. 68 'Before long the metal . . .' Galeano, 'Open Veins', p. 22.

p. 68 'And that was on top . . .' Galeano, 'Open Veins', p. 23.

p. 68 'By the early 1800s . . .' Timothy Walton, *The Spanish Treasure Fleets* (Florida: Pineapple Press, 1994).

p. 69 'It was a massive infusion . . .' The silver was 'free' in the sense that it was dug up by unpaid slave labour. Also, the Spanish Crown claimed a 27.5–40 per cent share of all silver shipments. See Pomeranz, *The Great Divergence*, p. 269.

p. 69 'We can think of this . . .' Pomeranz, *The Great Divergence*, p. 269ff.

p. 69 'The numbers vary by source . . .' The high number for 1492 is about 112 million, but the general 'consensus figure' for Latin America's population at the time is about 54 million. William Denevan (ed.), *The Native Population of the Americas in 1492* (Madison, Wis.: University of Wisconsin Press, 1992).

p. 69 'By the middle of the . . .' Galeano puts the figure at 3.5 million, but others put it at 4 million. See Jorge Brea, 'Population Dynamics in Latin America', *Population Bulletin* 58(1), 2003.

p. 70 'In the 1700s, Portuguese Brazil . . .' Galeano, 'Open Veins', p. 52.

p. 70 'By the end of the . . .' These figures probably do not capture the slaves that were smuggled illegally across the Atlantic until at least 1870.

p. 71 'Valued at the US minimum . . .' These figures come from a 1993 article in *Harper's* magazine. Note that the minimum wage is calculated at the 1993 rate, interest is calculated only through 1993, and the total figure is expressed in 1993 dollars. In other words, the updated figure would be much higher than this.

p. 71 'They have not disclosed . . .' '14 Caribbean nations sue Britain, Holland and France for slavery reparations', *Daily Mail*, 10 October 2013.

p. 71 'For example, sugar came to . . .' Pomeranz, *The Great Divergence*, p. 275.

p. 71 'If we add timber imports . . .' Pomeranz, *The Great Divergence*, p. 276.

p. 72 'Or even just a proportion . . .' Of course, it wasn't only Europeans who plundered Africa of bodies. In 'The Impact of the Slave Trade on Africa', Elikia M'Bokolo writes that 'The African continent was bled of its human resources via all possible routes. Across the Sahara, through the Red Sea, from the Indian Ocean ports and across the Atlantic. At least ten centuries of slavery for the benefit

of the Muslim countries (from the ninth to the nineteenth) . . .
Four million enslaved people exported via the Red Sea, another
four million through the Swahili ports of the Indian Ocean, [and]
perhaps as many as nine million along the trans-Saharan caravan
route.' *Le Monde Diplomatique*, April 1998.

p. 73 ' "The discovery of gold and . . ." ' Karl Marx, *Capital*, vol. 1 (1867),
chapter 3.

p. 75 'They also began to privatise . . .' In chapter 3 of *Capital*, vol. 1,
Marx notes that before the enclosure movement there were about
3 acres of agricultural land for every 1 acre of pasture, but the
enclosure movement reversed this ratio.

p. 75 'They had to increase their . . .' Ellen Meiksins Wood, *The Origin
of Capitalism: A Longer View* (London: Verso, 2002).

p. 75 'It meant that, for the . . .' See Karl Polanyi, *The Great Transformation* (New York: Farrar & Rinehart, 1944).

p. 76 'Thousands of protestors pulled down . . .' These rebellions are
listed in Simon Fairlie, 'A Short History of Enclosure in Britain',
The Land 7, 2009. Fairlie mentions a peasants' revolt in 1381 as an
early expression of resistance against enclosure, although enclosure was not the main issue at stake.

p. 76 'Between 1760 and 1870 . . .' Fairlie, 'A Short History of Enclosure'.
The parliamentary enclosures, as they are known, focused less on
wool and more on the 'improvement' of agricultural land.

p. 76 'By the middle of the . . .' I draw this conclusion from mapping the
word 'poverty' through Google Ngram, along with 'vagabond',
'pauper' and other common synonyms from the time.

p. 77 'The population of England's urban . . .' The proportion of the
population in England and Wales living in rural areas dropped
from 65 per cent in 1801 to 23 per cent in 1901, while in France it
was still as high as 59 per cent in 1901. Fairlie, 'A Short History of
Enclosure'.

p. 78 'This was the basic mechanism . . .' Of course, coercion was a central piece of this system as well, but as a background condition – it
kept the system in place and prevented rebellion against it.

p. 80 'In other words, the scarcity . . .' I take this contrast from Polanyi's
chapter heading: 'Habitation versus Improvement', in *The Great
Transformation*.

p. 80 'Ireland was exporting thirty to . . .' Seamus P. Metress and Richard A. Rajner, *The Great Starvation: An Irish Holocaust* (New York: American Ireland Education Foundation, 1996).

p. 81 'According to Locke, this added . . .' This logic was also developed by William Petty and John Davies, who were crucial to justifying the new imperialism.

p. 81 'These land grabs took . . .' For example, 1,000 Indians were killed in the Apalachee massacre of 1704, and another 1,200 or so were killed at Fort Neoheroka in 1713, to list two of the biggest massacres of that century.

p. 83 'Yet farmers found that . . .' Mike Davis, *Late Victorian Holocausts* (London: Verso, 2000), p. 290.

p. 83 'And with water sources enclosed . . .' Ibid., pp. 327–31.

p. 83 'The human toll was staggering . . .' Ibid., p. 7. Davis presents a number of different estimates based on different sources; 29 million is the high estimate.

p. 84 'During the period from 1875 . . .' Ibid., p. 299.

p. 85 ' "We are not dealing . . ." ' Ibid., p. 9.

p. 86 'It worked: India, once . . .' Ibid., p. 298.

p. 86 'By the time they left . . .' Angus Maddison, *The World Economy*, OECD, 2006.

p. 88 'And, as in India . . .' Davis, *Late Victorian Holocausts*.

p. 88 'In the middle of the . . .' Paul Bairoch, *Economics and World History* (Chicago: University of Chicago Press, 1995).

p. 88 'Even as late as 1800 . . .' Paul Bairoch, 'The Main Trends in National Economic Disparities since the Industrial Revolution', in Paul Bairoch and Maurice Levy-Leboyer (eds), *Disparities in Economic Development since the Industrial Revolution* (New York: St Martin's Press, 1975), pp. 3–17.

p. 88 'Indian artisans enjoyed a better . . .' Davis, *Late Victorian Holocausts*, pp. 292–3.

p. 88 'From 1872 to 1921 . . .' According to figures cited in Davis, *Late Victorian Holocausts*, pp. 311–12.

p. 92 'Ten million Congolese perished . . .' Adam Hochschild, *King Leopold's Ghost: A Story of Greed, Terror, and Heroism in Colonial Africa* (London: Pan Books, 2006), pp. 225–33.

p. 93 'And the costs of caring . . .' Harold Wolpe, 'Capitalism and cheap labor power in South Africa: from segregation to apartheid', *Economy and Society* 1(4), 1972, pp. 425–56; J. S. Crush et al., *South Africa's Labor Empire: A History of Black Migrancy to the Gold Mines* (Boulder, CO: Westview Press, 1991).

p. 94 'From the late 15th . . .' I am indebted to Naomi Klein for the concept of the sacrifice zone.

p. 94 'By contrast, incomes in Western . . .' Ha-Joon Chang, *Bad Samaritans* (New York: Bloomsbury Press, 2008), p. 25.

p. 94 'At the end of this . . .' Thomas Piketty, *Capital in the 21st Century* (Cambridge, MA: Harvard University Press, 2014), p. 69.

p. 95 'This agenda became particularly clear . . .' The Roosevelt Corollary was initially established to allow the US to respond militarily if Europeans invaded Latin America, which happened in 1902 when Britain, Germany and Italy blockaded Venezuela to demand debt repayment.

p. 96 'The first was that the . . .' One reason for this is that manufactured commodities have greater 'elasticity of demand', meaning that their prices rise as incomes rise. Another reason is that technological innovation makes primary commodities cheaper at a more rapid rate than manufactured goods.

p. 96 'This meant that they had . . .' Economists Raúl Prebisch and Hans Singer described this effect in 1950, in what is now known as the Prebisch–Singer hypothesis. The Prebisch–Singer hypothesis has been confirmed with recent evidence that the terms of trade for most commodities *do* deteriorate over time (while others are flat); see, for example, David Harvey et al., 'The Prebisch–Singer hypothesis: four centuries of evidence', *Review of Economics and Statistics* 92(3), 2010, pp. 367–77; and Rabah Arezki et al., 'Testing the Prebisch–Singer Hypothesis since 1650', IMF Working Paper, 2013. The Prebisch–Singer hypothesis fell into disuse during the period of globalisation beginning in the 1980s, when global South economies (with the exception of most African countries) began to export simple manufactures. Of course, the principle still applies, but today the unfair terms of trade are between the simple manufactures of the global South versus the complex manufactures of the West.

p. 97 'Together, these two patterns . . .' The term 'unequal exchange' was coined by Arghiri Emmanuel, and made famous by Samir Amin.

p. 97 'By the end of the colonial . . .' United Nations Development Programme, *Human Development Report 1999: Globalization with a Human Face* (New York: Oxford University Press, 1999), p. 38. If we use the Maddison Project data, the figures are slightly different: 6.3:1 in 1800 to 31.8 in 1960.

p. 97 'That is twice the amount . . .' Samir Amin, *Unequal Development* (New York: Monthly Review Press, 1976), p. 144.

Four: From Colonialism to the Coup

p. 99 'In 1910, the richest . . .' Thomas Piketty, *Capital in the 21st Century* (Cambridge, MA: Harvard University Press, 2014), p. 349. During this period (between 1870 and 1910), aggregate private wealth was six to seven years of national income in Europe (Piketty, p. 26). In the United States, this era saw the rise of powerful industrialists and financiers – John Rockefeller, Andrew Mellon, Andrew Carnegie, Cornelius Vanderbilt and J. P. Morgan – symbols of social inequality and known by their critics as 'robber barons' for the extent to which they made their riches through sometimes brutal monopoly power.

p. 100 'The following decade became known . . .' The accumulation of income and wealth among the rich was aided by tax cuts in their favour. The Coolidge administration cut taxes with the Revenue Acts of 1924, 1926 and 1928, reducing inheritance taxes and bringing the top marginal tax rate down to 25 per cent. These tax cuts were conducted according to the policy of Andrew Mellon, Secretary of the Treasury, one of America's richest men, who claimed (as Ronald Reagan did in the 1980s) that reducing taxes on the rich would yield higher tax revenues. Of course, some context is necessary. When the income tax was first established in 1913, the top marginal rate was only 7 per cent. It was raised to 77 per cent in 1916 to finance the war. The Coolidge tax cuts were dramatic, but only against the backdrop of wartime rates.

p. 100 'Once Europe withdrew from Africa . . .' Latin America was decolonised during the early 19th century, long before the rest of the global South, after a struggle for national independence led by figures such as Simón Bolívar. In the wake of decolonisation, however, most Latin American countries were controlled by autocratic governments, and by the early 20th century the United States began to exert a strong influence over the region.

p. 102 'These measures, he said . . .' Keynes outlined these ideas in 1933 in *The Means to Prosperity* (copies of which were sent to the governments of Britain and the United States), and more thoroughly in 1936 in his famous text *The General Theory of Employment, Interest, and Money.*

p. 102 'When Franklin Delano Roosevelt came . . .' The Works Progress Administration was established in 1939 to employ unemployed citizens in public works projects.

p. 102 'When the Second World War . . .' The Roosevelt administration raised the top marginal tax rate to 75 per cent in 1939, and then to 94 per cent in 1944. It remained above 90 per cent until the mid-1960s.

p. 102 'This new system relied on . . .' In the United States, the key piece of legislation was the National Labor Relations Act of 1935, which facilitated trade unions and collective bargaining.

p. 103 'In 1944, the Bretton Woods institutions . . .' While the Bretton Woods institutions were Keynesian in spirit, in reality Keynes himself disapproved. The problem with the World Bank and the IMF is that creditor nations (like the US) get all of the power, and can dictate terms to debtor nations. Keynes argued instead for an International Clearing Union – a kind of global central bank – which would automatically shift finance from surplus countries to deficit countries through a demurrage system. Keynes' proposal was defeated at Bretton Woods.

p. 103 'Middle-class women, for example . . .' Consider, for instance, Betty Friedan's critique of women's social subordination in her 1963 book *The Feminine Mystique.*

p. 104 'The progressive political parties that . . .' See, for example, Frederick Cooper, *Decolonization and African Society* (Cambridge: Cambridge University Press, 1996).

p. 105 'The policy suspended the long . . .' In 1933 the United States signed the Convention on the Rights and Duties of States. Article 8: 'No state has the right to intervene in the internal or external affairs of another.' Within a few years thereafter the United States relinquished its control over Panama and Cuba.

p. 105 'Founded in 1948, the Commission . . .' Prebisch ran the Commission from 1950–63. He developed his ideas about unequal exchange at the same time as Hans Singer, who was a student of Keynes – hence the double name of the Prebisch–Singer hypothesis. Prebisch's key work in this vein was *The Economic Development of Latin America and its Principal Problems* (New York: United Nations, 1950).

p. 105 'Prebisch argued that underdevelopment . . .' Prebisch made this argument in the Havana Manifesto, among his other publications.

p. 105 'In Argentina, for example . . .' While Perón and Prebisch shared the goal of achieving economic independence, Prebisch did not always agree with Perón's import substitution policies, which he felt were pursued at the expense of exports. See 'Raul Prebisch: Latin America's Keynes', *The Economist*, 5 March 2009.

p. 106 'These developmentalist policies mimicked . . .' Ha-Joon Chang, 'Kicking away the ladder', *Post-Autistic Economics Review* 15, 2002.

p. 106 'And they worked equally well . . .' Robert Pollin, *Contours of Descent* (New York: Verso, 2005), p. 133. Note that the 3.2 per cent figure excludes China.

p. 106 'And the new wealth was . . .' UN, *Human Development Report 1999/2000*, p. 39.

p. 107 'By the early 1980s . . .' According to the United Nations Population Division.

p. 107 'The same is true of . . .' Leandro Prados de le Escosura, 'World Human Development 1870–2007', *Review of Income and Wealth* 61(2), 2015, pp. 220–47.

p. 107 'During the same period . . .' The per capita income ratio of the US to Latin America shrank from 4.7:1 to 4.2:1, while the ratio of the US to the Middle East and North Africa shrank from 7:1 to 5.4:1 and the ratio of the US to East Asia shrank from 13.6:1 to 10:1. For South Asia, the ratio continued to grow. (GDP per capita, constant 2010 US$; data from World Development Indicators.)

p. 108 'Import substitution policies meant that . . .' Smaller, Western-based exporters of consumer goods were hurt by import substitution industrialisation (ISI) in the global South, as high tariffs excluded their goods. But larger exporters of heavy equipment benefited from ISI, for ISI governments were in need of such equipment. Foreign direct investors also benefited – in cases where such investment was allowed – for they got to reap the benefit of operating behind the barrier of a closed market. In fact, the United States government promoted ISI across the global South during the 1940s and 1950s, partly as a way of absorbing the surplus heavy manufacturing capacity left over from the Second World War, and partly to assist the interests of large US foreign investors. The preferred plan was to gradually shift global South countries from ISI to export-led industrialisation under a free-market model in hope that this would help global South countries to repay their debts, even if it meant making some US businesses uncompetitive. But protectionism in the US, which was difficult to dislodge at the time, precluded this option – so they chose instead to deepen ISI, while negotiating for the best possible terms. See Sylvia Maxfield and James Nolt, 'Protectionism and the Internationalization of Capital', *International Studies Quarterly* 34(1), 1990, pp. 49–81.

p. 109 'When President Dwight Eisenhower took . . .' My grasp of this narrative owes much to Naomi Klein's *The Shock Doctrine* (London: Allen Lane, 2007) and Noel Maurer, *The Empire Trap: The Rise and Fall of US Intervention to Protect American Property Overseas, 1893–2013* (Princeton, NJ: Princeton University Press, 2013).

p. 110 'Operation Ajax was one of . . .' The first successful attempt by the United States to overthrow a foreign government was in Cuba in 1933, when the US backed Fulgencio Batista in his uprising against the revolutionary government of Gerardo Machado. But this did not become a common strategy until after the Second World War, with the formation of the CIA.

p. 111 'Despite being offered full compensation . . .' John Perkins, *Confessions of an Economic Hit Man* (San Francisco: Berrett-Koehler Publishers, 2004), p. 73.

p. 111 'The new government quickly deregulated . . .' Perkins, *Confessions*, p. 73.

p. 112 'When opposition arose, it was . . .' This story is told most eloquently in the autobiography of Rigoberta Menchú, a well-known indigenous leader and winner of the Nobel Peace Prize. Rigoberta Menchú and Elisabeth Burgos, *I, Rigoberta Menchú* (New York: Verso, 1984). The 200,000 figure comes from Billy Briggs, 'Secrets of the dead', *Guardian*, 2 February 2007.

p. 112 'In 1964, in an operation . . .' See Phyllis Parker, *Brazil and the Quiet Intervention, 1964* (Austin, TX: University of Texas Press, 1979).

p. 113 'In response to growing citizen . . .' By the mid-1970s, Latin America was firmly in the hands of right-wing dictatorships. The dictatorships of Argentina, Chile, Paraguay, Uruguay, Brazil and Bolivia collaborated in Operation Condor, a clandestine campaign designed to assassinate leftist activists. Operation Condor had explicit US support (including technical and financial support) under Henry Kissinger. It is estimated that 60,000 assassinations were carried out. See Larry Rohter, 'Exposing the legacy of Operation Condor', *New York Times*, 24 January 2014.

p. 113 'The tactical support for many . . .' For example, Guillermo Rodriguez, the military dictator in Ecuador from 1972 to 1976, was trained at the School of the Americas.

p. 114 'When the CIA made it . . .' Sukarno had endorsed plans by the Indonesian Communist Party to arm workers and peasants as a people's militia. Suharto considered this a direct threat to the military's primacy.

p. 115 'In his place, Western governments . . .' Between 1962 and 1991, the US gave $1.03 billion in development aid and $227.4 million in military assistance to the Mobutu regime. Carole Collins, 'Zaire/Democratic Republic of the Congo', *Foreign Policy in Focus*, 1 July 1997.

p. 116 'During Mobutu's long reign . . .' Leonce Ndikumana and James K. Boyce, 'Congo's odious debt: external borrowing and capital flight in Zaire', *Development and Change* 29, 1998, pp. 195–217.

p. 116 '"We hereby commit ourselves to . . ."' This passage represents small portions of the text of the 'Common Man's Charter' with some sentences truncated and merged.

p. 120 'The elite – those whose wealth . . .' The argument that the elite class was looking for a solution to Keynesianism has been made compellingly by David Harvey in *A Brief History of Neoliberalism*.

p. 121 'These policies were improving people's . . .' Klein, *The Shock Doctrine*, p. 53.

p. 122 'Before long, the Chicago School . . .' Klein, *The Shock Doctrine*, p. 56.

p. 123 'Juan Gabriel Valdés, a Chilean . . .' Juan Gabriel Valdés, *Pinochet's Economists: The Chicago School in Chile* (Cambridge: Cambridge University Press, 1995), p. 13. Classes were also held at the Catholic University of Santiago, which partnered with the University of Chicago.

p. 123 'His victory was an impressive . . .' The International Telephone and Telegraph Company (ITT) paid out $700,000 to Alessandri, and the company's president paid an additional $1 million to the CIA to help manipulate the elections. ITT owned 70 per cent of Chilteco, the phone company that Allende would later nationalise (an investment of $200 million). Daniel Brandt, 'US responsibility for the coup in Chile', 28 November 1998, www.namebase.org. See also 'Covert Action in Chile 1963–73: Staff Report of the Select Committee to Study Governmental Operations With Respect to Intelligence Activities, United States Senate', https://archive.org/details/Covert-Action-In-Chile-1963-1973.

p. 124 'Allende's nationalisation and land reform . . .' Brandt, 'US responsibility for the coup'.

p. 124 'At the time, 20 per cent . . .' Klein, *The Shock Doctrine*, p. 64.

p. 124 'President Richard Nixon famously ordered . . .' This job fell to the Washington-based Ad Hoc Committee on Chile, which included major US mining companies operating in Chile, as well as ITT.

p. 125 'Two hundred thousand fled . . .' Klein, *The Shock Doctrine*, pp. 76, 107.

p. 126 'The CIA funded a group . . .' This group was led by Sergio de Castro and by Sergio Undurraga. They produced a 500-page economic plan for the new junta to implement. Eight of the ten principal authors of the plan had studied at the University of Chicago. Seventy-five per cent of the funding for this work was coming directly from the CIA. Sergio de Castro became a senior economic adviser in the new regime. Klein, *The Shock Doctrine*, p. 77ff.

p. 126 'To quell it the Chicago . . .' 177,000 industrial jobs were lost in Chile between 1973 and 1983.

p. 126 '"an orgy of self-mutilation"' Cited in Klein, *The Shock Doctrine*, p. 77ff.

p. 126 Eventually things got so bad . . .' For instance, Pinochet sacked Sergio de Castro, one of the leading Chicago Boys, who was Finance Minister at the time.

p. 127 'The poverty rate was 41 . . .' Andre Gunder Frank – one of Friedman's students – was deeply disturbed by these events. He wrote an Open Letter to Arnold Harberger (one of the lead economists of Project Chile) and Milton Friedman, pointing out that on Friedman's version of the 'living wage', a Chilean family would spend 74 per cent of its income on bread. Under Allende, these basic expenses – bread, milk and bus fare – claimed only 17 per cent of a family's budget. Frank went on to become one of the main Latin American economists behind dependency theory.

p. 127 'And hunger was widespread . . .' The figures I cite here come from: James Petras, Fernando Ignacio Leiva and Henry Veltmeyer, *Democracy and Poverty in Chile: The Limits to Electoral Politics* (Boulder, CO: Westview Press, 1994); and Alvaro Díaz, *El Capitalismo Chileno en Los 90: Creimiento Economico y Disigualdad Social* (Santiago: Ediciones PAS, 1991).

p. 127 'Real wages declined by 40 . . .' Klein, *The Shock Doctrine*, p. 96.

p. 127 'Arnold Harberger, the economist in . . .' According to Harberger's CV, which is available online through his UCLA profile.

p. 128 'According to standard Keynesian theory . . .' The relationship between inflation and employment is the basic principle of the Philips Curve.

p. 128 'For one, Nixon was engaged . . .' See, for example, Paul Krugman, 'The stagflation myth', *New York Times*, 3 June 2009.

p. 129 'Not because it was correct . . .' The prize was established in 1968 as the Swedish National Bank's Prize in Economic Sciences In Memory of Alfred Nobel. It is unrelated to the original prizes established by Alfred Nobel himself in 1895, although it is granted at the same ceremony.

p. 129 'The argument held a great . . .' As I mentioned above, the share of national income that went to the top 1 per cent of earners fell dramatically during the post-war decades. This didn't hurt them a great deal so long as economic growth remained strong, since they were getting a still-large share of a fast-growing pie. But when growth stalled and inflation exploded in the 1970s, their wealth began to collapse in a much more serious way.

p. 130 'He even managed to abolish . . .' The Financial Services Modernization Act of 1999 abolished the Glass–Steagall Act.

p. 131 'CEO salaries grew by . . .' *Executive Excess 2006*, the 13th annual CEO compensation survey from the Institute for Policy Studies and United for a Fair Economy.

p. 131 'According to US Census data . . .' US Census Bureau, Historical Income Tables: Families.

p. 131 'As it turns out, making . . .' As Ha-Joon Chang has so aptly put it.

p. 131 'In fact, quite the opposite . . .' Robert Pollin, *Contours of Descent* (New York: Verso, 2005), p. 133.

p. 134 ' "We thought that an acceleration . . ." ' Prebisch, 1980, pp. 15, 18, cited in Kevan Harris and Ben Scully, 'A hidden counter-movement? Precarity, politics, and social protection before and beyond the neoliberal era', *Theory and Society* 44(5), 2015, pp. 415–44.

Five: Debt and the Economics of Planned Misery

p. 138 'It drove right to the . . .' For more on this movement, see Vijay Prashad's excellent book, *The Darker Nations: A People's History of the Third World* (New York: The New Press, 2007).

p. 139 'The idea was to create . . .' Vijay Prashad, *The Poorer Nations: A Possible History of the Global South* (London: Verso Books, 2013).

p. 140 'Outraged by this incursion . . .' This shipment was known as Operation Nickel Grass.

p. 140 'In response, the Arab coalition . . .' Egypt's Sadat managed to convince Saudia Arabia's King Faisal to make this move.

p. 140 'Desperate for a quick solution . . .' Lizette Alvarez, 'Britain says US Planned to seize oil in '73 crisis', *New York Times*, 2 January 2004.

p. 141 'As a result of the oil . . .' The $450 billion figure reflects petrodollar influx into OPEC as of 1981.

p. 142 'Loan pushers were trained . . .' John Perkins offers a troubling account of his time as a loan pusher during those years, in his bestselling book *Confessions of an Economic Hit Man*.

p. 142 'These "juicers" created a strong . . .' Perkins, *Economic Hit Man*.

p. 142 'By 1982, total debt stocks . . .' In 2013 dollars, according to World Development Indicators (DataBank).

p. 143 'Through the miracle of compound . . .' In 2013 dollars, according to World Development Indicators (DataBank).

p. 143 'And that's exactly what happened . . .' Average interest rates on new loans to global South countries shot up from 5 per cent in 1970 to more than 10 per cent in 1981.

p. 143 'In 1982, Mexico took . . .' In current dollars.

p. 144 'In other words, the IMF . . .' I am indebted to my colleague David Graeber for this comparison.

p. 144 'This is how the plan . . .' The IMF had been using conditional lending since 1952, but it wasn't until the late 1970s that this power was leveraged to impose a specific economic ideology around the world. This idea was first hatched by World Bank president Robert McNamara (formerly president of Ford Motor Company, and then Secretary of Defense) in 1979. The goal was to begin to dismantle developmentalism and get indebted countries to focus on exports again. In 1980 the World Bank's first Structural Adjustment Loan was approved for Turkey – Loan 1818, for $200 million. The idea was picked up and supported strongly by Ronald Reagan.

p. 145 'This was a big blow . . .' As the Phillips Curve states, higher inflation correlates (in the short term) with higher employment.

p. 148 'These "innovative debt products" . . .' See World Bank Treasury, List of Selected Recent Bonds, http://treasury.worldbank.org/cmd/htm/World_Bank_Bond_Issuances.html.

p. 148 'And yet such invasive conditions . . .' I am indebted to Ha-Joon Chang for this illuminating comparison.

p. 149 'During the 1960s and 1970s, global South . . .' These figures exclude China. Robert Pollin, *Contours of Descent* (New York: Verso, 2005), p. 133.

p. 149 'The region went into a long . . .' For perspective on the impact of structural adjustment on Africa, see: H. White, 'Adjustment in Africa: a review article', *Development and Change* 27, 1996, pp.

785–815; B. Riddel, 'Things fall apart again: structural adjustment programs in sub-Saharan Africa', *Journal of Modern African Studies* 30(1), 1992, pp. 53–68; Howard Stein and Machiko Nissanke, 'Structural adjustment and the African crisis: a theoretical appraisal', *Eastern Economic Journal*, 1999, pp. 399–420.

p. 149 'The GNP of the average . . .' Ha-Joon Chang, *Bad Samaritans* (New York: Bloomsbury Press, 2008), p. 28.

p. 149 'the number of Africans living . . .' World Bank, World Development Indicators, 2007.

p. 151 'We can get a better . . .' The figures I cite here come from the chapter titled 'SAPing the Third World', in Mike Davis, *Planet of Slums* (London: Verso, 2006), unless indicated otherwise.

p. 151 'By the end of the 1990s . . .' James Petras and Henry Veltemeyer, 'Age of reverse aid: neoliberalism as catalyst of regression', *Development and Change* 33(2), 2002, p. 287.

p. 151 'In Brazil, wages fell by . . .' According to the ILO; see Martin Khor, *States of Disarray: The Social Effects of Globalization* (Geneva: UNRISD, 1995), p. 45. See also Davis, *Planet of Slums*, p. 166: the average income of working people fell by 40 per cent in Venezuela, 30 per cent in Argentina and 21 per cent in Brazil and Costa Rica.

p. 152 'In Latin America in 1980 . . .' Petras and Veltemeyer, 'Age of reverse aid', p. 287.

p. 152 'In Rio, inequality rose from . . .' Davis, *Planet of Slums*, p. 166.

p. 153 'By 1992, some 146 IMF . . .' Davis, *Planet of Slums*, p. 166. See John Walton and David Seddon, *Free Markets and Food Riots: The Politics of Global Adjustment* (Hoboken, NJ: John Wiley & Sons, 2011).

p. 154 'Structural adjustment allowed the West . . .' Ha-Joon Chang, *Kicking Away the Ladder: Development Strategy in Historical Perspective* (London: Anthem Press, 2002).

p. 154 'In the United States . . .' And the Foreign Sovereign Immunities Act of 1976.

p. 155 'Middle- and low-income countries . . .' 'Analysis of World Bank voting reforms', Bretton Woods Project, 30 April 2010.

p. 156 'This minority (and white) control . . .' The term global apartheid was first introduced by Gernot Köhler in 1978.

p. 156 'There have long been calls . . .' For instance, the demands made in the Charter for Global Democracy (Charter99), signed in Vienna in 1999.

p. 156 ' "Today I resigned from the staff . . ." ' I first came to learn about Budhoo's letter from Naomi Klein's *The Shock Doctrine* (London: Allen Lane, 2007).

p. 157 'But it was little more . . .' Geske Dijkstra, 'The PRSP approach and the illusion of improved aid effectiveness: lessons from Bolivia, Honduras, and Nicaragua', *Development Policy Review* 29, 2011, pp. 110–33.

p. 157 'Once they understand the consequences . . .' This appears to be the position of William Easterly in his book *The White Man's Burden* (Oxford: Oxford University Press, 2007).

p. 158 'This is what economists call . . .' David Harvey, *A Brief History of Neoliberalism* (Oxford: Oxford University Press, 2005).

p. 159 'Capitalists tend to prefer such . . .' The Supreme Court case *Dodge v. Ford Motor Company* is often invoked to force companies to prioritise short-term shareholder returns over other concerns.

p. 160 'To get a sense of . . .' World Bank Treasury, Annual Borrowing Program, http://treasury.worldbank.org/cmd/htm/AnnualBorrowing Program.html.

p. 160 'On top of this . . .' Petras and Veltmeyer, 'Age of reverse aid', p. 286.

p. 160 'Through these "tied aid" arrangements . . .' James Bovard, 'The World Bank vs. the Poor', Cato Policy Analysis No. 92, 1987.

p. 161 'What is more, American companies . . .' Harvey, *A Brief History of Neoliberalism*, p. 30.

p. 161 'The World Bank alone privatised . . .' World Bank, Private Participation in Infrastructure Database, http://ppi.worldbank.org/.

p. 162 ' "We believe that providing clean . . ." ' 'The World Bank botches water privatization around the world', *Alternet*, 22 September 2008.

p. 162 'It is not a real solution . . .' I am indebted to David Harvey for this insight.

p. 163 'Rather, the statement of purpose . . .' IBRD Articles of Agreement, http://siteresources.worldbank.org/EXTABOUTUS/Resources/ibrd-articlesofagreement.pdf.

p. 164 'In 1960, the richest fifth . . .' United Nations Development Programme, *Human Development Report 1999: Globalization with a Human Face* (New York: Oxford University Press, 1999), pp. 104–5.

p. 165 'South Asia, where structural adjustment . . .' The ratio of per capita income in the US to that in Latin America grew from 6:1 to 8.5:1, the ratio of the US to the developing countries of the Middle East and North Africa grew from 15.1:1 to 20.8:1, and the ratio of the US to sub-Saharan Africa grew from 26.9:1 to 51.5:1. For South Asia the ratio shrank from 86.5:1 to 73.2:1. The absolute gap in per capita incomes, however, grew for all regions during this period vis-à-vis the United States. The gap between the US and Latin America grew by 66 per cent. For the Middle East, North Africa and sub-Saharan Africa it grew by 60 per cent. For South Asia it grew by 56 per cent. (GDP per capita, constant 2005 US$; data from World Development Indicators.)

p. 165 'If workers in the developing . . .' Samir Amin, *Unequal Development* (New York: Monthly Review Press, 1976), p. 144.

p. 166 'The best way to think . . .' Gernot Köhler, 'Unequal Exchange 1965–1995: World Trend and World Tables', 1998, wsarch.ucr.edu/archive/papers/kohler/kohler3.htm. See also Gernot Köhler and Arno Tausch, *Global Keynesianism: Unequal Exchange and Global Exploitation* (New York: Nova Science Publishers, 2002). Köhler calculates unequal exchange in 1995 as $1.752 trillion in current dollars. See note in Chapter 1 for more on Köhler's methods and the meaning of unequal exchange.

p. 166 'Altogether, during the whole period . . .' All of these figures come from the World Bank's World Development Indicators, accessed through DataBank, and are reported in 2013 dollars.

p. 167 'Lebanon, for instance, spends 52 . . .' New Economics Foundation, 'Debt Relief as if Justice Mattered', 2008.

p. 168 'The rest was piled up . . .' J. W. Smith, *The World's Wasted Wealth* (Sun City, AZ: Institute for Economic Democracy Press, 1994), p. 143.

p. 168 'External debt as a percentage . . .' External debt stocks (percentage of GNI), World Bank, International Debt Statistics.

p. 171 '"There's no better way . . ."' David Graeber, *Debt: The First 5,000 Years* (New York: Melville House, 2011), p. 5.

p. 171 'In all of these cases . . .' In other words, in order win debt relief a country must first agree to submit to IMF structural adjustment.

p. 172 'One of the key tenets . . .' Amartya Sen, *Development as Freedom* (New York: Oxford University Press, 1995).

p. 172 'The World Bank itself defines . . .' World Bank, 'What is Development?' http://www.worldbank.org/depweb/english/beyond/beyondco/beg_01.pdf.

Six: Free Trade and the Rise of the Virtual Senate

p. 174 'Ever since the 14th century . . .' See Ha-Joon Chang, 'Kicking away the ladder', *Post-Autistic Economics Review* 15, 2002.

p. 174 'The system was rigged . . .' See Perry Anderson, *American Foreign Policy and Its Thinkers* (New York : Verso, 2014).

p. 177 'If Portugal is better at . . .' And Portugal should focus on wine even if it can produce cloth more cheaply than England, presuming its comparative advantage over England in wine is greater than that in cloth.

p. 178 ' "We are told that free . . ." ' These words come from a speech by Karl Marx that he delivered before the Democratic Association of Brussels on 9 January 1848.

p. 179 'Comparative advantage isn't given . . .' The economist Arghiri Emmanuel has probably done the most to develop this view, arguing that wages and prices are set by historical-political factors. This view became a cornerstone of dependency theory.

p. 180 ' "But," Chang argues, "if I drive . . ." ' Ha-Joon Chang, 'My six-year-old son should get a job', in *Bad Samaritans* (New York: Bloomsbury Press, 2008), chapter 3.

p. 181 ' "Likewise," Chang says, "industries . . ." ' Chang, *Bad Samaritans*, pp. 65–6.

p. 182 '$374 billion per year . . .' This is the figure for agricultural subsidies in OECD countries in 2010, according to data published by the OECD. Subsidies given directly to farmers totalled $227 billion in the same year. Agricultural subsidies also hurt small farmers *within* rich countries, as the vast majority of subsidies go to big agribusiness. In the US, 20 per cent of recipients receive 89 per cent of subsidies.

p. 183 'If they decide to break . . .' I am indebted to Yash Tandon for the example of the cotton four. Yash Tandon, *Trade is War: The West's War Against the World* (New York: OR Books, 2015), p. 41ff.

p. 183 'Indeed, a study conducted . . .' Cited in Chang, *Bad Samaritans*, p. 69.

p. 184 'They placed special quotas on . . .' The quota system was known as the Multi-Fiber Arrangement, and was first put in place in 1974.

p. 184 'At the same time, Western . . .' Preferences were organised through the Generalized System of Preferences (GSP) and the US-initiated African Growth and Opportunity Act (AGOA), of which Swaziland became a beneficiary in 2000.

p. 185 'The WTO upheld their argument . . .' This was according to the Agreement on Textiles and Clothing (ATC), which was implemented in 1995 and phased in over ten years.

p. 185 'As one might imagine, this . . .' I develop this argument in 'Neo-liberal plague: the political economy of HIV transmission in Swaziland', *Journal of Southern African Studies* 38(3), 2012, pp. 513–29.

p. 188 'As a result of TRIPS . . .' Meena Raman, 'WIPO Seminar Debates Intellectual Property and Development', Our World is Not For Sale, 10 May 2015.

p. 189 'During the AIDS crisis . . .' See Peter Mugyenyi, *Genocide by Denial: How Profiteering from HIV Killed Millions* (Kampala: Fountain Publishers, 2008).

p. 190 'It was only in 2003 . . .' The Doha Declaration on the TRIPS Agreement and Public Health was signed in November 2001 in order to allow Least Developed Countries (LDCs) to produce generic drugs for internal consumption in the case of emergency public health crises. Nevertheless, the Doha Declaration failed to benefit countries that lacked the capacity for pharmaceutical production (like Swaziland), for TRIPS still prevented the *importation* of generic drugs. It was not until the WTO succumbed to pressure and signed the General Decision of August 2003 that poor nations were allowed to import generics.

p. 190 'But we know that . . .' Dylan Gray, 'Big pharma's excuses for the monopolies on medicine won't wash', *Guardian*, 22 February 2013.

p. 191 'As for the argument about . . .' The pharmaceutical industry spent $27 billion on marketing in the US in 2012. Nine of the ten largest companies spent more on marketing than they did on research and development. Ana Swanson, 'Big pharmaceutical companies are spending more on marketing than research', *Washington Post*, 11 February 2015.

p. 191 'In the consensus process . . .' Peter Drahos, 'When the weak bargain with the strong: negotiations in the World Trade Organization', *International Negotiation* 9(1), 2003, pp. 79–109.

p. 191 'This is why so many . . .' Richard H. Steinberg, 'In the shadow of law or power? Consensus-based bargaining and outcomes in the GATT/WTO', *International Organization*, 56(2), 2002, pp. 339–74.

p. 194 '"Twenty-five per cent of the population . . ."' Lara Carlsen, 'Under NAFTA, Mexico Suffered, and the United States Felt Its Pain', *New York Times*, 24 November 2013.

p. 194 'NAFTA led directly to the . . .' Robert Scott, 'Heading South: US–Mexico Trade and Job Displacement after NAFTA', Economic Policy Institute, 3 May 2011.

p. 194 'NAFTA proved to be a powerful . . .' The statistics I have listed in the previous paragraphs come from Public Citizen's 'NAFTA's Legacy for Mexico' report, unless otherwise stated.

p. 195 'After all, it had the effect . . .' Noel Maurer, *The Empire Trap: The Rise and Fall of US Intervention to Protect American Property Overseas, 1893–2013* (Princeton, NJ: Princeton University Press, 2013).

p. 196 'The judges in these hearings . . .' White & Case and Shearman & Sterling are two of the most prominent ISDS firms.

p. 197 '"When I wake up at night . . ."' Cited in Sebastian Perry, 'Arbitrator and counsel: the double-hat syndrome', *Global Arbitration Review* 7(2), 2012.

p. 197 'The highest award so far . . .' 'The arbitration game', *The Economist*, 11 October 2014.

p. 198 'Alfred de Zayas, a UN . . .' 'Secret negotiations on trade treaties, a threat to human rights – UN expert', United Nations Human Rights, 23 April 2015.

p. 201 'Sitting in their high-rise . . .' I am indebted to Noam Chomsky for the term 'virtual senate', which I believe he coined in an article titled 'The high cost of neoliberalism' published in the *New Statesman*.

p. 202 'The *Doing Business* report has . . .' World Bank, *Doing Business*, 2014, http://www.doingbusiness.org/~/media/GIAWB/Doing%20 Business/Documents/Annual-reports/English/DB14-Full-Report.pdf.

p. 203 'Countries are rewarded when they . . .' The 'getting credit' indicator also ranks countries based on their credit registries. The more data a country publishes about each citizen's credit history, the higher they rank. In other words, *Doing Business* seeks to extend the US credit score system across the entire world: ideally, every citizen will be ranked by a number that allows banks to assess their credit 'worthiness'. So people who end up defaulting on student loans or predatory mortgages get frozen out of the system, ruining their lives. This is a powerful way to render citizens docile and obedient to the banks.

p. 203 'And the "registering property" indicator . . .' Oakland Institute, *(Mis)Investment in Agriculture* (Oakland, CA: The Oakland Institute, 2010).

p. 204 'An official review of the report . . .' As noted in the Independent Review Panel report of the *Doing Business* Indicators.

p. 205 'As for the jobs that . . .' 'An 80-hour week for 5p an hour: the real price of high-street fashion', *Guardian*, 8 December 2006.

Seven: Plunder in the 21st Century

p. 207 'In 2002, the United States . . .' Officials in the George W. Bush administration had prior knowledge of the Venezuela coup, met with coup leaders in the weeks leading up to the action, and provided training and support to some of the individuals and organisations involved.

p. 207 'and in 2004 helped topple . . .' Aristide – a priest beloved of the poor – was deposed in a coup backed by the Bush administration and by France, who were incensed by his attempts to raise the minimum wage for garment factory workers and his calls for debt cancellation and colonial reparations. Paul Farmer, 'Who removed Aristide?', *London Review of Books*, 28(6), 2004, pp. 28–31. Interestingly, when Aristide's successor ended up raising the minimum wage anyhow, to $0.61 per hour, US companies like Levi Strauss and Hanes got the State Department involved, which forced Haiti to reverse the decision. Dan Coughlin and Kim Ives, 'WikiLeaks Haiti: let them live on $3 a day', *The Nation*, 1 June 2011. That same year, the US State Department manipulated Haiti's elections to swing in favour of their preferred candidate. Center for Economic and Policy Research, 'Clinton emails reveal "behind the doors actions" of private sector and US embassy in Haiti elections', 2015.

p. 207 'In 2009, the elected leader . . .' Zelaya had taken steps to impose environmental regulations on the mining industry, regulate trade and raise the minimum wage, all of which enraged the multinational companies operating there.

p. 208 'Honduran indigenous activist Berta Caceres . . .' Nina Lakhani, 'Berta Caceres cour papers show murder suspects' links to US-trained elite troops', *Guardian*, 28 February 2017.

p. 208 'As a result, external debt . . .' Katie Allen, 'World's poorest countries rocked by commodity slump and strong dollar', *Guardian*, 10 April 2016.

p. 208 'Structural adjustment programmes are still . . .' Fortunately conditionality has been relaxed a bit since the 2009 G20 Summit, which raised this as an issue. But as yet there is still no non-conditional borrowing facility available to global South countries.

p. 208 'And sometimes creditors take even . . .' John Nichols, 'Just in time for the July 4 break, Congress imposes "colonialism at its worst" on Puerto Rico', *The Nation*, 2 July 2016.

p. 209 'In 2003, the United Nations . . .' United Nations, *United Nations Convention against Corruption*, 2004, p. iii, http://www.unodc.org/documents/treaties/UNCAC/Publications/Convention/08-50026_E.pdf.

p. 209 'According to the World Bank . . .' Jim Yong Kim, 'Anti-corruption Efforts in a Global Commitment to Act', Speech in Washington, DC, 30 January 2013, http://www.worldbank.org/en/news/speech/2013/01/30/world-bank-group-president-jim-yong-kim-speech-anti-corruption-center-for-strategic-and-international-studies.

p. 210 'By contrast, the Washington-based . . .' Dev Kar and Devon Cartwright-Smith, *Illicit Financial Flows from Africa: Hidden*

Resource for Development (Washington, DC: Global Financial Integrity, 2010), p. 1.

p. 210 'According to GFI, each year . . .' Actually $1,090.1 billion. This figure comes from Dev Kar and Joseph Spanjers, *Illicit Financial Flows from Developing Countries: 2004–2013* (Washington, DC: Global Financial Integrity, 2015). Forty-five per cent of flows end up in tax havens, and 55 per cent end up in developed countries, according to GFI web page 'Illicit Financial Flows', www.gfintegrity.org/issue/illicit-financial-flows. The measurement of illicit financial flows is hotly debated. One scholar has disputed the GFI methodology (Volker Nitsch, 'Trillion dollar estimate: illicit financial flows from developing countries', *Darmstadt Discussion Papers in Economics* 227, 2012). There may be good reasons to question GFI's large numbers, but for now the OECD's official position is that 'there is general consensus that illicit financial flows likely exceed aid flows and investment in volume' (OECD, *Illicit Financial Flows from Developing Countries: Measuring OECD Responses* (Paris: OECD Publishing, 2014)).

p. 210 '($99.3 billion in 2013)' $99.3 billion is the figure used by Kar and Spanjers, *Illicit Financial Flows*, p. 15, for ODA to developing countries in 2013. Note that this is lower than the $135 billion in ODA estimated by the OECD for the same year.

p. 210 'And these outflows have been . . .' Kar and Spanjers, *Illicit Financial Flows*, p. vii.

p. 210 'Between 2004 and 2013, developing . . .' Kar and Spanjers, *Illicit Financial Flows*, p. vii.

p. 211 'In 2013, hot money accounted . . .' Kar and Spanjers, *Illicit Financial Flows*, p. 10.

p. 211 'In 2013, trade misinvoicing accounted . . .' Kar and Spanjers, *Illicit Financial Flows*, p. 10.

p. 212 'Because of the rapid expansion . . .' Christian Aid, *Death and Taxes: The True Toll of Tax Dodging* (London: Christian Aid, 2008), p. 2. Also see World Health Organization, 'International Corporations', http://www.who.int/trade/glossary/story057/en/.

p. 212 'Analysts have recorded some flagrant . . .' Nicholas Shaxson, *Treasure Islands: Tax Havens and the Men Who Stole the World* (London: Vintage Books, 2011).

p. 213 'That means *another* $879 billion . . .' Raymond Baker, *Capitalism's Achilles Heel: Dirty Money and How to Renew the Free-Market System* (Hoboken, NJ: John Wiley & Sons, 2005), pp. 170–1.

p. 213 'Already the world's poorest region . . .' Kar and Spanjers, *Illicit Financial Flows*, p. 12.

p. 214 'In total, developing countries may . . .' This figure includes $1.3 trillion in hot money, $6.5 trillion in reinvoicing, and $6.5 trillion in transfer mispricing during the decade 2004–2013. Kar and Spanjers, *Illicit Financial Flows*, p. vii.

p. 214 'But the WTO argued that . . .' World Trade Organization, 'Technical Information on Customs Valuation', http://www.wto.org/english/tratop_e/cusval_e/cusval_info_e.htm. The relevant passage reads: 'customs valuation shall, except in specified circumstances, be based on the actual price of the goods to be valued, which is generally shown on the invoice'.

p. 215 'Today, at least 30 per cent . . .' Matthew Valencia, 'Storm survivors', The Economist, 16 February 2013, http://www.economist.com/news/special-report/21571549-offshore-financial-centres-have-taken-battering-recently-they-have-shown-remarkable.

p. 215 'There are three main categories . . .' Nicholas Shaxson, *Treasure Islands*.

p. 219 'By 2008, the IMF had . . .' Fred Pearce, *The Land Grabbers: The New Fight Over Who Owns the Earth* (Boston: Beacon Press Books, 2012), p. 23.

p. 219 'The rising price of oil . . .' Pearce, *The Land Grabbers*, pp. 22–3.

p. 220 'In other words, people who . . .' Pearce, *The Land Grabbers*, p. 25. On p. 26, Pearce states: 'In 2003, there had been $13 billion in agricultural commodity funds. But by 2008, many commentators put the figure at over $300 billion.' Also see Frederick Kaufman, 'The food bubble', *Harpers*, July 2010.

p. 220 'World food prices continued to . . .' This according to the FAO's world food price index graph.

p. 220 'According to UN sources . . .' Olivier De Schutter, cited in Pearce, *The Land Grabbers*, p. 24.

p. 220 'A land purchase qualifies as . . .' This is the definition used by the Land Matrix (www.landmatrix.org).

p. 222 'Early estimates from the World Bank...' Pearce, *The Land Grabbers*, p. ix. On transparency issues, see Josie Cohen, 'What's in a number? Why the struggle to quantify the global land grabbing crisis is part of the problem', *Global Witness*, blog post, 11 March 2014, https://www.globalwitness.org/en-gb/blog/whats-number-why -struggle-quantify-truncated/.

p. 222 'While the majority of the land-grabbers ...' 'Land grabs: the facts', *New Internationalist*, May 2013, p. 17.

p. 222 'Number of land grabs since 2000' Map generated by the Land Matrix (www.landmatrix.org). Data accurate as of January 2017.

p. 222 'This explains why 66 per cent ...' This is according to the Land Matrix's first data, in 2012. It claimed 124 million of 203 million hectares was grabbed in Africa – over 4 per cent of the continent's total land area. Seventy per cent of the deals reported by the World Bank in 2008–9 were in Africa. Fred Nelson, 'Who owns the Earth? A review of Fred Pearce's *The Land Grabbers*', *World Policy Blog*, 5 October 2012, http://www.worldpolicy.org/blog/2012/10/05/who-owns-earth-review-fred-pearces-land-grabbers.

p. 223 'And more often than not...' Two-thirds of countries that are giving away land are suffering from hunger problems. 'Land grabs: the facts', *New Internationalist*, May 2013.

p. 223 'In Liberia, 75 per cent...' 'Land grabs: the facts', *New Internationalist*, May 2013.

p. 224 'In Côte d'Ivoire, these deals...' 'The G8 and land grabs in Africa', *GRAIN*, 11 March 2013, https://www.grain.org/article/entries/4663-the-g8-and-land-grabs-in-africa.

p. 224 'Land is not the only ...' In both land and seeds, countries are made to draw up registries that lay bare the investment opportunities that corporations can take advantage of. 'The G8 and land grabs in Africa', *GRAIN*, 11 March 2013.

p. 224 'In Papua New Guinea, more ...' Pearce, *The Land Grabbers*, chapter 16.

p. 224 'So many Cambodian peasants have ...' Pearce, *The Land Grabbers*, chapter 17.

p. 224 'Across South East Asia...' Pearce, *The Land Grabbers*, chapter 18.

p. 226 'Examples from Ethiopia and Peru . . .' Joseph Holden and Margarethe Pagel, 'Transnational Land Acquisitions', *EPS PEAKS*, January 2013, http://partnerplatform.org/?azrv33t9.

p. 226 'Even at conservative estimates . . .' According to a study by IFPRI, cited in 'Outsourcing's third wave', *The Economist*, 1 May 2009.

p. 228 'Rich industrial economies are responsible . . .' About half of these emissions come from the United States.

p. 228 'Yet, according to data from . . .' This data comes from the 2010 report of the Climate Monitor. The Monitor includes an additional category of 'other industrialized' countries, which accounts for the remainder.

p. 230 'Much of this has to do . . .' Suzanne Goldenberg, 'CO_2 emissions are being "outsourced" by rich countries to rising economies', *Guardian*, 19 January 2014.

p. 230 'The United States remains the . . .' Duncan Clark, 'Which nations are most responsible for climate change?', *Guardian*, 21 April 2011.

p. 230 'And yet the costs of climate . . .' 'A bad climate for development', *The Economist*, 17 September 2009.

p. 231 'According to *The Economist* . . .' 'A bad climate for development', *The Economist*, 17 September 2009.

p. 231 'In Africa, the growing period . . .' According to an IPCC study, noted in John Vidal, 'Climate change will hit poor countries hardest, study shows', *Guardian*, 27 September 2013.

p. 231 'By 2080, agricultural production could . . .' 'A bad climate for development', *The Economist*, 17 September 2009.

p. 231 'Oxfam predicts that, as a . . .' Oxfam, *Growing Disruption: Climate Change, Food, and The Fight Against Hunger* (Oxford: Oxfam Publishing, 2013).

p. 231 'Present estimates suggest that by . . .' 'A bad climate for development', *The Economist*, 17 September 2009.

p. 232 'Meanwhile, my home country of . . .' Climatefairshares.org.

p. 233 'If we want to have . . .' Carbon Countdown, Carbon Budget 2016 Update, Carbon Brief, www.carbonbrief.org.

p. 233 'At our current rate of . . .' 'The sky's the limit: why the Paris Climate Goals require a managed decline of fossil fuel production', *OilChange*, September 2016.

p. 233 'And yet instead of reducing . . .' 'Global Carbon Emissions', Co2Now.org, http://co2now.org/Current-CO2/CO2-Now/global-carbon-emissions.html.

p. 233 'Governments are still subsidising . . .' Damian Carrington, 'Fossil fuels subsidized by $10 million a minute, says IMF', *Guardian*, 18 May 2015.

p. 234 'According to a 2012 report . . .' World Bank, *Turn Down the Heat: Why a 4°C Warmer World Must Be Avoided*, Working paper 74455 (Washington, DC: World Bank, 2012).

p. 234 'According to the Intergovernmental Panel . . .' NASA, 'The consequences of climate change', http://climate.nasa.gov/effects/.

p. 235 'Problems like this, which have . . .' International Energy Agency, 'Scenarios and Projections', http://www.iea.org/publications/scenariosandprojections/.

p. 236 'As Naomi Klein puts it . . .' Naomi Kleim, *This Changes Everything* (London: Penguin Books, 2015), p. 21.

Eight: From Charity to Justice

p. 241 ' "People find themselves surrounded . . ." ' From Oscar Wilde, *The Soul of Man under Socialism*, 1891. Slightly paraphrased for clarity.

p. 243 'Starbucks has given charity . . .' For example, in 2012 the Starbucks Foundation gave a $500,000 grant to Project Concern International to assist a water and sanitation programme in the Sidama Zone of southern Ethiopia. But according to an Oxfam report in 2005, Starbucks's trading practices cost Ethiopian growers about $90 million per year. Starbucks prevented efforts by the Ethiopian government to trademark three of its local coffee beans, which would have allowed Ethiopian growers to claim a greater share of profits on international sales.

p. 243 'Coca-Cola gives a bit of charity . . .' 'Coca-Cola accused of funding Columbian death squad', TeleSUR, 1 September 2016.

p. 245 'By implying that debtors have . . .' This moral framing around debt is a complete inversion of what every ancient philosophical tradition proclaims: that usury is the sin, not indebtedness.

p. 245 'This sounds like a lot . . .' NEF, *Debt Relief as if Justice Mattered* (London: New Economics Foundation, 2008).

p. 245 'Another recent report finds that . . .' Save the World's Resources, *Financing the Global Sharing Economy* (London: Share the World's Resources, 2012), p. 145.

p. 249 'Instead of requiring across-the-board . . .' Joseph Stiglitz has made interesting proposals for reforming this imbalance.

p. 252 'For countries where wages are . . .' See Thomas Palley, 'A global minimum wage system', *Financial Times*, 18 July 2011. Also see Jason Hickel, 'It's time for a global minimum wage', Al Jazeera English, 10 June 2013.

p. 253 'There is no evidence that . . .' The evidence suggests that raising the minimum wage has no negative effect on employment. See John Schmitt, *Why Does the Minimum Wage Have No Discernible Effect on Employment?* (Washington, DC: Center for Economic and Policy Research, 2013). See also International Labour Organization, *Global Wage Report 2008/9: Minimum Wages and Collective Bargaining* (Geneva: International Labour Office, 2008).

p. 253 'In fact, you could raise . . .' Robert Pollin et al., 'Global apparel production and sweatshop labour: can raising retail prices finance living wages?', *Cambridge Journal of Economics* 28(2), 2002, pp. 153–71.

p. 253 'It might sound like a . . .' See 'C131 Minimum Wage Fixing Convention', 1970.

p. 254 'This could be done by . . .' Like the Brussels Definition of Value, which was abolished by the WTO.

p. 254 'Requiring global financial transparency would . . .' The United States, Britain and the European Parliament are already taking steps in this direction. In the US, the Incorporation Transparency and Law Enforcement Assistance Act eliminates anonymous shell companies by making beneficial ownership information available to law enforcement agencies. States can use this Act to require that this information be made publicly available.

p. 255 'The weight of evidence suggests . . .' Frances Moore Lappé, Jennifer Clapp, Molly Anderson, Richard Lockwood, Thomas Forster, Danielle Nierenberg, Harriet Friedmann, Thomas Pogge, Dominique Caouette, Wayne Roberts et al., 'Framing Hunger: A Response to the State of Food Insecurity in the World 2012', June

2013, http://www.ase.tufts.edu/gdae/pubs/rp/framinghunger.pdf; Frances Moore Lappé, Jennifer Clapp, Molly Anderson, Richard Lockwood, Thomas Forster, Danielle Nierenberg, Harriet Friedmann, Thomas Pogge, Dominique Caouette, Wayne Roberts et al., 'How we count Hunger Matters', *Ethics & International Affairs* 27(3), 2013, pp. 251–259.

p. 256 'And if the top 10 per cent . . .' These estimates come from British climate scientist Kevin Anderson (www.kevinanderson.info).

Nine: The Necessary Madness of Imagination

p. 262 'Scientists tell us that even . . .' These figures comes from the Global Footprint Network database.

p. 262 'Forty per cent of our planet's . . .' Ian Sample, 'Global food crisis looms as climate change and population growth strip fertile land', *Guardian*, 31 August 2007.

p. 262 'Or look at fish: around . . .' Gaia Vince, 'How the world's oceans could be running out of fish', *BBC Future*, 21 September 2012, http://www.bbc.com/future/story/20120920-are-we-running-out-of-fish.

p. 262 'Haddock have fallen to 1 per cent . . .' George Monbiot, 'The great riches of our seas have been depleted and forgotten', *Guardian*, 7 September 2012.

p. 262 'Scientists tell us that up . . .' S. L. Pimm, G. J. Russell, J. L. Gittleman and T. M. Brooks, 'The future of biodiversity', *Science* 269, 1995, pp. 347–50.

p. 265 'Species biodiversity will have declined . . .' OECD, 'Biodiversity chapter of the OECD Environmental Outlook to 2050: The consequences of inaction', http://www.oecd.org/env/indicators-modelling-outlooks/biodiversitychapteroftheoecdenvironmentaloutlookto2050theconsequencesofinaction.htm.

p. 265 'Stocks of all presently fished seafood . . .' Charles Clover, 'All seafood will run out in 2050, say scientists', *Telegraph*, 3 November 2006.

p. 265 'Most major metal reserves will . . .' 'A forecast of when we'll run out of each metal,' Visual Capitalist, 4 September 2014, http://www.visualcapitalist.com/forecast-when-well-run-out-of-each-metal/.

p. 266 'Nor will it do much . . .' 'Only 60 years of farming left if soil degradation continues', Reuters, 5 December 2014.

p. 266 'Unfortunately, it no longer holds . . .' Lew Daly et al., *Does Growth Equal Progress? The Myth of GDP* (New York: Demos, 2012).

p. 266 'Because past a certain point . . .' As the economist Herman Daly has put it. See for example: 'Sustainable development: definitions, principles, policies', *Mechanism of Economic Regulation* 3, 2013, pp. 9–20.

p. 268 'If we bring it back . . .' Thomas O. Wiedmann et al., 'The material footprint of nations', *Proceedings of the National Academy of Sciences of the United States of America* 112(20), 2013, pp. 6271–5.

p. 268 'If we use this approach . . .' Stefan Giljum et al., 'Global patterns of material flows and their socio-economic and environmental implications: a MFA study on all countries world-wide from 1980 to 2009', *Resources* 3(1), 2014, pp. 319–39.

p. 268 'And it is still going up . . .' Friends of the Earth Europe, *Overconsumption? Our Use of the World's Natural Resources* (Brussels: Friends of the Earth Europe, 2009), p. 26.

p. 269 'And of course the great . . .' N. H. Stern, *The Economics of Climate Change: The Stern Review* (Cambridge: Cambridge University Press, 2007).

p. 269 'We would need to create . . .' Kevin Anderson, 'Talks in the city of light generate more heat', *Nature* 528, 21 December 2015.

p. 270 'Deforestation is a major cause . . .' US Environmental Protection Agency, 'Global Greenhouse Gas Emissions Data', https://www.epa.gov/ghgemissions/global-greenhouse-gas-emissions-data, accessed 4 February 2017.

p. 270 'As the soils deplete . . .' 'Deforestation and its extreme effect on global warming,' *Scientific American*, https://www.scientificamerican.com/article/deforestation-and-global-warming/.

p. 270 'Livestock farming alone contributes more . . .' Carbon Countdown, Carbon Budget 2016 Update, Carbon Brief, www.carbonbrief.org.

p. 271 'Now, let's accept that poor . . .' Richard G. Wilkinson and Kate Pickett, *The Spirit Level: Why More Equal Societies Almost Always Do Better* (London: Allen Lane, 2009).

p. 271 'Kevin Anderson and Alice Bows . . .' Kevin Anderson and Alice Bows, 'Beyond "dangerous" climate change: Emissions scenarios for a new world', Philosophical Transactions of the Royal Society 369, 2011, pp. 20–44.

p. 272 'In this scenario, poor countries . . .' Then they will have to reduce emissions aggressively from 2025, cutting by about 7 per cent each year until net zero in 2050, with assistance from rich countries.

p. 272 'And poor countries are going . . .' The rate necessary for them to achieve net zero emissions by 2050, assuming maximum reductions from clean energy technologies and efficiency improvements.

p. 272 'We already have plenty of . . .' Daniel W. O'Neill, 'The proximity of nations to a socially sustainable steady-state economy', *Journal of Cleaner Production* 108, 2015, pp. 1213–31.

p. 273 'After that, what makes us . . .' Benjamin Radcliffe, 'A happy state', *Aeon*, 17 September 2015. See also Richard Wilkinson and Kate Pickett's *The Spirit Level*.

p. 273 'We should look at societies . . .' P. Edward, 'The Ethical Poverty Line: a moral quantification of absolute poverty', *Third World Quarterly* 27(2), 2006, pp. 377–93.

p. 273 'A similar majority also believe . . .' Reported in Jennifer Elks, 'Havas: "Smarter" consumers will significantly alter economic models and the role of brands', *Sustainable Brands*, 15 May 2014.

p. 277 'It made headlines in 2012 . . .' Jaromir Benes and Michael Kumhof, *The Chicago Plan Revisited*, IMF Working Paper WP/12/202 (New York: International Monetary Fund, 2012).

p. 278 'According to a recent report . . .' US advertising expenditure data available at: http://purplemotes.net/2008/09/14/us-advertising -expenditure-data/.

p. 278 'This frenzy of advertising has . . .' Betsy Taylor and Dave Tilford, 'Why consumption matters', in Juliet B. Schor and Douglas B. Holt (eds), *The Consumer Society Reader* (New York: The New Press, 2000), p. 467.

p. 279 'This may sound impossible, but . . .' Neal Lawson, 'Ban outdoor advertising', *Guardian*, 20 April 2012.

p. 279 'Research by the New Economics Foundation . . .' Anna Coote et al., *21 Hours: Why a Shorter Working Week Can Help Us All to Flourish in the 21st Century* (London: New Economics Foundation, 2010).

p. 280 'Unlike microfinance, which has had . . .' Maren Duvendack et al., *What is the Evidence of the Impact of Microfinance on the Well-Being of Poor People?* (London: EPPI-Centre, Social Science Research Unit, Institute of Education, University of London, 2011).

p. 281 'If growth is a substitute . . .' Rob Dietz and Daniel W. O'Neill, *Enough is Enough: Building a Sustainable Economy in a World of Finite Resources* (New York: Routledge, 2013).

p. 282 'Forty per cent of agricultural soil . . .' World Economic Forum, 'What if the world's soil runs out?', *Time*, 14 December 2012.

p. 282 'In fact, industrial farming has . . .' Oliver Milman, 'Earth has lost a third of arable land in past 40 years, scientists say', *Guardian*, 2 December 2015.

p. 282 'A recent study published by . . .' Andreas Gattinger et al., 'Enhanced top soil carbon stocks under organic farming', *Proceedings of the National Academy of Sciences of the United States of America* 109(44), 2012, pp. 18226–31.

p. 282 'An article in *Science* suggests . . .' R. Lal, 'Soil carbon sequestration impacts on global climate change and food security', *Science* 304, 2004, p. 5677.

p. 282 'And new research from the Rodale . . .' Rodale Institute, *Regenerative Organic Agriculture and Climate Change* (Kutztown, PA: Rodale Institute, 2014).

p. 282 'And it comes with a very . . .' R. Lal, 'Soil carbon sequestration impacts'.

p. 284 '"Come, then, comrades, the European . . ."' Frantz Fanon, *The Wretched of the Earth: Pref. by Jean-Paul Sartre*, trans. Constance Farrington (New York: Grove Press, 1963).

Acknowledgements

Legend has it that Eduardo Galeano wrote *Open Veins of Latin America* in only three months, during the evenings after coming home from his day job as an editor. Isabelle Allende mentions this tantalising titbit in her foreword to the book, and when I first read it I was inspired. Galeano's rendition of Latin American history resonated with me; I was impressed by the data he marshalled as evidence and longed for his reporting to extend beyond Latin America's shores and cover the rest of the South. That's what I had in mind when I first sat down to write what eventually became *The Divide*. But I am not Galeano, neither in literary talent nor in pace. While I too wrote mostly on the side, tending by day to my research and teaching obligations at the London School of Economics, this book ended up taking much longer than three months. Still, I owe Galeano for giving me the foolish courage to try.

I also owe many others. To this day, when I sit down to re-read Aimé Césaire's *Discourse on Colonialism*, I can't help but feel that he said in 1950 everything that I have tried to say in this book, everything that has bubbled within me for so long, only more brilliantly. So too with figures like Frantz Fanon, Mahatma Gandhi,

Walter Rodney, Julius Nyerere, and many others. And then there are those who said more with their lives than with their words – who risked everything in the struggle for a fairer world, and were killed for their efforts. From Patrice Lumumba to Salvadore Allende, all the way up to Berta Cáceres – I count them among my ancestors. They continue to guide and inspire me.

Each chapter that appears in this book draws on thinkers and writers much greater than myself: Raúl Prebisch, Andre Gunder Frank, Gernot Köhler, Samir Amin, Sanjay Reddy, Frances Moore Lappé, Thomas Pogge, Peter Edward, David Woodward, Lant Pritchett, Mike Davis, Immanuel Wallerstein, Ellen Wood, David Harvey, Naomi Klein, Susan George, William Easterly, Joseph Stiglitz, Ha-Joon Chang, Nicholas Shaxson, Fred Pearce, Bill McKibben, David Graeber, Herman Daly, Vandana Shiva, and countless others whose names appear in the text and the notes. I cannot list them all. I can only hope I have done justice to their work.

Many friends and colleagues have helped me along this journey. Martin Kirk – my occasional co-author – read an early draft of the manuscript and has offered helpful feedback at a number of junctures. Alnoor Ladha and /The Rules team provided a nourishing and challenging intellectual community wherein I was able to explore and develop many of the ideas that appear in these pages. Rebecca Reid helped me with research in the early stages of the project. Alice Pearson proved to be a helpful interlocutor throughout. Bibi van der Zee at the *Guardian* and my editors at Al Jazeera English helped me work out my thoughts in columns that ended up providing the basis for certain sections of the book. Ha-Joon Chang was gracious enough to advise me – and believe in me – when I started to think about publication. Zoe Ross has been supportive and enjoyable to work with – the best agent I could have asked for. My editor, Tom Avery, with his careful reading and keen sense for language and narrative flow, has made this book much stronger and more readable than I could have done on my own. And the team at W. W. Norton has been delightful to work with: Ashley Patrick, Jeff Shreve, and Francine Kass, who oversaw the art for the cover.

I researched and wrote this book while on an Early Career Fellowship from the Leverhulme Trust, whose support I gratefully acknowledge. I take full responsibility for whatever faults it bears. And there are no doubt many. For one, I cannot help but feel I have left far too much out – important stories neglected for the sake of brevity: the Great Bengal Famine of 1770, for instance, during which ten million Indians were sacrificed for the sake of the British East India Company's profits; the Sykes–Picot Agreement by which Europe carved up the Middle East; the French colonisation of Indochina; the Vietnam War, which saw the United States commit its full military might to destroy a peasant insurgency asking for land reform; and the seemingly endless foreign military interventions that have been conducted in the Middle East over the past two decades. All of this – and more – belongs to the story this book sets out to tell.

I must thank my parents for their constant support, which in this case came in the form of kindly asking after the book and then suffering my descriptions of action-packed days spent moving pixels around on a computer screen. Really, writing can be a lonely process. But I have been fortunate to have my partner, Guddi, beside me throughout. During long conversations in the kitchen around our little wooden table, mugs of tea in hand, she helped me shape ideas into arguments and stories, and slogged her way through drafts so shabby I am ashamed they ever existed. I am endlessly grateful for her patience, intellectual companionship and unflagging support – all of which she extended while getting on with a career much more important and demanding than my own. It's safe to say that without her I would be a completely miserable bugger.

Index

Numbers in *italics* refer to graphs and tables.